To Janet —
Thank you for your help in writing this. You made the writing more fun.
Best of luck in your quests.
Marilyn

For Love And Money, The Brazil Affair

The True Story of a Family's Quest

Marilyn Kelley

Hope you enjoy our story.
Marilyn Kelley

ISBN: 1484809122
ISBN-13: 9781484809129

For John, Lynne, Evan, Diane and Heather

Was I deceived or did a sable cloud
Turn forth her silver lining on the night?
–MILTON

Author's Note

This story is true. I have changed the names of our friends and enemies as well as the names of companies and organizations whose mention may cause embarrassment or lawsuits.

Scenes where I was not present are based on information I received from family members—and one acquaintance—and are related in their voices. For scenes where I was present, I have relied on my diary, notes and vivid recollections. Though scenes and conversations can't be depicted exactly as they occurred, they convey the true essence of the characters and of what happened.

Chapter 1
Marilyn Kelley

If you had told me in 1972 that in less than two years I would be living in Brazil with my husband and four daughters, socializing with criminals, I would have called you crazy.

Why would we leave Greenwich, Connecticut, where we lived a relatively pleasant life? We loved our three-story Victorian, with its porte-cochere, three-car barn-garage, huge backyard, and old apple tree for the girls to play in, in spite of its constant need of repair. Our social life revolved around a small club on Long Island Sound, where we swam, sailed, played tennis, and partied. Though many club members held high positions in publishing, advertising, finance, and politics—including a Connecticut senator and a US president's speech writer—most left their status at the door. Some of these people were our close friends.

To an outsider, our life might have appeared idyllic. Yet behind the door of that big old Victorian, our family was falling apart. Office politics at work had ignited Jack's Irish temper. At home he yelled, slammed doors, threw chairs. I was thinking of taking our daughters, ages eleven to seventeen, to my mother's in Kansas City when school ended in June.

Then Jack was fired.

He couldn't find another job in New York. He grew desperate. After four months of unemployment, he suspected he'd been blackballed in New York by his former employers. He also knew he had alienated his family with his angry outbursts over the past year. We struggled to make his severance check last and worried about losing our house.

Then, while flying to Miami for a job interview, he met Jerry Green.

Chapter 2
Marilyn

I was at the kitchen sink when I heard Jack come through the back door, home from Miami. I'd pulled my hair back in a ponytail and had put on mascara. For luck, I'd added two squirts of Estee Lauder. Unsure of his mood, I did not turn around.

He came up behind me, wrapped me in his arms, and kissed my neck. Then he turned me around and gave me a long kiss. "Hi," he said. His vivid blue eyes sparkled.

I laughed. "I guess it was a good trip."

He pressed himself against me. "You better believe it, baby." He looked around. "Are the kids home from school yet?"

"Not yet. But anytime now."

He took my hand. "Come on. I want to be alone with you." He led me out the back door.

Reluctantly, I followed. "What are we doing? Did you get the job?"

Jack was quiet until we reached our Volkswagen Bug. He opened the passenger door. "Get in. I'll tell you all about it."

I had no idea what he had in mind. He was always full of surprises. "Can't you tell me at home?"

"I don't want any interruptions." He grinned.

"The station wagon is more comfortable."

"Uh-uh. I feel like I'm eighteen again. And if I was eighteen, I'd be driving the Bug. Get in." Excitement lit up his handsome face.

This was the old Jack, full of hope and aspirations. Irresistible, then and now. I climbed into the small blue car.

He turned right at the end of the driveway and headed north toward Westchester County Airport, where he and his brother kept their Cessna 172.

"Are we going flying?" I asked.

"Nope."

"Well, then, where?"

"Just around. I want to tell you about my trip. I think I found a solution to our problems."

Maybe he had good news. "Well, hurry up and tell me."

"You won't believe it. I can hardly believe it myself."

"Tell me, damnit." He had always loved to tease me.

He grinned. "You sure you want me to?"

"Jack! Come on!"

"Okay, okay." He took a deep breath. "Yesterday," he began in a grand manner, "I met a very interesting man. He could change our lives."

My hope faded. "What is he, a magician?"

"Not exactly. I met him on the plane to Miami. Nice guy. He told me about his business. He said he needed help. I said I was interested. We had a long meeting this morning. He gave me more details. Then he offered me a partnership."

It sounded crazy. But Jack often met interesting people in his travels. "And?"

"I said I'd think about it."

I wanted to be optimistic, but this seemed too far-fetched. And yet . . . "Wait a minute. What kind of business? In Florida?"

"A little farther south. Brazil."

"Bra*zil*!" I turned to see if he was kidding.

"Brazil," he said, smiling.

Disappointed, I slumped against the back of my seat. "You're right. I don't believe it."

During the next fifteen minutes, Jack talked about the international entrepreneur he had met. Jerry Green was in the import/export business and traveled to Europe, Africa, South America, even the Far East. He told Jack he was working on various enterprises in Brazil: selling shrimp out of Recife, shipping beef to Taiwan and the Philippines, leasing used fiberglass airboats for use on inland waterways. But the most promising of all the enterprises was gold.

By the time Jack finished talking, we had reached the field next to the airport, near Westair, where the Cessna was tied down. The early June sun was bright as our little car bounced over the rutted dirt road used for emergencies.

"What do you think?" Jack asked.

I was silent for a few minutes, trying to gather my thoughts. It was a wild idea. I didn't know anything about Brazil, except that I liked the song "The Girl from Ipanema."

"Well," I said, "it would be a gamble. Taking the kids to a foreign country. What if it doesn't work out? What would it do to the girls? Still, we have to do something. And soon too." I stared out the window. "I'd like to meet the guy. At least learn more about it." Laughing, I added, "Actually, it would be quite an adventure."

Jack's tone softened. "This would really change our lives." He put his hand on my knee. "Maybe we could get back to the way we used to be." A note of mirth entered his voice. "No more commuting! The damn New Haven Railroad can fly away for all I care!"

"You'd be home at a decent hour. I wouldn't have to cook an early dinner for the kids."

"Hell, you wouldn't have to cook at all. You could hire somebody else to do it." He drove into the tall grass, stopped the Bug, and turned off the engine. The only sound was the swish of the wind in the grass. He grabbed me and kissed me. "I've been such a bastard, Mare. You'll never know how sorry I am. Maybe we've been going in the wrong direction. Maybe we need a change like this."

"We do need a change. Because if things go on the way they are, you're going to lose us."

"I know, I know. And I can't blame you." He sighed. "I need to get away from New York."

We grew quiet, Jack's arms resting lightly around me. We had fallen in love in high school. I was a cheerleader, he was a football player. We took walks and dreamed about our future. Even then his Irish heritage came through in his emotions and humor. He was handsome—tall and strong, with blue eyes that sent thrills through me. After Jack had spent two years at college in Vermont, where he played defensive right end, and I had finished my freshman year at a school outside of Boston, our separations grew too painful. We eloped. I was nineteen, Jack was twenty-one.

We rented an apartment in New Rochelle. Jack drove a nursery school bus and sold silverware to brides-to-be while he took classes at Iona College. I worked in New York as a secretary at a radio and TV station rep, which sold commercial time to advertising agencies.

Eventually Jack took a night job as a page at NBC in New York. Since I worked days and Jack worked nights, most of our conversations were by phone, when Jack would call me from work every evening. We didn't realize how poor we were, but one thing was certain: we were in love. A year after I started working, our daughters began to arrive, like little step stools, four in five and a half years. People would say we looked too young to have so many children, and we'd say we'd gotten married at the eighth-grade prom. After Jack finished his required year as a page, he took a job at a station rep, the same business I had worked in, selling commercial time to ad agencies. Fortunately, he was a good salesman, since we were now living on one income. I had a new full-time job at home.

Over the years, the growing pressures of business and raising four daughters provoked Jack's frequent outbursts. I knew the responsibilities of supporting a family of six weighed heavily on him. He worked hard and changed jobs a few times to improve his position and income and was doing well at Taylor & Co. Some called him the Heir Apparent for the president's job. Carl Magnus, his boss and friend, grew distant, apparently threatened by Jack's success. He kept a bottle of vodka in his desk drawer to ease the pressure. Eventually, he fired Jack. Rudy Schultz, a supposed friend, who recently had eased himself into the president's chair, made little effort to save Jack's job. Now with his former employers working against him to save their own reputations—they needed an excuse to let a good manager go—it was almost impossible for him to find a job in New York. Even his old lunch buddies didn't return his calls. It seemed loyalties changed for the sake of self-preservation.

Was I guilty of the same thing? Planning to leave him for the sake of the children?

These were my thoughts as we sat parked in the tall grass. A small plane revved its engine in the distance, preparing for takeoff. Abruptly, Jack straightened up. "Do you realize how much money we could make?" he said.

His mood had shifted from serious to lighthearted.

"How much?" I asked. "How much?"

"I don't know. A lot more than I made selling television ads."

"*Sounds* like a great opportunity. But I think we should sleep on it."

"Yeah. For about thirty seconds."

"Jack! I mean it."

"Oh, baby, don't fret."

I could tell he was feeling good now, better than he'd felt in months. Years, maybe. His mood was light, as if he'd been set free.

He struggled in the cramped front seat to maneuver his tall frame over the stick shift, displaying the grace of a fat lady in a tight skirt. When he finally reached me, he gave me a short kiss. His expression was playful as he unzipped my jeans.

"Wait," I said. "What if somebody comes over here?" My enthusiasm for what he had in mind was minimal, his past behavior still fresh in my mind.

"Don't worry. Nobody uses this road." He lowered his body onto me.

"Are you sure?" I grunted. "You're squishing me."

"I'm sure." He tried to shift his weight and banged his knee on the window handle. "Ouch, damnit!"

Now half-willing, I made an astute observation. "Jack, this won't work."

"Oooh, yes it will." As gently as possible, he tried to pull down my jeans and undies at the same time.

"Ow! You're breaking my back."

"Oops, sorry."

I squirmed under him.

"Ouch!" Through clenched teeth, he asked with utmost politeness, "My sweet, could you please get your knee out of my groin?"

"And where would you suggest I put it, Romeo?"

"Anywhere but there, my dearest."

I giggled as we struggled to change positions.

"Aaagh!" he yelled.

"Now what?"

"Somebody goosed me!"

"The gear shift!"

My giggles ballooned into guffaws that swiftly captured my husband's funny bone. The pitch of our combined laughter bounded up the scale to a gleeful, pulsing soprano, our haw haw's and hee hee's throbbing noisily at high C. Wedged between the dashboard and the passenger seat, we laughed helplessly until tears rolled down our cheeks. We laughed at our ridiculous entanglement; we laughed away months of pent-up frustration and bitterness; we laughed at the giddy prospect of a brighter future. We laughed and laughed.

"Jack, Jack," I gasped, when finally I could speak. "This really won't work!"

"Be*leeeve* me, it will," he said. By now he was kneeling on the floor, one long leg hooked around the stick shift, his other leg bent sharply in a V with the foot jammed under the glove compartment. "This *will* work, damnit, if I have to break both my legs to do it!"

And somehow . . . it did work.

It wasn't the most passionate lovemaking we'd ever experienced. It could have been the most excruciating, though no bones were broken. Perhaps it was the most needed.

Jack popped open the passenger door and strained to extricate his twisted body. "God," he grunted, as he tried to straighten his legs. "This must be what they mean by 'bent out of shape.'"

We laughed again.

Chapter 3
Marilyn

Jack picked up Jerry Green at LaGuardia Airport the following week. When the girls and I heard the crunch of tires on the driveway, we raced to the front door to meet the man about whom Jack had been talking nonstop.

I extended my hand to Jerry, apprehensive, afraid he might be too good to be true. "It's nice to meet you," I said, noting his pale blue see-through shirt and his oiled hair, a style unique among our friends. He was at least six foot one, like Jack, with tanned skin and eyes the color of root beer.

Pom Pom, our brown miniature poodle, jumped up and down to say hello. Jerry bent to pet her and rub her belly, and she wiggled happily.

The dog likes him, I thought. *A good sign.*

Jack introduced our daughters, in order of size. Jerry smiled broadly at each of them as they were presented. He shook hands first with Lynne, seventeen. "How do you do?" she said quietly. She studied Jerry with her huge blue eyes, making a quick judgment, and then stepped away, unimpressed. Next came Evan, fifteen, who raised her freckled face to Jerry, shyly greeted him, and then turned to me and rolled her eyes. Thirteen-year-old Diane, whose love of fun matched her father's, stepped forward. "*How* do you do?" she said, wearing an impish grin that suggested she in no way took this man seriously. And finally, Heather, eleven, a petite composite of all her sisters. She raised a limp arm to shake hands, her giggles rendering her helpless to do anything more. Jerry laughed too. "Oh, what a cute little face." He pinched her cheek, and Heather pulled away, rubbing her cheek and frowning.

Lynne glared at Jerry. "Hmmph," she mumbled. She nodded at her sisters, and they bounded off in their own directions, their haste bordering on rudeness.

Watching my daughters disappear, I made a mental note to work on their manners. And if Jerry was again overcome by Heather's "cute little face," I would casually mention that Heather disliked pinches.

I led Jerry and Jack into our cream-colored living room. An earlier resident had taken down the wall between the front and back parlors, and they were now one long room. The front of the house was where we kept the piano and more formal furniture, and the back end was more inviting with its fireplace and built-in bookshelves. Our guest quickly surveyed the room and nodded his approval. "Lovely," he said.

"Please sit down," Jack said, since Jerry seemed to be waiting to be asked.

He chose a seat near the fireplace, then turned to me and smiled. "I have a little gift for you." He reached into his pocket and brought out a small white square of cloth. "Open your hand." He laid the cloth in my palm and then sat back to watch me open it.

I could feel the men's eyes on me as I held my palm open and carefully lifted each corner of the cloth. A strangely-shaped gold nugget sat in the center.

"That is what gold looks like when it comes out of the ground," Jerry said.

I weighed it in my hand, surprised that a piece of gold no bigger than the tip of my pinky could be so heavy. It had a dull finish, unlike gold jewelry, and was the shape of a dried lima bean, dented and irregularly shaped. I smiled at Jerry. "I've never seen raw gold before. Thank you." I passed it to Jack, who inspected it carefully.

"You'll see plenty more." Jerry's voice was confident. "You should ask Jack to have that put on a chain for you. As a reminder of what is to come."

I glanced at Jack. As I guessed, he looked annoyed at Jerry's suggestion of what he should do for his wife.

Appearing not to notice, Jerry looked around the room. "You have a lovely home, at least from what I've seen. How long have you lived here?"

"About eight years," I said.

"It must be nice to stay in one place that long. It seems like I've been on the go ever since the war." He began to talk about his World War II days, when he was a member of the US armed services, as he called it, working behind German lines for the OSS, the forerunner of the CIA. "I still have shrapnel in my leg from an old war wound. It sets off the metal detectors they use to spot hijackers at airports." He laughed. "You should see the commotion that causes." He took a wallet from his back pocket, pulled out a card, and proudly held it up. "The State Department gave me this. It gets me through to the gate for international flights. Without setting off the alarm." He passed it to each of us. Though it was no bigger than a driver's license, his connection to the State Department made me believe there was much more to learn about this man.

"And speaking of traveling," he said, "you would love Brazil." He talked for a few minutes about the exotic animals, including the barracuda in a river near his home and the three-toed sloth in his yard, and then he returned to his war stories.

I studied Jerry while he spoke. His voice was moderate, never rising, yet somehow more intense in the dramatic parts. His demeanor was polished, like his nails, and he gave off an aura of importance that made me feel privileged to have him in our living room. He was not good-looking by my standards, but I found his ebony hair and intelligent brown eyes attractive in an earthy way. His full lips and remarkably large teeth worked together to enunciate every word. I watched, engrossed, as he spoke.

Jack leaned forward, his arms on his thighs, seeming to devour the tales of Jerry's war escapades. Though he had been too young to participate, he was fascinated with World War II and admired men who had seen action. His older brother was one of them, a fighter pilot who had spent a year and a half in a German prison camp. Based on Jerry's war experience, we guessed he must be about fifty, the same as Jack's brother.

* * *

That evening, Jack and I took Jerry to dinner at the Breezy Harbor Club on Long Island Sound. After holding out as long as we could, Jack had reluctantly downgraded us to house membership, which meant we could eat there but not use the other facilities. The change would be effective the end of June, only two weeks away. The beginning of school vacation.

We sat with Jerry in the Victorian clubhouse dining room, overlooking the Sound. In the distance, the wind pulled a race of tiny sailboats across the horizon. Jerry drank in the view. "Well," he said, "here I am in Connecticut again. I was born here, you know. In Berlin."

"I didn't know there was a Berlin, Connecticut," I said.

"Yes indeed. I was born there." He also told us he had attended boarding school in Switzerland while his parents ran a successful import/export business out of Panama. After World War II, he and a friend had operated a prosperous sweater factory in Trenton. "Things were doing fine until the union and the mob moved in. So," he said, "we closed it down."

He noticed one of the diners at a table across the room. "Isn't that Frank Goldberg, the movie producer?"

"Do you know him?" Jack asked, surprised.

"My associate and I tried to do business with him a few years ago when we were acquiring old films for television syndication. Which maybe you can help us with. But Frank. Tough?" He laughed. "We were lucky to get out of there with our skin! Besides which, the man has a very foul mouth."

"That's Frank," Jack said, "with his F word."

Jerry Green's acquaintance with Frank Goldberg was one of many new facts we added to our list that evening.

Chapter 4
Jack Kelley

So far Jerry's visit was going well. Marilyn hadn't threatened to hire a divorce lawyer or have me committed. I think she was intrigued by Jerry, like I was. The man's interests were broad. He'd obviously done his homework on running a business in Brazil. I had come home from Miami thinking that all his enterprises sounded like reasonable ventures that would generate needed income. Despite the necessary fact-finding that lay ahead, the idea of living and working in Brazil, building an international business, gave me more energy than I'd felt in months. Especially after eleven hard years at Taylor & Company. All the late nights entertaining clients. The office politics. The damage to my home life. I had sensed Marilyn might take the girls and go to her mother's. I was definitely ready for a change. I would do anything to keep our family together.

* * *

The morning after our dinner at the club, I drove Jerry to City Island—a small spot of land with marinas and restaurants on Long Island Sound, between New Rochelle and the Bronx—to look at fiberglass airboats. An airboat's engine and propeller are mounted above board, so it can skim over shallow water, mud, and even marshland as fast as fifty-five miles per hour. This would be a boon for Brazilian farmers who now traveled over muddy terrain by horse or jeep. An airboat would cover the same territory in less than half the time.

The plan was to buy them used and lease them to the farmers. Eventually, we could expand all over South America.

We picked up brochures for further study.

The following day Jerry and I visited the New York showroom of a good friend of mine, Vince Warner. His family owned a large furniture manufacturing company. Vince said he'd welcome another source of hardwood to use in their furniture frames. Brazilian lumber was plentiful. The arrangement would be good for Vince, good for Jerry, and good for me.

Despite these trips, Jerry and I spent much of his week-long visit in the cool of our living room. Jerry would sit in what had become his favorite green chair, legs stretched out in front of him. Always in a long-sleeved shirt, with his Gucci loafers and Rolex watch. I paced back and forth in less formal attire—red sailing pants and a polo shirt. Sometimes, Marilyn would sit in the matching green chair, listening and asking questions.

We talked about potential businesses. One thought gave birth to another. I'd always been an idea man. It would be nice to have help with one or two of them. I suggested making bodysuits—leotards with a snap crotch to wear under skirts or pants—for a friend who had recently started designing and producing them. Another possibility was to open a Cessna distributorship. I dreamed of flying my own plane to businesses in out-of-the-way places, and I could see the benefit for others in South America to do the same. Jerry suggested importing government-subsidized prefab housing for the Brazilian military and starting a fast-food business.

"They sell fresh fruit juice and ices from open storefronts," he said. "You walk right in off the sidewalk. Jinx Falkenberg, the radio personality, and her brother started a chain called Bob's a few years ago, where they sell American hamburgers and soft drinks. They're making a bloody fortune. And believe me, there's plenty room for more. The sidewalks in Rio are always crowded. It never gets cold there." He laughed. "It gets hot as Hades, but they still have to eat."

As enticing as some projects seemed, we both agreed that gold should be the number one priority. When we met in Miami, Jerry had told me confidentially that gold would be decontrolled in about four years. Once it went on the open market, the price would rise from its current thirty-five dollars an ounce to five or six hundred. He said his information came from reliable sources. When I asked who, he said he had contacts in the US government. It went with the territory.

He proposed we get a license to trade gold, start buying it at today's prices, store it and wait. Once it was decontrolled and the price skyrocketed, we'd sell at a huge profit. All legal, he assured me.

When I told Marilyn about the project, she was skeptical. She thought it sounded too good to be true.

I asked Jerry one afternoon to explain his calculations to her.

He leaned back in his chair and said, "My associate in Munich will buy up to thirty kilos of unrefined gold per month. Which is a lot of gold, by the way." He pulled a small calculator from his pocket. "Let's be conservative. A mere fifteen kilos would bring in $37,049 at Germany's price of $93.38 an ounce. Every month. Twelve months a year."

"That's Troy ounces?" I asked. "Twelve ounces to the pound?"

Jerry smiled his approval. "Yes indeed. And in *five* years, you can figure five or six times that much."

Marilyn still looked doubtful. She told me later she thought Jerry's numbers were too precise. Would it really be that easy? Or was he making it up?

When she asked Jerry about a profit, he said that after labor costs, production and transportation, we would make 20 percent. With the help of his trusty calculator, he established that even if we sold only five kilos a month, we'd make $10,000. Times twelve. "But remember," he said, "that's the tip of the iceberg. We'd save the bulk of it until trading began on the *open* market, wait for the price to reach five hundred at least, and *then* start selling." Pleased, he reached down to scratch the dog's ears.

I couldn't help but smile.

His plan was to first form a corporation to buy and sell precious and semi-precious stones and minerals. Then I would go to Washington to apply for a trader's license.

Jerry would work on the Brazilian end. "We'll make Pedro Da Silva an officer of the corporation. He's the man who works for me in Belèm. He'll apply for the license in his name, since licenses are issued only to Brazilians. And that," he said, "will put us in the gold business."

* * *

To me, the plan sounded logical and well thought out. But wanting to know more about Jerry himself, I invited him for lunch at the Breezy Harbor Club. We sat on the porch with a view of the harbor. Yachts rocked at their moorings and small waves blinked in the sun like sequins in a spotlight.

I began the conversation by saying, "You know, Jerry, you're a very intriguing guy. I must admit, that's an attractive feature. But from the viewpoint of doing business, it's a major concern. I mean, what do you *really* do? You say you have business interests all over the world. But for all I know, that's bullshit. You're asking me to be your partner and move my wife and four daughters from a safe, reasonably good life in Greenwich USA to an unpredictable South American environment. I need to know more. I need to trust you completely."

For a long minute, Jerry stared at the water. "I don't often talk about it. And you'll understand why, once I do." He hesitated, appearing reluctant to go on. "I . . . uh . . . occasionally do consulting work for the US government. My OSS background and my present need to travel worldwide for business make it a perfect fit."

I leaned forward. "Okay. Tell me more."

"Well." He looked around to see if anyone was near. "I contribute information to one of the intelligence bodies that reports to the executive and judicial branches." He lowered his voice even further. "Undercover work."

"Come on, Jerry. Be more specific."

Jerry's face was somber. He related a story about the failed Bay of Pigs invasion and how the Kennedy brothers reneged on their promise to supply air cover and sea support to the Cuban exiles. "The Kennedys pulled their support. *After* the action had begun. And here it is, 1973, twelve years later, and the full story still hasn't come out. I have access to such information." He paused. "The Cubans were mad as hell. And they haven't forgotten, either. That's something we have to watch."

I slapped the table. "What does that have to do with you?"

"As you know," Jerry said, a slight edge to his voice, "I've been traveling to South America. Right now, communist guerrillas are infiltrating new territory. Every day Salvador Allende is closer to handing over Chile to the communists. Believe me. I know. I've been there." He relaxed. "So you see why I have to be closed mouth about my travels."

I drummed my fingers on the table. "Come on, Jerry. It's me, Jack. Your potential partner. I have a lot to lose."

Jerry frowned. He slid a spoon back and forth between his fingers and stared at it, as if an answer would appear. Then he leaned forward and spoke quietly. "Do you remember about a year ago when Henry Kissinger took a spur-of-the-moment trip to Miami?"

"Vaguely."

"Well, my friend, I was one of the people who met with him there. Once in a while the data I contribute to the government require further detailing, and I get an invitation I can't refuse." He chuckled at his little mafia joke. "Such as meeting with Dr. Kissinger in Miami. Naturally, I can't tell you much, except it was South-America related. So. If you find my behavior a little mysterious at times, I hope now you'll understand why."

I lit a cigarette. "Keep going."

Jerry cleared his throat. "Here's something else that will send chills down your spine. I've been told by a reliable source that the Russians have established nuclear warheads in Egypt's Alexandria Harbor. The way they operate is to create a distraction in one place and then quietly infiltrate someplace else. Very disheartening, I'm afraid. But you didn't hear about the warheads here. As a matter of fact, it would be best if you forgot it altogether."

I squinted at the water, saying nothing, my cigarette burning in my fingers. As far as I knew, that story hadn't made the press.

"I'm sorry, my friend," Jerry said. "I have to be secretive about my comings and goings. I can't jeopardize my contacts or myself." He stared intently at me. "I hope you understand."

I faced him, keeping my expression noncommittal.

Jerry continued. "And as far as my business is concerned, well . . . you already know about that. Come to Brazil and see for yourself. In fact, I wouldn't have it any other way. And then, I sincerely hope you'll join me. I think we would work well together." He leaned back and smiled. "My little consultancy is a nice bit of synergy, wouldn't you say? It helps me *and* it gives me a chance to help the State Department."

If Jerry was telling the truth—and his unpublicized information indicated he was—the business should be golden anywhere in the world. I wanted badly to believe he and the business were legitimate. Working with a man in Jerry's position appealed to my entrepreneurial spirit, as well as to my sense of adventure. Not to mention my need for income. And keeping the family together.

"It's all very interesting," I said. "But I need time to think."

"Take all the time you need," Jerry said. "And if you want references, I've got them."

"Good. I'd like to see them."

He took a business card from his wallet and gave it to me. "You can contact the Mellon Bank in Pittsburgh. Ask for this man. His number's there. And you can call Mr. Fitzgerald at the New York Trust Company in Manhattan."

I wrote Fitzgerald's name on the back of the card.

"You'll rest easy after you speak with them," Jerry said.

That night in bed, I told Marilyn about Jerry's "other life." "He doesn't want anyone to know this. For obvious reasons." I paused. "I'll bet he's with the CIA."

"It would make sense." She was quiet, thinking. "It's impressive," she said. "But let's wait and see how the references turn out."

Chapter 5
Marilyn

The next morning, Jack went upstairs to his den to call the names Jerry had given him. I was in the kitchen, cleaning up after breakfast. I felt a presence behind me and spun around, surprised to see Jerry standing there holding a small bundle. He asked if I knew of a laundry nearby.

I later regretted my offer to take care of it for him, when I stared at the vivid imprint my iron had left on the sleeve of his blue shirt. *I've ruined his shirt. He'll think I'm just a flighty housewife.* I shook out the shirt and neatly folded it, the damaged sleeve out of sight. If I was lucky, Jerry wouldn't need to wear it before he left—and hopefully not at a meeting with Henry Kissinger.

Jack received a glowing report from Jerry's references. He called Howard Fox, an attorney friend who worked for a prestigious Manhattan law firm, and asked him to dig a little deeper to see if there was anything Jerry wouldn't want him to know.

* * *

When the men weren't talking business, Jerry entertained Jack and me with stories of his world travels. Though he tried to make friends with the girls, they went out of their way to avoid him, their hostility barely concealed.

"He's gross," our youngest daughter, Heather, said. "He always pinches my cheek." She rubbed the side of her face. "It hurts."

One day Lynne, our oldest girl, came into the kitchen and asked me why we would want to live in Brazil. She sat down at the table and I joined her. She wore her usual ragged jeans and drab-colored shirt.

"It's a great opportunity," I said. "One that will help the whole family."

"Hmmph."

I looked into her big blue eyes, considering what to tell her. Lynne was mature for seventeen, wise in some—though not all—ways. "You know," I began, "how Daddy was when he worked at Taylor? Losing his temper all the time? Over lots of things?" I avoided mentioning her hippy friends.

"Oh, yeah," she said emphatically. She shivered and pulled her knees up, wrapping her arms around them.

"That was terrible and I'm sorry you had to go through it." I still resented Jack for his temper displays. "I'm not making excuses for your dad. But I do know that his job was unbearable. Carl Magnus turned on him, and so did Rudy Schultz."

"Wow." She leaned forward, her eyes keen, hoping for a bit of inside gossip. "But you guys went to the Giant games with the Magnuses. I thought you were friends."

"So did I."

"And we used to go skiing with the Schultzes."

"I know. I know. So you can imagine how Daddy felt. Betrayed. Hurt. Angry. Frustrated. Unfortunately, he took out his feelings on us."

"Yeah!" She thought for a minute. "But can't he find another job in the United States?"

"He's been looking everywhere, but nothing has worked out. He was getting worried that he couldn't take care of us for much longer. That's a pretty scary feeling when you have five people relying on you."

Lynne sighed deeply, as if carrying her father's burden.

"Then Jerry came along and offered Daddy a partnership in his business." I took hold of Lynne's hands. "With Jerry, he can have a whole new career and be much happier. No more temper. Plus, he'll make a good income. It'll be better for all of us."

"We'd have to move, right?"

"Probably. But I'm not sure when. So we won't worry about that yet." I looked at Lynne's troubled face. "We don't have a lot of choices, honey. We just want to do what's best for our family. You girls matter more than anything in the world."

I squeezed her hands. "We'll be fine. You'll see." Ninety-five percent of me believed that.

Later that night, I told Jack I was worried about the girls. "I hope they can adjust to all the changes we have to make. Like maybe moving to Brazil."

On the other hand, moving to Brazil might be just what we needed. The Greenwich kids lived in a culture of money and privilege. Drinking and drugs were popular, and many had their own cars. Lynne commuted to school in our old VW, which the police discovered was used to smoke pot during breaks. One of Evan's sixteen-year-old friends would visit her carrying a 2 liter pitcher of beer that he sipped from like a mug. Diane liked to test her limits as well. The most frightening was taking her little sister for a joyride in our Toyota at age fourteen. And that just scratched the surface of what we *knew* was going on. It would be fair to say that our daughters' antics contributed to Jack's angry outbursts.

"If we move to Brazil," Jack said, "the girls will have so much to see and do, they won't have time to be homesick." He hugged me. "Don't worry, my little worrier. Kids are resilient."

* * *

Toward the end of Jerry's visit, Jack's lawyer friend, Howard Fox, called. "The man seems to be okay," he reported. "I see no problems in doing business with him."

It was all Jack needed to hear. He and Jerry planned Jack's first visit to Brazil. He would see Jerry's enterprises for himself.

Chapter 6
Jack

The 707's wheels touched down on the short Belèm landing strip at daybreak. Belèm was in northern Brazil on the Amazon River. I grabbed my aluminum carry-on with my .45 automatic hidden under the false bottom Jerry had helped me build. As I reached the plane's door, a blast of intense heat hit me. A mass of tall tropical trees stood along the runway, erect as soldiers on guard. Thin sun rays pierced their dense canopy and lit millions of floating specks. Somewhere in that fertile darkness, a choir of birds offered their welcome. The Amazon jungle at sunrise.

Jerry met me at the gate and introduced me to a young man. Pedro Da Silva shook my hand. His eyes reached the level of my chest. "Alo, Kel-lay."

"You've just heard your last name pronounced in Portuguese," Jerry said.

"I wouldn't have recognized it." Maybe the language difference would be tougher than I expected.

"Da Silva will be our Brazilian liaison, so to speak," said Jerry. "As an officer of our corporation, he'll provide the required Brazilian signature on all legal documents."

Da Silva's coloring made him a pint-sized Brazilian copy of Jerry—a small ranch house standing next to a two-story colonial. He drove us to the small estate the Greens were renting.

"This used to be a private club," Jerry said proudly as we walked toward a white stucco building with a red tile roof. A matching outbuilding stood nearby.

Jerry introduced me to his wife, Starr. She was as fair as Jerry was dark. A tall blonde with blue eyes, long shapely white legs, and brightly painted toes. Very attractive.

The Greens gave me a quick tour of their newly renovated, spacious three-bedroom home. The coolness of the stucco walls and tile floors were a welcome relief from the tropical heat.

Afterwards, everybody relaxed in the shade by the large pool. We drank strong Brazilian coffee and ate pastries made by the servants, who lived in the outbuilding. I watched two Indian girls, about eleven or thirteen, the ages of my youngest daughters, scrubbing the tiles around the pool in slow circles of suds.

"Aren't they a little young for that?" I asked.

Some, Jerry told me, were even younger. Their families couldn't afford to feed them, so the children were let out to work for a small wage, three decent meals a day, and a clean place to sleep that didn't leak when it rained.

While Jerry told stories about life in Brazil, Starr gazed at him in a way that left no doubt about how she felt. She had been a showgirl at the Latin Quarter in New York. Also the Coca Cola girl in magazines and on national billboards.

Why had she given up a promising career to follow Jerry to Brazil? For love? Or money?

While Jerry talked, Da Silva sat up straight, his face bright as he listened, though he spoke little English. I smoked Winstons between bites of sweetness and sips of muddy energy. I wondered if Jerry was everyone's hero.

By bedtime, the temperature had dropped quite a bit, much to my relief. I had a feeling air conditioning was out of the question in that part of the country.

* * *

In the morning, Jerry and I flew to Macapà, two hundred miles west of Belèm, to see the gold mine. The pilot easily set down the small plane on a strip that was no more than a dirt road.

Off to one side, a short muscular man stood next to a jeep, waiting. Jerry introduced me to Victor Heusi. "Victor and I met in Africa," Jerry said. "He's a veteran of the French Foreign Legion. And, a fellow Knight of Malta."

I knew that the Knights of Malta dated back to medieval times and was a benevolent organization working for the good of mankind. The men's membership was reassuring.

Heusi pressed his coarse, powerful hand against mine while he squinted at me through one good eye. The other eye, a pupil-less pale blue disk, gravitated to the right as if to view the wide jagged scar that snaked along that side of his weather-beaten face. A battle-worn leather holster with a .38 revolver rested on the hip of the former mercenary. A mean-looking bastard if ever there was one.

Heusi took us for a jarring ten-minute ride through fields and high thick brush. When we reached a clearing at the edge of tall dense trees, he stopped the jeep and everybody got out.

Huesi's lack of height did not diminish his toughness. It compacted it. His faded khaki shirt barely contained his thick barrel chest, and his huge biceps and triceps bulged beneath the torn-off sleeves. We stood and talked near a makeshift table and two wooden folding chairs. Huesi's rumbling voice plowed through the air like a tank through the jungle, punctuated by a rolling, gurgling cough. Enhanced, no doubt, by the dirty hand rolled cigarettes he chain-smoked. He spoke English—one of fourteen languages—with barely a trace of an accent. A hard-nosed intelligence shone through the tough exterior, and his good eye, brown and glinting, hinted at a zest for fun. I hated to think what his idea of fun might be.

Heusi led us down a path that had been cut through thick jungle to the spot in the river where a group of native men worked. This, Huesi said, was where he had recently discovered a large deposit of gold with the help of the Indians he employed. "They have great lung power," he said. "They can dig and scrape on the river bottom for minutes at a time with only a mask and a snorkel." He pointed to a wooden trough. "We set up this sluice to sift the gold from the silt and the pebbles."

We watched the workers carry their baskets up from the river. They were dressed in G-strings and wore their masks and snorkels on top of their heads. They emptied their baskets into the sluice and then headed back to the river for another dive.

Huesi said, "We're going to add a dredge to speed things up."

Jerry said, "That's where our money would go. The dredge would increase our production substantially. We'd stockpile most of it until the price went up, though we'd sell some to keep the mine going and establish good relations with clients. We'd transport the gold up the river by boat to Belèm. There it would be transferred to storage or to the buyer. As I said, "We'd be in the gold business from the ground up. It will take some capital and hard work, but the reward will be well worth it." Beaming at the burly soldier of fortune, Jerry said, "Of course, we have the right person managing the operation." Then he made an astonishing announcement. "Victor is also my partner in the Macapà gold mine."

Minutes later, Huesi excused himself to talk to the Indians. By then, I was ready to explode with the obvious question: "Why the hell would you team up with a man like Victor Heusi?"

"Very simple, my friend." Jerry appeared smug as he listed the reasons. "Nobody dares cross Victor. That is, if he values his life." He watched with admiration as his partner talked and gestured to his engrossed audience. "Victor understands the jungle like he was born here. The Indians obey him like he's some kind of god. He's got them spooked with that wandering eye and that fancy scar. He treats them well, though. Also—and this is very important—he's honest. I trust him completely. Even with my life. And I know few men I can say that about."

Point taken. And it works two ways. "I guess," I said, "the criteria for choosing a partner in the jungle are different than in the boardroom."

"That they are, my friend. That they are."

"On second thought," I said, "a man who takes nobody's shit, commands respect, knows his way around, is fair, honest and trustworthy . . . The corporate world would do well to use the same criteria."

If those had been the standards at Taylor & Company, I might still be sitting in the general sales manager's office concentrating on selling TV ads. In fact, my whole corporate experience made the Brazil deal even more appealing. It made forming a partnership with Victor Huesi a good move.

Jerry and I finished our visit and left for Belèm that evening. On the plane, I leaned back against the seat and closed my eyes, remembering our conversation in the living room about potential income. *This could happen.*

* * *

The next morning began at 9 a.m.—7 a.m. New York time, since Brazil is farther east than the United States. "We're going to see Carlos Alberto, my lawyer," Jerry said. "He knows his way around and he'll be helpful in our dealings. Who's good. Who's bad. Contracts and such." He gave me a sympathetic smile. "I have to warn you, though. His whole family will probably be there. They've never seen an American before." He added quickly, "Besides me."

Alberto lived on a prosperous Belèm street lined with stucco houses colored in pinks, tans, yellows, and whites, all with red tile roofs. The yards, full of tropical plants and trees, were surrounded by high stucco walls, twelve to eighteen inches wide and thickly blanketed on top with hearty doses of broken glass. *Where are the people?* I wondered. Guard dogs ran loose inside many of the yards. Others had heavy iron gates to guard the openings, some electric, some manned by guards.

"The residents are forced to barricade themselves inside their gates because of the constant robberies," Jerry explained. "Poverty is everywhere. It breeds thieves."

Would Belèm be a safe place to live?

A guard let us through the gate to Alberto's home. He waited for us at the front door. His slow-blinking eyes had long lashes that gave him a calm, innocent look. He spoke softly and slowly, English obviously not his first language. He led us inside to a room full of excited relatives. They quickly surrounded me, nudging each other to get a better look. Alberto introduced me to his parents, his in-laws, his sisters, his brothers, and his cousins, who all came in a variety of sizes. They stared at me and talked in Portuguese. The women giggled. The men shook my hand and smiled. Or grunted. Or bowed. I nodded politely.

Afterwards, Da Silva drove Alberto, Jerry, and me to lunch in downtown Belèm, where I had my first sight of a South American seaport. We ate at the rooftop restaurant of one of the city's three high-rise buildings. From the thirteenth floor, Belèm looked like a photograph in *National Geographic.* Red tile roofs. Milling crowds.

After a meal of fried white fish, stewed okra, and a popular black bean dish called *feijoida,* the men took me on a tour of Belèm.

Among the people out in the scalding heat were native Indians and barefoot women carrying bundles on their heads. The Indians' wide eyes, flat noses, and straight, shiny hair made them easily distinguishable from the blacks of African heritage. I was told that their dark skin put the blacks on the lowest rung of the social ladder and made them the poorest. They were forced to exist on a yamlike food that was cheap. And fish, which was plentiful. All fried in animal fat, which in turn made them fat. Soda was popular on all social levels. Judging by the empty cans littering the sidewalks, Coke was the favorite.

Food stalls lined the street. Piles of mangoes, papayas, pineapples, bananas, grapefruit, oranges, lemons, and limes were arranged in bright colors worthy of an artist's canvas. The fruit surrounded a blender with jaws waiting to chew up any combination and spit out a tasty drink. Some stalls sold only *cafèzinho*—coffee served in demitasse cups half-filled with sugar, the energy of Brazil. My first sampling of the muddy brown syrup sent a jolt of high propane surging through my veins. If I accompanied the coffee with a few Brazilian cigarettes—which could only be described as tough—I felt like I'd been plugged into a light socket. I understood why the Brazilians always seemed ready to explode.

In the heat, everybody's shirts were soaked in minutes. Except Jerry's. He never seemed to sweat. In Brazil, Miami, or Greenwich. With his dark coloring, he could have passed as a Brazilian. Considering his undercover work, I wondered if he'd ever played that role.

We walked past countless shacks on stilts. Crowded together, the shacks spilled out over the river, like pictures I had seen of Hong Kong. I wondered how anybody could live in such hovels. Once the sun baked the corrugated metal roofs, they must have been like ovens.

The absence of running water and electricity forced the inhabitants to dump, drink, and bathe in the same muddy part of the Amazon. But nobody got sick. They'd been doing it for centuries.

As we neared the docks, my sense of smell was brutally attacked by a pile of rotting garbage, moistened by a tropical rainfall and then seasoned by the sun. While I gagged, my Brazilian friends barely seemed to notice the stench.

Unaware of my digestive troubles, Jerry explained that Belèm was the major seaport for northeastern

Brazil. The main export was raw lumber from the jungle, which arrived via the Amazon River.

In very poor English, and with Jerry's help, Alberto told me that one of Belèm's major imports was contraband. He sadly shook his head, his long eyelashes lowered. Jerry added, "Unfortunately, it brings the riffraff."

Then Alberto pointed out a four-story wooden warehouse built over the water where, Jerry explained, German U-boats reportedly refueled during World War II out of sight of US planes that were on their way to Recife—a coastal city on the easternmost bulge of Brazil—and then to Dakar, Africa. He said many Germans returned to Brazil after the war. Their influence could be seen throughout the country.

A wealth of history was waiting to be discovered in Brazil, and I was eager to share it with my family. To get them into a totally different environment and away from the pressure of corporate life.

After our tour of the city, we returned to Alberto's house. Jerry and Alberto excused themselves, leaving Da Silva and me alone on the veranda.

We smiled at each other as if to say, "Now what?"

I spoke slowly and loudly. "Do you speak English?"

Da Silva answered, "*Sim. Un poco.*"

"You know Green long time?" Jerry had informed me that Brazilians called men by their surnames and women by their given names.

"Mmm." Da Silva nodded and smiled. "Grrreen good *homen.*" He inhaled deeply and his chest expanded. "Grrreen *esplendido*! *Magnificente*!"

"Why you say that?"

"Grrreen *muito importante.* Grrreen *muito grande.* Brraseel Aerro Forrrsay *es taxi para* Grrreen. Grrreen *aqui.*" He flung an arm to the right. "Grrreen *ali.*" He flung an arm to the left. "*En* Aerro Forrrsay plane. *Comprende?*"

I guessed what Da Silva was trying to say: Green used the Brazilian Air Force as a taxi service. "*Si.*" Spanish, but close enough.

Da Silva smiled slyly and tapped his finger to his head. "I know *porque.*"

I winked. "*Porque?*"

"*Porque.* How you say? Bee-uze-ness."

"Business," I said.

"*Sim, sim.*" Da Silva's head bobbed enthusiastically. "Grrreen bee-uze-ness . . . *Frances* planes *para Brasil. Agora* . . . *Frances* planes *Brasil* planes." He held up his hands in a gesture of *Voila!*

Slowly I spelled it out. "Green . . . did business . . . with the French . . . to buy planes . . . for the Brazilian Air Force?"

"*Sim. Sim,*"Da Silva crowed. "Grrreen *e Brasil governamente* . . ." He almost purred as he crossed the first two fingers of both hands to show Jerry's relationship with the Brazilian government.

"Aaah, Grrreen." Da Silva sighed fondly. "Hymie Bonjay."

"Hymie Bonjay," I said, puzzled. "Hymie Bonjay." I shook my head.

Da Silva held up seven fingers and shook them at me. "Oh oh *siete.* Oh oh *siete.*"

"Oh oh. Seven. Oh oh seven. Oh!" I said. "Double oh seven. James Bond. Well, of course."

When Jerry and Alberto joined us on the veranda, I half-expected Da Silva to genuflect.

I wondered about the ratio of truth to fiction in this tale. Had Da Silva, undisguisedly enamored of Jerry, embellished the facts? Or had Jerry, aware of Da Silva's admiration, padded the story for Da Silva's listening—and telling—pleasure?

One more possibility did exist: the story was true.

* * *

The next day was Sunday. Jerry and Starr invited about twenty friends, including wives and children, for a barbecue. Jerry flipped beef ribs and hamburgers on the grill and proved to be as gracious a host as he had been a guest in Greenwich. In spite of the heat, he appeared as cool as ever.

Most of the men spoke English well enough to talk freely. While the children swam or played games under the almond trees, the women sat by the pool and chatted among themselves. They seemed averse to speaking with me. Was it lack of English? Or lack of status?

Jerry told me that some of the guests were Belèm city officials. Others were higher-ups from the state of Para. "They're in uniform," he added, "because, as you know, Brazil is a military dictatorship." His eyes moved slowly over the guests. "We also have a number of Brazilian army and air force officers. You'll see ranks of major and colonel." He nodded toward a man in civilian clothes and lowered his voice. "That man is a general. His military escorts are out in front with his car."

I nodded, duly impressed.

Some officers were eager to talk, even brag. And judging from what they told me, most appeared to be in intelligence, giving even more credence to Jerry's confidential disclosures about doing odd jobs for the US government on some of his business trips.

One story the officers told was especially interesting. As the men explained, the state of Para covered most of the jungle as well as the territory north of the

Amazon leading to the Guianas. A few years past, as the story went, Che Guevera and a group of his men made a nighttime landing in Para, in the dense jungle near the Amazon shore. They planned to set up a base of operations where they would train a group of guerrillas to aid Castro's encroachment into South and Central America. The officers laughed at Castro. "We call him the Paper Tiger," one said.

According to the men, the Brazilian military learned of the plan and prepared a surprise welcome for their unannounced guests. When Guevera and his men arrived, the Brazilians wiped out the entire force, with the unfortunate exception of Guevera himself. Still, it was a great victory, they proclaimed.

To my knowledge, that event never made the US news. But the officers' rendition of the ambush was elaborate enough for me to believe it had actually happened.

By the end of the barbecue, I was convinced that Da Silva had told the truth. Jerry Green was indeed connected, somehow, some way, to the military intelligence arena, as he had confided back in Greenwich.

* * *

The following day, Jerry and I took a thousand-mile flight on Varig, the national airline, traveling southeast along the Brazilian coast to Recife. We planned a two-day visit with the owners of the fishing enterprise Jerry had mentioned in earlier conversations. Their trawlers dragged mostly for shrimp to sell to the United States, Japan, and Taiwan. Jerry was in the process of acquiring additional export licenses for them.

The English-speaking Brazilians received us warmly. I found their long-established operation busy and healthy. They said they would be happy to have help expanding their markets even further.

"While we're at it," Jerry said to me, "we would simultaneously broker beef." Because Recife was at the easternmost tip of Brazil, it had its own history as the landing place for African slaves a century earlier, and more recently—like Alberto had said—as the jumping-off spot in World War II for US aircraft on their way to Dakar. I saw several old fighter planes still parked at the airport.

Our next stop, four hundred miles down the Atlantic coast from Recife, was Salvador, the charming capital of the state of Bahia, with its largely black population, beautiful beaches, native food, and attractive hotels. Like Belèm, this seaport's major enterprise was lumber, but in a more finished state. Surrounded by the smell of freshly cut wood, I met the owners of a busy sawmill, where large saws turned mahogany and teak logs into beautiful slabs of wood. Raising his voice above the saw's whine, Jerry said, "We could acquire a large supply of lumber here to build low-cost housing for the Brazilian military. A lucrative proposition for us that would help the Brazilians."

From Salvador, we traveled nearly eight hundred miles farther down the coast to Rio de Janeiro. I couldn't help but gawk like a tourist. Mountains and ocean surrounded a busy city crammed with humanity. It seemed to vibrate with tension. Was it too little space? Too much coffee? Or hot South American blood?

On Rio's streets, Volkswagen Beetles were the most popular autos, with Renaults and small Brazilian-made Fords mixed in. The cars darted everywhere, colliding, drivers shouting and shaking fists, and then—with new dents—speeding off again. "Everybody on the road is called Fittipaldi," Jerry explained, "after Emerson Fittipaldi, the race car driver."

We stayed in Copacabana at the Trocadero Hotel on Avenida Atlantica, the boulevard that skirted Rio's beaches in half-moon curves from Leme, through Copa, Leblon, Ipanema, and over to Baha. The four-lane thoroughfare was divided in half by wide center islands paved with small black and white mosaic tiles. Each block was set in a different pattern tarnished with city grime. A blend of pounding waves, car engines, and horns formed a restless background din.

Jerry introduced me to some of his Rio associates and then privately warned me not to trust them. An obvious skepticism existed between Jerry and these men. It heightened my awareness of the growing friendship between my potential business partner and myself.

Jerry's acquaintances boasted that Brazil was a sanctum of corruption. Though not all Brazilians were corrupt, they said, the depravity ranged from poor beggars on the street all the way to high levels of the military dictatorship. "It is the way of life!"

Alberto, who had come down from Belèm, told of a scam he had heard about. His big eyes and long lashes gave him a guileless, vulnerable look, which I suspected he used to his advantage. He related the tale in meager English. Jerry, obviously familiar with the story, filled in the many gaps.

The gist of it was: A freighter loaded with coffee left Santos, near Sao Paulo, and headed up the coast. The captain and the crew—partners in the plan—sailed to Paramaribo, unloaded the coffee, and returned to sea. When they were between Salvador and Recife, they sent out an SOS. The captain radioed that they had a fire aboard and were doing all they could to save the ship and its cargo. Then they scuttled the vessel and watched it sink as they floated safely in their lifeboats. A short time later, they were rescued by a passing ship. The captain, crew, and their partners resold the coffee. The owners of the freighter and of the coffee collected their insurance. Everybody was happy—except, of course, the insurance company.

At the end of Alberto's story, the four other men admired the brilliant scheme. One wore a mocking grin when he said, "*Gracas a Deus* no man lost in grrreat trrragedy!"

I shook my head in disbelief. "Ees South American way to do bee-uze-ness," the men explained. Jerry frowned and said nothing.

Later he reiterated his advice. "You should avoid these people. They are not the type of Brazilians you and your family want to associate with. In South America, we occasionally have to deal with undesirables to fulfill our business obligations. Unfortunately, it's part of the culture."

Many challenges lay ahead. Maybe I should have said good-bye to Jerry and grabbed the next flight to New York when we returned to Belèm that night. But it wasn't my nature to run from a challenge. Besides, this was the best opportunity I had to keep my family together.

* * *

The next morning, I sat with Jerry and Starr by their pool, enjoying the early sun before its intensity forced us to retreat to the shade. Jerry, as usual, was telling stories of his travels. I half listened while I waited for my call to Connecticut to go through—a long, tedious process in that part of the world.

Finally. I went into the house to talk to Marilyn. Once she had assured me the kids were fine, I said, "You should see the Greens' setup. And you'll like Starr."

"That helps," she said. "But more important, have you seen the businesses Jerry mentioned?"

My wife. Always the practical one.

I told her about the fishing and lumber enterprises. "They're successful, ongoing businesses. I saw the fishing boats and the sawmills. I saw how they operate. I met the owners. They seem competent. Efficient."

"What else?" she asked.

The doubt in her voice made me realize how much I wanted this deal to work. I needed to convince her it was the right move.

"We visited the gold mine in Macapà, and I saw how they mine gold. I met Jerry's partner. I'll tell you about him later. What a character."

"But can you trust him?"

"I really think so. He seems like an honest guy. A Knight of Malta." What more could I say? "It's a successful, working mine, Mare. I saw them carry the gold from the river."

"Really? You saw them?" I detected a note of hope.

"Yeah. It's quite a process," I said, encouraged to go on. "They have plans to increase production and make it a successful, ongoing business. "And as far as Jerry goes, his 'other life' seems to be true. I met a group of Brazilian military officers at the Greens' barbecue. They told some stories that confirm what Jerry told me. And his assistant, Pedro Da Silva, added a few more pieces that fit right in. I'll give you details later."

It was time to close the deal, so I said, "I'd say Jerry's reliable and the businesses are real. So . . . we're at the big decision point. What do you want to do?" I held my breath.

"What do *you* want to do?"

"I want to get out of New York, Mare. It's killing me. It's killing us."

"I know," she said. "I know."

"I want to do something different. Show the kids another part of the world. Help the Brazilians. Get out of the rut we're in. Plus, generate a good income."

She was quiet. I sat down and then stood back up.

"Well," she finally said, "you say the business looks good. Jerry's authentic, based on what you've learned. Plus the lawyer's investigation."

"That's right." My grip on the phone grew tighter.

"I want us to be happy together," she said. "We really do need a change. For everybody's sake. I know I'm ready. And you are too." She paused. I didn't speak. Finally she said, "I think we should do it."

I laughed out loud.

"I don't know about you, but my pioneer spirit's calling."

I wanted to hug her. "Mine too, Mare. Big time."

"Living in a foreign country. What a great experience for the kids."

"I can't wait for you and the girls to see this place. So big and beautiful." I pictured my four beautiful daughters running around, discovering new places. Everybody happy.

"This will change our lives, Jack."

"That it will." *Thank God.* It was settled. "Okay. I'll tell Jerry."

"Great. It's a deal."

"Mrs. Kelley, we are about to embark on a new adventure."

"I can't wait," she said. "You know what? We're going to be okay!"

"You better believe it, baby." *We're going to be great!*

* * *

We were about to change a once-in-a-lifetime opportunity into a reality. I walked outside to gather my thoughts before I spoke to Jerry. I lit a cigarette and wandered toward the back of the Greens' yard, into the shadows of the almond trees. As I watched my smoke wind around the leaves, I pictured myself standing in my own yard, planning the next flight to the Macapà gold mine—in my Cessna 185—while my family explored their new home, awed by the jungle, a new and different culture, the vast tropical beauty.

Glory!

When my cigarette was finished, I walked back to the pool to accept Jerry's offer.

He rose from his chair and shook my hand, smiling. "Welcome, partner. It's a pleasure to have you aboard. I know we'll do big things together."

Starr congratulated us. "It'll be wonderful having the Kelleys in Brazil."

The three of us began making plans. We agreed it would be convenient for us to live in Belèm, close to Jerry and close to the projects, especially the gold mine. The fishing business would be next, and then the cattle business.

Though it needed work, the estate next to the Greens' was available. It had a guest house, a huge pool tiled in yellow mosaics, a playground, a stable for twenty horses with room for chickens, an orange grove, and a soccer field. Something for everybody and then some.

But there was one major problem. No English-speaking school. Too big an adjustment for Evan and Lynne in their last two years of high school, with college looming.

"The language problem. It's a tough one," Jerry agreed. "Don't worry, my friend, we'll do what's best for your daughters."

* * *

Marilyn and I were aware there could be enormous consequences to our decision. As far as culture, society, and life in general were concerned, Brazil was as far from Greenwich, Connecticut, as it was from Mars. Yes, it would be an enriching experience. But to pull the girls from all that was familiar and throw them into a foreign world while they were on the rough road to womanhood might harm them in ways we couldn't imagine. I would go out of my way to avoid that end.

Nobody told us it would be easy. I hoped we were doing the right thing. All I had ever wanted was to make a good life for my family.

Chapter 7
Marilyn

When Jack pulled into the driveway, home from Brazil, I ran out to meet him. For the first time in over a year, I was happy to see him when he returned from a trip. He hugged me and then stared at the house. Our old Connecticut Victorian, a massive grande dame, wore two faces: one beaming with charm, the other leering with the never-ending need of repair. "I'll miss this old ark," he said. "But I'll be happy to say good-bye to the cracking plaster and crumbling chimneys."

I barely had time to agree with him before the girls came rushing out. Jack seemed surprised at their welcome. A few months ago, they might have gone to their rooms to avoid him. He embraced each daughter and put his arms around as many of us as he could, and we all walked into the house together.

I had waited for Jack to get home so we could tell the girls together. All six of us gathered in the living room. Shadows of leaves danced on the cream-colored walls. Gold fabric, tied back, hung at the eight tall windows along one side and the front of the long room. Jack leaned on the mantel and I sat nearby, feeling apprehensive. The girls were lined up on the sofa, except for Diane, our third daughter, who lay on the floor, raised on elbows, toes tapping the carpet. Pom Pom, our poodle, was part of the group, bouncing from one to the other. Even Jasmine, our calico cat, joined us, rubbing against everybody's legs, tail pointed heavenward.

"Well, girls," Jack said, "I've got some exciting news. We're moving to Brazil."

The news hung in the air like a cloud of smoke after the fireworks. The girls looked at one another, eyes wide with wonder, and then the questions began. "Why do we have to move to Brazil?" "Do the natives wear bones in their hair?" "Do they speak English in the schools?" "Can our friends visit us?" "Boys too?" "We have to bring the animals." In the end, they reluctantly admitted that it sounded *sort* of exciting. Maybe they'd like Brazil. Maybe they wouldn't.

* * *

Soon after Jack returned from Brazil, Jerry came to Greenwich to help us plan our move. When he walked in the door, Pom Pom jumped up and down with delight. Jerry pursed his full lips and sent her kisses. The four girls were immediately repulsed and disappeared. They thought he looked like a greaser with his heavy gold ring and gold neck chain. Besides, he was basically mucking up their lives. Yet they enjoyed the stories he told on the rare occasions they joined us. Their favorite was about a water buffalo in Brazil that allowed a huge anaconda to wrap itself around his chest, preparing to strangle him to death. "But that big old buffalo wasn't as dumb as he pretended to be," Jerry told them. "He waited until the snake was wound up tight around his middle. And then . . ." He paused, gazing from one to the other. They barely moved. "That old buffalo took in a huge deep breath that seemed to go on forever. And all of a sudden, there was a great explosion—it sounded like a storm of bullets—and a hundred bloody pieces of snake shot into the jungle in all directions."

"Gross!" the girls exclaimed, pleasantly disgusted.

* * *

One morning, Jack went upstairs to his den to make phone calls. I was left alone with Jerry, a good time to ask a question that had been weighing on my mind. We sat in the living room in the matching green chairs. "I've been wondering . . ." I hesitated, suddenly awed by the man and his background.

"Yes?" he said.

"I've been wondering . . . Of all the people you've met in your travels, why did you choose Jack to be your partner?"

Jerry didn't hesitate. "He's smart, he's aggressive, he's got an entrepreneurial spirit, he's easy to get along with, and—this is most important—he's pu-re." He pronounced the last word in two syllables.

"Pure?"

"Yes. He's clean. He has no record. Which is imperative when you're dealing on an international level. You've got to be clean."

Though I was surprised at Jerry's answer, I never asked how he knew Jack was clean. I assumed he had investigated Jack through his government contacts.

It bothered me somewhat, but I had to concede that Jerry had as much right to check *his* potential partner's history as Jack did.

* * *

Jerry pitched in to help organize the big move, and the three of us often chatted over coffee in the dining room. The walls were covered in red flocked wallpaper. A portrait we had found at a thrift shop of a stern-faced woman we called Aunt Bruce peered down from her heavy gold frame over the mantel. Jack usually paced, carrying his coffee cup.

One day, the subject was schools. The Belèm schools spoke strictly Portuguese and were not geared for college. Jerry suggested a boarding school in the States. Or in Switzerland. Preferably Switzerland: English was spoken, the education was unsurpassed, and the girls would be mingling with the cream of society—royalty, sons and daughters of diplomats, children of industrialists.

I had a brief fantasy of my daughters lounging by the pool of an Italian villa. Or having tea with a duchess in an English castle. Or skiing in the Swiss Alps with a handsome scion of an old European family.

No. Switzerland was too far way. What about Rio?

Jerry wore the expression of a concerned uncle. "Rio has a number of private schools. That might be our best solution." He gave us a sympathetic smile. "Don't worry. Believe me, I understand how you feel. I'm a parent too."

He told us he had a twenty-one-year-old son in the merchant marines on Long Island, and a seventeen-year-old daughter who lived with her mother in upstate New York.

"Now, back to the subject of schools in Rio," he said. "I'll have my people check them out for you. It shouldn't take long."

We felt more comfortable knowing Jerry had his own parental concerns. He would be more compassionate about the girls. Lynne, our firstborn, intelligent, sensitive, trying nobly to be the son her father never had; Evan, the quiet diplomat, her sisters' favorite, never giving her parents trouble; Diane, charming and strong-willed, the only one who could provoke her mother to anger; Heather, full of laughter, a friend to animals, a thief of hearts: our darling daughters.

This move would turn their lives upside down. It needed to be as painless as possible—a huge task, a burden of love, deserving every effort.

Chapter 8
Jack

Jerry sat in his favorite chair in our long room and handed me a sheet of letterhead from his briefcase. Printed across the top was: Watkins, Thomas and Witherspoon, Chartered Accountants; Post Office Box 6101; Road Town, Tortola; British Virgin Islands, West Indies. The bottom name on the roster, Robin Eyres, was handwritten in the center of the page.

As Jerry explained it, we would get an attorney in Tortola to set up a holding company. Brazil only allowed a family to take $25,000 a year of earned income out of the country, and the potential for our business was far above that. Robin Eyres would handle incoming letters of credit ranging from $9,600 to $499,000 for a fee of $200 a year. At half a million and up, the fee went to $352.40. As long as 50 percent of the profits emanated from outside the United States, we could pay income tax to the British Virgin Islands at 12 percent. The US rate was at least four times that much.

"Is this legal?" I asked. "Sounds too good to be true."

"I told you, my friend, we won't do anything illegal. This is established procedure for many corporations that do business outside the States. And the British West Indies is happy to cooperate. They end up holding a lot of money."

"It seems like a good arrangement for the British Virgins and the corporations," I said. "But I'm surprised the US tolerates it. They must be missing out on millions."

"The US doesn't like it, but that's the law."

We named the new holding company The Meridian Corporation. We added Ltd., since it was British.

* * *

A few mornings later, Jerry and I sat in the living room.

I held a yellow legal pad on my lap. Projects—8/12/73 headed the first page. Underneath I had written:

Meridian Corp.

Power of attorney for Marilyn

Pistol permit

Treasury Dept.—application for gold license

Jerry said, "I have another item for your list." He had taken up my habit of pacing. "I'm afraid the time has come when I must ask you for . . . funds. Because, as you well know, it takes money to make money. And I think you'll agree that expenses should be shared as well as profits." His full mouth found its familiar pursed position.

I had been wondering when he would broach the subject of money. "How much are we talking about?"

Jerry stopped pacing to lean on the mantel. "Oh, about a hundred thousand."

I whistled softly. "That's a lot of cash! Far more than I had in mind." I had no intention of investing that kind of money—even if I had it—and I did not believe Jerry expected me to. So, let the negotiation game begin. My years of selling TV time and programs had prepared me well. I remained silent.

"Of course, you wouldn't have to put it all up at once," Jerry said.

I stretched out my legs, relaxed, and kept my mouth shut.

"Maybe we could start with . . ." He searched the air for a figure. "Seventy-five."

It was better, but not good enough. I looked out the window. "I was thinking of quite a bit less."

"We could start with fifty, I suppose. At least it's a start." Jerry stopped pacing and sat down opposite me.

The amount still seemed large, but I didn't argue. I knew I had to invest something. It depended on how much I needed to keep for living expenses from my severance and profit sharing. "Where exactly would this money go?"

"The mining company in Macapà. Gold is where we should put our money. And with a healthy injection of capital, the mining company will be able to increase production, like we discussed at the site. As you know, the more gold we can stockpile, the more money we'll make when the market opens up. I plan to put in additional money of my own."

"Assuming I put my money in the Macapà gold mine," I said, "who would do the accounting?"

Without hesitating, Jerry answered, "Victor Heusi. And you know how I feel about him."

"What percentage would fifty thousand get me?"

Jerry paused to think. "Considering what Victor and I have already invested, time and moneywise, I would say your share would be a quarter. Twenty-five percent. Of course, if you put in additional funds, your share would go up."

I stared at the fireplace for a moment. "All right, Jerry. I'll go along with that. I'll invest in the mining operation. And I should emphasize that I'm doing this in good faith. I believe in what we're doing. The potential for success is there. I want to be part of it. So, I'll work on getting the funds together. Then what happens?"

"Here's what you do. What New York bank do you use?"

"Chase Manhattan."

"Good. What you do is open an account at Banco do Brasil at 550 Fifth Avenue and transfer funds out of Chase. Better put in a little over fifty thousand. For bank fees, et cetera. Then, have it transferred to my account in the same bank, but in the Belèm branch. Here . . ." He pulled his wallet from his back pocket and extracted a folded piece of paper. "Let me give you my account number."

I copied the number and returned the paper. "The only problem I can foresee is what happens to my fifty thousand if something happens to you."

"In case something happens to either of us, we should each have a piece of paper to cover ourselves." He reached for my yellow pad. "Let me borrow that for a minute." He wrote:

To whom it may concern

The amount of 100,000 (one hundred thousand) dollars less transfer and exchange charges requested by the Brazilian government are in case of my demise the property of Jack Kelley and shall be treated as such.

I hereby instruct my executor to return these funds to him at his request and according to govt regulations.

Aug 12, 1973 Jerry Green

He handed the paper to me. "Please note that I have used the amount of one hundred thousand dollars rather than fifty thousand in *my* good faith that: one, you will invest the remaining fifty thousand in the near future; and two, that I will not meet my demise before that occurs."

"So I noticed."

"Next time you go downtown, maybe you could get a copy made for me."

"Okay," I said. "And I would like another piece of paper from you stating that in case of your demise, my share of everything we've built together will remain mine, and that I also have first option to purchase your share from Starr."

"Good idea. And I'd like the same from you."

"Fine," I said. "We can do that right now."

When we had finished, I went back to my list of projects. At the bottom I wrote *Transfer funds,* followed by *International driver's license.* Then, I added *Plane.*

* * *

Transfer funds loomed the largest on my project list. Handing over that kind of money to somebody—to anybody—was a staggering proposition. It would be my formal, and formidable, commitment. A few doubts still lingered at the back of my mind. Had I been too quick in my agreement? Had my desire to get out of broadcasting and improve my home life prejudiced my decision? I certainly hadn't rushed into this. I had done my homework. I had thoroughly investigated the details, with the help of my lawyer and my visit to Brazil. The timing was good, personally and professionally. I had to believe I was making the right move. All the facts pointed in that direction.

Putting aside the transfer of funds for now, I called Robin Eyres at the accounting firm in Tortola to incorporate the Meridian Corporation. Eyres would contact the lawyer and get things in the works "straightaway." *Bloody good!* My pistol permit and the power of attorney for Marilyn were being processed. I had incorporated the company for the gold venture and was waiting for the trade license application I had requested from the US Treasury Department.

My favorite item, *Plane,* kept grabbing my attention. It didn't cost to dream. I spent a few hours studying the brochure of the Cessna 185. The taildragger was more difficult to land, with its third wheel on the tail instead of the nose, but I didn't begrudge the extra practice hours I would need. The single-engine aircraft could take off and land on short strips and bumpy surfaces. Where I was going, it was the only plane to have.

I kept coming back to *Transfer funds.* I decided to hold back ten thousand until the income began. Finally, after a week, I braced myself for the trip to New York to conduct the transfer. It was a simple transaction, really, over quickly, but even so, a lump the size of a baseball lodged in my throat. Forty thousand dollars. Today that would be equal to $212,400. A hell of a lot of money.

Chapter 9
Marilyn

Flitting in and out of Greenwich like Mary Poppins and her umbrella, Jerry returned a few weeks later. For once, the girls were pleased to see him: piles of clothes in Germany's latest styles were draped in appealing combinations on the sofa.

In a grand send-off for their adventure—and obviously knowing the way to a woman's heart—Jerry had brought outfits for the girls to wear in Brazil. There were bright turquoise and orange coveralls with blouses to match, and shirts of all styles and colors.

He gave me a silk burgundy blouse and a pair of gray slacks that fit like the skin on a banana. "I have a good eye," he boasted, as I blushed. "That's the way the girls in Brazil wear their pants." Jack frowned and loudly cleared his throat.

When we ladies had finished parading through the living room in our new outfits, Jerry lay a small folded piece of cotton in my hand. Inside lay a polished purple amethyst, a small yellow topaz, and a piece of raw gold. "A small memento from Brazil," he said. "And there's plenty more where that came from."

* * *

One evening over cocktails and dinner, we introduced Jerry to Jack's mother, brother, sister-in-law, and two sisters. They couldn't help disapprove of the polished stranger, for he was taking us away. Yet they also admired him, even seemed awed at times, for he appeared to know something about everything. This, in turn, made them skeptical.

The ladies were lit up with the special glow that women radiated when an attractive man was in the room. And therein lay another paradox, for Jerry's features, taken separately, were unexciting. Yet when combined, they created an alluring package filled with charm, mystique, and sex appeal.

By the end of the evening the general consensus was that Jerry Green was something special. The entire enterprise received everybody's support. With maybe one or two reservations.

News of our plans swiftly traveled through Greenwich.

Vince and Jane Warner, our close friends, invited us and Jerry to one of their small cocktail parties. The conversation buzzed all evening about Jack Kelley's new partner. He was nothing like the typical Greenwich gent who made the local cocktail circuit or walked down Greenwich Avenue. And it was a safe bet that his suitcase had never carried parrot-green pants or a pink Izod shirt. His entire demeanor was different . . . although nonetheless attractive, for it was difficult to find fault with him. He was aloof but not snobby, smart but not condescending, self-assured but not egotistical (though an ego was plainly in residence). He was a man of vision as broad as his background, and definitely one to recognize and respect. He had little in common with the men of Greenwich; he came from a different mold. The contrast worked as much in his favor as against it.

After the party, we took Jerry and the Warners out to dinner. Something intangible, difficult to identify, kept Jerry Green from fully fitting in.

* * *

The household hummed whenever Jerry was on the premises. Things got done. Problems too close for Jack and me to view rationally found solutions.

What about knives and forks? A toaster? An iron? Pots and pans? Sheets and towels? "Brazil's electrical outlets are a different size," Jerry said, "so you should buy new appliances after you get there. I wouldn't worry about anything but sheets and towels. For some reason, you can't find good linens there. Which reminds me, if you see any decent king size-sheets, Starr and I could use them."

The most crucial problem, however, was school, with only three weeks left until the September start. Lynne and Evan had to be settled *somewhere* to ease their entry into college.

"We'll get them enrolled in a private English-speaking school in Rio," Jerry said. "They can go as soon as the school year starts. After I go to Florida and then to Belèm to see Starr, I'll meet you in Rio, Jack. We'll take care of the school problem. Then when the rest of the family moves to Belèm, the younger girls can go to the local public school. At their young ages, they'll pick up Portuguese fast." He smiled consolingly. "Don't worry, Mom and Dad, we'll have it organized in no time. No time at all."

"Good," I said. "School is top priority." Both Jerry and Jack were pacing the living room by now. I sat in my chair with my feet tucked in so as not to trip them.

"And after we get that settled," Jack said, "I want to go to Belèm and talk to the architect about starting work on the house."

"Then we'll fly to Macapà and get going on the mining enterprise," Jerry said, pacing toward the fireplace. "By the way, any word on the gold license?"

"I wrote for an application from the Treasury Department two weeks ago, but no word yet. I'll call them."

"I knew it would take time. Washington moves at a snail's pace." Jerry stopped pacing and smiled. "But we'll get there. Never fear."

Soon after, he was gone. We had a week to ourselves before Jack went to Brazil again.

* * *

Before he left, Jack told me what he had done.

"You *what?*" I was stunned. "You *gave* him forty thousand dollars? All that money? Just like *that?*" I snapped my fingers. "For God's sake, you didn't even have the courtesy to discuss it with me!" I glared at him. "I suppose you used your profit sharing?"

He nodded.

"Forty thousand dollars! That doesn't leave much to fall back on." Fear shot down my spine.

"We'll manage. I thought you believed in the venture too."

"I didn't know you had to invest so much in the beginning."

"Just think about it. You didn't expect to get into the business for nothing, did you? You have to put in *something*. If you thought otherwise, you were deluding yourself." He was definitely on the defensive. "It takes money to make money, you know that. I didn't fork over forty thousand dollars to Jerry Green because I like his smile. I invested in the mining company in Macapà. And I'm sure we'll be rewarded many times over. Once we get our license and start trading gold, that forty thousand dollars, *times two*, will be back in your pocket before you know it." He put his hands on my shoulders. "Just relax and let me do the worrying. Okay?"

I pulled away. "I can't even put into words how angry I am."

"He wanted fifty."

"Oh. That makes it okay?"

"No."

"So you owe him more. Where are you going to get it?"

"The sale of the house."

"We need that money to live on."

"Plus proceeds from the business."

"Hah. When does that start?"

"Soon."

"I hate what you did, Jack. Going behind my back."

"I'm sorry, Mare. I didn't know what else to do."

"Tell me the truth," I said, eyeing him with suspicion. "Are you keeping anything else from me?"

"No," he said quietly. "That was it. I knew you'd balk at the forty, and I didn't have time to argue. I had to do it and that's all there was to it. What's done is done!" he said with finality.

I stewed for about a day and a half, speaking to Jack only when necessary. But I knew that holding a grudge would be counterproductive. Besides, it was too late to change course now. Somewhere in my subconscious I had known the business would require a sizable investment. What I hated was the way Jack had gone about it. I felt left out.

A sense of foreboding filled me. I wondered if we would ever see that money again.

* * *

"I love you guys," Jack said to us as he left for the airport amidst noisy good-byes. "Take care of each other." He hugged me once more and kissed me quickly, a man with a mission. "Hang loose, kid. I'll call you when I have news about school. And don't worry!" the boundless optimist told the constant worrier.

Chapter 10
Jack

Rio!

The airport was swarming with people. The air smelled of sweat. The language was foreign. People's tongues clicked like machine guns.

From the airport, my Volkswagen taxi hummed past the mountain that held Corcovado. The awesome ninety-eight-foot statue of Jesus Christ stood among the clouds, arms outstretched. Guarding Rio. We circled Lagoa, a residential section on a small lake. Eventually we stopped in front of the Trocadero Hotel in Copacabana, where Jerry and I had stayed on my first trip to Rio. The Trocadero was a small, modern hotel popular with Brazilians. It sat on Avenida Atlantica a few blocks south of the Palace, an older, larger, more ornate hotel that appealed to internationals.

After checking in, I took a brisk swim in the cool August ocean, had lunch in my room, and then took a nap. I was refreshed and ready when Jerry called. Two minutes later he was at my door, looking the same as always. Cool. Fresh. In control. "Hello, my friend," he said. "*Como vai?*"

"*Muy bien, amigo. Entrar, por favor.*"

"Hey, not bad. I think it's Spanish, but it'll pass."

"Stick around. It can only get worse! When did you get in?" I asked.

"I arrived yesterday from Belèm. Starr sends her regards, by the way. And then I had the dubious pleasure of spending the afternoon with our corrupt friends." He shook his head, disgusted. "I advise you to see as little of them as possible."

I recalled the story of scuttling the coffee boat. "Based on what little I know, it sounds like good advice. So, what did you find out about schools?"

"My sources tell me there are two schools of quality in Rio. However, the only school that teaches in English is the American School. Which, I understand, has a good reputation."

"Sold," I said. "The choice is easy when there's only one game in town."

"It's a good choice. You can rest easy with it," Jerry said. "I'll make an appointment."

* * *

Our taxi passed a clump of *favellas* at the bottom of a mountain in Gavea, an inland section of Rio. The slums seemed to sprout in unexpected places, like weeds through cracks in the sidewalk. The Volkswagen Beetle labored under our weight as it chugged up the mountain road to the school. As we drove higher, the houses grew more substantial. Banana trees, palms, and jacaranda provided shade.

Finally, the car pulled to the side of the road and let us out. I stared at a large rambling glass and stucco tree house nestled against the jungle-covered mountain. It zigged and zagged to fit the winding contour. My disbelieving eyes read the sign across the top: *Escola Americana Estrada en Gavea.*

We followed a curving sidewalk that bridged a ravine, while jungle birds warbled and cawed. "Wait'll the kids see this!" I said. "They'll think they're in Disneyland."

We found the main office and approached the secretary. "We-are-here-to-see-the-prin-ci-pal," I said in a slow, jerky monotone.

"Of course," she answered brightly. "You must be Mr. Kelley."

I had forgotten I was in the *American* School. "Guilty as charged," I admitted sheepishly. "And this is Jerry Green."

She led us to an office marked Principal, Senior School, and introduced us to Mr. Battista.

"Sit down. Sit down. Make yourselves comfortable." Antonio Battista spoke perfect English and seemed pleased to have us there. He tipped his chair back and lit a cigarette.

I felt comfortable immediately. "It's certainly a pleasure to meet a Brazilian who speaks better English than I do."

Antonio laughed heartily, and his fresh draw of smoke spurted out in short gusts. "Don't let the name fool you. My parents came from Portugal, but I grew up in Bridgeport, Connecticut."

"I'll be damned. I live right down the road. In Greenwich." It was a good beginning.

Antonio explained that school had started in the middle of August to take advantage of the cool weather, and they had their long vacation in December and January when it was the hottest. Then he took us on a tour. We walked along an open corridor where we could lean over the filigree concrete block rail, touch the mountain, and see its slope disappear under the school. Looking into the rooms, I noted that the classes were small. "Half the students, grades one through twelve, are American," Antonio said. "Most of the rest are Brazilian. We have some from other South American countries and even a few from Europe. They seem to socialize within their own ethnic groups."

Back in Antonio's office, I asked him to tell me more about the students.

He said most of the students, except for the Brazilians, had fathers who came to Brazil to work, either as diplomats, international bankers, corporate executives, or for the US army. The Brazilians—who were mostly from Rio—came to improve their chances of getting into an American college. "The requirements to enter a Brazilian university are so tough, they have a better chance in the States, where the schools have foreign quotas to fill."

"Can I assume the girls will get into a US college if they graduate from the American School?" I asked.

Antonio's eyes sparkled as the teacher in him emerged. "You can assume as much *if* their grades and their SAT scores are good enough, and their records are satisfactory."

"Naturally." I liked Antonio. I gave him a brief description of my new business, mentioning the gold mine, shrimp, and lumber. Jerry leaned forward while I spoke, as if ready to correct me. Once I switched the subject to my family's situation, he relaxed and whistled quietly to himself.

Antonio lit another cigarette. "So. Your girls need a place to live."

"Do you have any ideas, I hope?"

"We have an English teacher in the Senior School who's a possibility." Antonio pulled a file from his desk drawer. "Her name is Prudence Pommerly. She's single. Overweight. I figure there's no rush of amorous Brazilians breaking down her door. She's new this year, so I don't know her very well, but her credentials are good. Before teaching here, she was a secretary to a diplomat at the UN." A grin lit up his face. "A couple of teenage girls might add a little spice to her life."

"I can guarantee it," I said. "Her UN experience will be very helpful."

"Let's go find her." Antonio led the way to the teacher's lounge.

I easily spotted Prudence Pommerly. Antonio introduced Jerry and me to the lady and explained the situation.

"Very interesting." Prudence Pommerly had a voice that would make a contralto green with envy. "You must understand," she trilled, "your girls will have to adhere to some very strict rules."

"You're singing my song," I said with enthusiasm. "I'm happy to know you feel the same way I do."

"How long do you anticipate they'll be staying with me?"'

"Ideally, until the rest of the family arrives. A few months or so."

"We'll wait and see how it goes," she said, as though she had just eaten a lemon.

I hoped that somewhere behind the austere facade flickered a spark of humor. We settled on the price of room and board and other details before Jerry and I left. I promised to have the girls there within two weeks.

* * *

The next day I visited the American Consulate to learn Brazilian immigration requirements. Brazil was not overly welcoming to new residents. They required proof that I had a way to earn sufficient income to support myself and my family. They also wanted a certified letter from the police chief in Greenwich for *each* member of the family—including eleven-year-old Heather—stating that none had a police or criminal record, and that none of us had any outstanding warrants or criminal proceedings against us. We all needed birth certificates. The girls and the animals also needed certificates of vaccination.

I was exhausted when I returned to the hotel. I lay on the bed and placed a call to Greenwich. It took twenty minutes for the operator to make the connection.

When Marilyn answered I asked how things were going.

"Oh . . . fine."

She didn't sound fine. "What's the matter?"

"Just little aggravations not important enough for long distance. What's happening down there?"

"I miss you."

"I miss you too. Come on. What else?"

"Well, your two oldest daughters are enrolled in the *Escola Americana Estrada en Gavea* and can start as soon as they get here."

"Oh, God. I don't know what to do first. They have to get shots, they need passports, I have to buy them luggage, and what kind of clothes do they need? Do they wear uniforms or pants or skirts or what, and do they need sheets and towels, and what about lamps?"

I laughed at the frenzy that always seized my bride when under pressure. "Slow down, sweetheart," I said in Humphrey Bogart style. "There's no need to get in a 'twit.'" Her word. "We'll take things one at a time. First get their passports. Then their shots. And then their airline tickets. Then go buy them some good luggage. Something tough. All they need to bring are jeans, a couple sweaters, and a bathing suit. We'll get everything else down here."

"What do their rooms look like? Can they be together?"

"Well. There's good news and bad news. The bad news first: it's not a boarding school, but—"

"What? Oh my God! What are we going to do?"

"Just calm down and let me give you the good news. I found a very nice lady, an English teacher at the school. She used to work at the UN, which qualifies her to handle two teenage girls, I think, although a stint in the army would have been better."

"Do you really think the girls will be safe with her? I mean, will she be understanding when they're homesick? Or is she a tyrant? What kind of morals does she have?"

"She seems okay, honest. I'm more concerned about *her* than I am the girls. They're tough. And don't forget, they've got each other." I told her about Antonio Battista from Bridgeport.

"I'll be damned."

"Jerry and I are going to Macapà and Belèm. I'll call you from Belèm to find out when the girls will arrive. I wish you were all here already."

"Me too. I guess we'll just have to think ahead to when we'll all be together." She sighed. "There's so much to do first."

"I know. Don't worry. I'll help." But after I hung up, my brain spun with all that had to be done.

* * *

Jerry and I bypassed Macapà and went directly to Belèm. Something was brewing, but Jerry wasn't volunteering any information.

I met with the architect and we compiled a list of sixty items that would make our future home habitable.

The architect would need two months just to put together an estimate. With the slow pace of progress in the tropics, I couldn't even guess when the construction work would be finished. Where the hell would we live in the meantime?

I sat alone by the Greens' pool, lost in my thoughts. For a while I had had the feeling I was being watched. At first glance I saw nothing. But the feeling persisted, compelling me to look more carefully into the trees. There, finally, I discovered a three-toed sloth watching me from a low limb. A cute little thing, about twenty-four inches long, he looked like a monkey. He and I just stared at each other for a while, until the sloth decided to move closer. He traveled along the limb, placing one paw in front of the other as slowly as he could go and still be moving. I inched cautiously toward the little creature until he was close enough to touch. He stared woefully. I stroked him. He didn't move. I picked him up. He looked at me with the saddest eyes in the world.

"What's the matter, little fella? Being slow isn't all bad. Remember the tortoise and the hare." I put him back in the tree. The little guy blinked through his incredibly sorrowful eyes.

He was only one of the many creatures that came to the Greens' yard. Even the Indian girls couldn't identify all of them.

Over the next few days I had plenty of time to contemplate my residential dilemma and look for animals while Jerry talked on the phone and made frequent trips to town alone.

One day, after a lengthy phone call, he joined me at the pool. He was in a pensive mood. "You know, my friend, Chile has big problems. *Big* problems. And that means trouble for all of South America and the United

States as well. It looks like Salvador Allende is getting ready to deliver his country into communist hands. That damn Marxist has put Chile right where the communists want it—on the verge of military and financial collapse. It's just waiting there, ripe and ready for the communists to walk in and take it over. The consequences are horrendous. It would give the Reds another stronghold on our side of the world. And make it that much easier to infiltrate the rest of South America. I don't have to tell you what that would mean for the US." He stared into space.

"The whole world is one big boiling pot," he went on. "It's not enough to have the communists sneaking into our own backyard. We've got to keep our eye on the Middle East as well. That's another trouble spot. When you've got madmen like Gaddafi in Libya running some of those countries, you've got large trouble brewing." He tapped his fingers together. "Muammar al-Gaddafi. Did you know he had syphllis? He'll get crazier as time goes on." He lapsed into silence.

Finally he smiled. "But don't worry about Chile. It won't fall to the communists. Within a few days, the problem will be resolved."

"Oh?" I asked. "What makes you so sure?"

Jerry was smug. "Trust me, my friend."

While I waited for the outcome on the political front, I resolved the residential problem. The whole family would live in Rio for the first year. It would take at least that long to get the Belèm house ready, and I wouldn't have the trouble of finding a more permanent home for Lynne and Evan. All the girls would attend the American School. It was the best solution.

* * *

Four days after our conversation about Chile, Jerry spent the morning on the phone. Finally he came outside to the pool, all smiles, big teeth shining. "Let's take a ride downtown."

After too many idle hours over the last week and a half, I was more than ready.

In the car, Jerry was ebullient. He laughed and made jokes as if all his cares had vanished, and smiled mysteriously as though he were delivering me to a great surprise.

In downtown Belèm, a feeling of jubilation was in the air. Crowds were celebrating in the streets, cheering wildly. Happy faces everywhere. "*Allende es morto! Allende es morto!*" they shouted.

Jerry looked at me with an I-told-you-so satisfaction.

A chill went through me as I watched the happy, perspiring Brazilians who had spilled into the blistering streets.

Grinning from ear to ear, Jerry explained that Allende had been assassinated. Shot in a military coup led by a conservative named Augusto Pinochet, who would immediately begin a new dictatorship. The communists had lost. South America had bought more time. Everybody was full of hope.

I wondered what Jerry's role had been.

Chapter 12
Marilyn

Down in the kitchen, I prepared dinner for Lynne and Evan's last meal in Greenwich. I was tired, a nice tired, filled with a sense of accomplishment. It had been a harrowing two weeks.

Amidst the scramble of getting passports, shots, plane tickets, and new luggage, I had even managed to buy them new underwear. An adventure of this magnitude definitely merited new underwear.

An underlying somberness wafted in and out of our laughter as the four girls and I exchanged reminiscences during our candlelight dinner in the dining room. Pom Pom, sensing the mood, moved from one of us to the other, looking up at our faces, wagging her tail.

After dinner, Lynne's and Evan's boyfriends arrived, ready to drive the girls to the airport in the family station wagon. Lynne's friend, Pete Sullivan, a poor boy growing up in a rich town, came in, his lucid blue eyes full of angry defeat. Evan's friend, Jeff Perillo, who came from a well-to-do family, walked into the kitchen slouched like an S, his face flushed. I gave them each a hug to let them know I understood. They knew.

Then it was time to say good-bye. Everybody, including the dog, walked outside.

I fought a moon tide of tears. Folding first one and then the other of my precious daughters into my arms, I wondered how they could have grown up so fast and when I would hold them again. Their young bodies quivered with excitement. *Please, dear God,* I prayed, *take care of my children.*

Evan and Lynne hugged and kissed their abnormally quiet younger sisters while the boys loaded the suitcases into the car. Then the four teenagers got in: Pete in the driver's seat, Lynne by his side, Evan and Jeff in the back. The car rolled down the long driveway, its horn bleating good-bye.

It was quiet then.

The three of us who were left trudged into the house, Diane and Heather tucked under my arms and Pom Pom, her stubby brown tail drooping, trailing behind.

The house echoed with a feeling of emptiness.

We went to bed early. I tried to reassure myself that my children would be fine. I had had no choice but to let them go. Still, I choked back tears. My little girls. They were so young. I had raised them to be independent, but were they prepared to live alone in a foreign city? Would their judgment be tainted by all sorts of temptations? What if they got involved with the wrong people? Would Prudence Pommerly help them? Would they find friends in school? They had each other, but they were so different. Would they go their separate ways or stick together? They needed each other now. So many things could happen.

Dear God, I prayed, *don't let them be hurt by our decision. Please keep them safe.*

Chapter 13
Evan

Of all people to be stuck with in a foreign country! Lynne and I had nothing in common. We didn't think alike, dress alike, act alike, or even *look* alike. I had Daddy's Irish skin with freckles, and my hair was brown. Lynne had blonde hair and Mom's tan skin. The only thing we had the same were blue eyes. That was it. I was a preppy. Lynne was a hippy. And just because my sister was sixteen months older didn't mean she could boss me around.

We didn't talk much on the way to the airport. We were too bummed out. Lynne and I didn't want to go to Brazil, and Pete and Jeff didn't want us to go either.

At the airport, we checked our suitcases and then the four of us waited for the boarding signal. It was hard to find the right words. Everybody giggled a lot, kind of nervous. Lynne and I said we were afraid the boys wouldn't be faithful, and they said the same about us. We all promised we would be loyal.

Pete was the first to give in, big tough Pete. When he tried to talk, a tear ran down his cheek, and he choked on his words. It was enough to make us all break down. Something terrible and unfair was happening, and we had no power to stop it. We held each other as tight as we could and cried without shame, sobbing our hearts out. Each of us was saying good-bye to our first love. I think we all knew deep down we had experienced something special that could never happen again. We clung to each other until the last possible minute, when Lynne and I had to board the plane for another continent.

After a bonecrushing hug and kiss, we parted silently and walked through the gate to an uncertain future.

The flight left at one a.m. It was nine hours long—plenty of time to sleep, but we were too wired. We didn't want to leave home and everybody we knew. And yet, Rio de Janeiro was waiting for us. The glamour. The freedom. But living in a strange place without our parents, sisters, or friends would be scary. We had no idea what to expect.

The plane was uncomfortable, like a sardine can, and I was smushed against Lynne. Everyone was smoking and talking loudly and we didn't sleep much. We must have finally fallen asleep sitting up. When I woke, our shoulders were touching and our heads were together. It was funny the way our long hair had gotten tangled, Lynne's blond strands mixed up with my brown ones.

Chapter 14
Lynne

In the Rio airport, Evan and I were carried along in a line of strangers. We couldn't understand what anyone was saying. I felt lonely. Finally, we had our passports and immunization slips checked. Then I saw Daddy. He looked tall and handsome. It didn't even matter that Jerry Green was with him.

An overloaded VW taxi took us to the Trocadero Hotel on Copacabana beach. We dropped off our stuff at the hotel and then went shopping. Daddy bought us embroidered shirts and surprisingly *tight* pants, platform shoes with *high* heels—*opa!*—big handmade leather pocketbooks with flaps, muslin bed sheets of bright red and turquoise, and dark green towels splashed with bright fuschia flowers that would have made our mother cringe. Jerry was part of the shopping trip, plowing through piles of clothes and towels, having fun too. The last thing Daddy bought each of us was a small notebook to keep track of our expenses so we could budget our money.

We had our portraits done in charcoal by a sidewalk artist. Evan's and mine looked just like us, but Daddy's was a caricature. We laughed at it.

The first time we noticed the view was when we got back to the Trocadero and looked out the picture window in our room. The beach stretched as far as we could see in both directions. Waves with foamy white edges raced toward shore and slammed onto the sand. Beautiful mosaic sidewalks lined the golden beach. Right off the coast sat a few small islands, their low peaks rising from the sea. Rio! Wow! If our friends could see us now.

* * *

Prudence Pommerly filled the doorway when she met us at her apartment in Ipanema. Evan and I weren't prepared for such a big lady, and we burst out laughing. It was not the way to make a good first impression, but we couldn't stop giggling.

Miss Pommerly pretended to ignore our rudeness and invited us in. "You must meet Cornelius," she warbled, her double chin rippling, as she scooped up a huge long-haired tiger cat that started to purr immediately. "He's a *very* important member of the family." Then she introduced us to her maid, Gina, who looked no older than Evan and me. Gina nodded shyly and muttered something in Portuguese, and then she took off for the kitchen.

"Let me show you your room," Miss Pommerly said. With Cornelius under her arm, she waddled down a short hallway, her full skirt swishing earnestly from side to side.

We followed her to a small room that held one four-drawer dresser, a mirror, an ugly print of a woman, and a double bed.

My heart sank. *How can Evan and I share the same room and the same bed when we're not even friends? How can we live with a weird lady like Prudence Pommerly?*

Evan's face was like a statue. "Hmmph," was all she said.

Miss Pommerly disappeared and left us alone with our father.

He put an arm around each of us. "I'm sorry I couldn't do better, guys. It was the only game in town. But," he promised, "it won't be for long. And remember, December will be here before you know it." We must not have looked too happy, because he said, "If you two weren't in your last years of high school, we wouldn't be doing this."

This was bad. Three whole months. With that fat, stuffy lady and her spoiled cat.

A long sigh came from Evan.

Daddy gave us a squeeze. "You guys are tough. You can handle anything. Just make sure you stick together and take good care of each other."

I wondered if he knew we weren't exactly crazy about each other.

"Come on," he said, "let's go back to the hotel. You can stay with me until I leave Rio." He walked down the hall. We followed quietly.

"I hope this works," said Prudence Pommerly as we left the apartment.

* * *

In the morning, Daddy took Evan and me by taxi to *Escola Americana do Rio de Janeiro en Gavea.* The long trip seemed short on our first day. Our nervous chatter tumbled with giggles, drowning out the traffic's noise.

The taxi chugged up the mountain and let us off in front of the school. We couldn't believe how much it looked like a scene from a fairy tale, which helped to calm us down. We took a minute to look around and listen to the jungle birds before going inside to the principal's office. Antonio Battista was a cheerful man. He welcomed us heartily and got right to work, studying our transcripts and making out our schedules.

"We don't offer the selection that Greenwich High does," he said, "but we have one course that isn't in Greenwich's curriculum." He raised his eyebrows and looked questioningly at us, just like a teacher. "Portuguese," he said. "Which, as you may know, is a combination of French, Spanish, and Italian. All descended from Latin." He gave Daddy a sympathetic smile. "But you girls are young. You'll pick it up fast.

"Since school has been in session almost four weeks, I would suggest you both have some tutoring to help you catch up." Evan and I exchanged a loaded glance. "The sooner you learn the language, the less overwhelming everything else will seem." He smiled, trying to make us feel good. It didn't work.

After we said good-bye to Daddy, Mr. Battista took us to our classrooms. As Evan left me to join her class, I was surprised by a sharp pang in my chest.

All the teachers and students gave me a friendly welcome and put me at ease. Maybe things would turn out better than I had expected. Which could mean anything really, for I hadn't known what to expect.

The next day, Daddy moved us into Prudence Pommerly's apartment and got ready to catch the night flight home. Our conversation was full of instructions, the *don'ts* outweighing the *do's* by two to one.

"If you have any problems, go to Antonio Battista," Daddy said. "He's promised to look out for you. And remember, you can call home anytime. We're only a phone call away."

We each gave him a big bear hug, as if that would make him stay longer.

Chapter 15
Jack

Jerry and I left Rio together, Jerry on the night flight to Belèm and I to New York. I had the whole night on the plane to sleep, but my mind wouldn't quit. It tore me apart to leave Lynne and Evan alone in Rio. It was necessary, yet I felt like I was deserting them. Was I doing the right thing? They were enrolled in a good school. But what was Prudence Pommerly *really* like? Why should she give a flying damn about two young strangers? Would they go to Antonio if they had a problem?

I trusted my girls. I had faith in God. With His help and the telephone, we would get through the next three months.

And Jerry. His insider Allende information confirmed his international intelligence connections. But as far as business was concerned, little had been accomplished. The thought troubled me. I would demand some answers the next time Jerry came to Greenwich.

Another chore lay ahead. Engineer the move from our chock-full, three-story, twelve-room house. Because of my traveling, Marilyn would be in charge. I'd help all I could.

* * *

It was 10:30 a.m. when I walked through the back door. I'd been away for more than two weeks. Marilyn looked as delectable as a piece of apple pie with whipped cream on top.

"Oh, did I miss you!" I said, and then I kissed her. For a minute, I felt like I didn't have a care in the world.

The mail waiting for me contained one envelope that had a sobering effect: my first bank statement from Banco Do Brasil S.A. It showed a beginning balance of $40,250.00. And an ending balance of $202.00.

Gone. Forty thousand dollars.

It was enough to send my stomach down to my shoes. But I was determined to view the transaction as a positive signal that progress had begun. With a healthy injection of capital, the gold mine could go into full-swing production. On the home front, one third of the family had already been relocated. That was progress.

A sudden burning spasm grabbed my abdomen, and I doubled over in pain. After twenty or thirty seconds, the pain vanished. I straightened up and caught my breath. I had had twinges in my gut during the Taylor office battles and once in Belèm, but nothing like this. Stress. It had to be stress. I had neither the time nor the desire to wonder what else it could be. Once the whole family was in Brazil and some of the projects were moving forward, I would be able to relax.

Chapter 16
Lynne

Daddy was gone.

When he was here, Rio was the most exciting place in the world. Now it was noisy and overwhelming. Living with Prudence Pommerly, a lady we didn't know—and didn't want to know—Evan and I were basically on our own. We had no choice but to stick together.

Everything was so different. Even taking a city bus home from school was scary. If we got lost, our Portuguese was too feeble for us to ask directions.

School was better than we had expected, though we weren't working very hard: too many distractions, too many adjustments. Luckily, most of the teachers were American—except my physics and calculus teacher, a retired admiral in the Brazilian navy who had a heavy accent, which made physics even harder. Evan's social science teacher—his name was Wally—was Brazilian too. Evan said that when he got excited, his English would run together, and after a bunch of garble, he would ask, "You can will understand?" He was skinny and wore glasses, and his eyes kept going to Evan's chest. He gave her the willies.

Sometimes monkeys swung through the trees outside the classrooms. They screeched and chattered, and everybody chirped back at them, hoping they would come and play. All our work stopped then, but nobody minded, not even the teachers. At least for a few minutes.

Butterflies bigger than bluejays flitted along the open-air halls. Their wings were thinner than paper and colored in luminous shades of sky blue, lavender, and turquoise; they looked like indigo handkerchiefs fluttering through the air on a playful breeze. What a school! The Greenwich kids would never believe it.

The students were friendly, especially the Americans. It helped to laugh a lot.

Every day after school we rushed home, put on our bathing suits, and went to the beach. We tied our beach towels around our waists like the Brazilians and walked the five blocks of city sidewalks, shaded by palms and banana trees, through all kinds of smells: sewer smells, sweet smells, smells of garbage and car exhaust. We hopped from one foot to the other to keep the hot pavement from burning our feet through our rubber flip-flops while we waited for a lull in the speeding traffic to cross the double boulevard. We saw men carrying purses, which was understandable: their pants were too tight to slip a thin dime into their pocket. And the string bikinis, called *tangas,* that Brazilian girls wore were just three dots of fabric held together by strings. They made Evan's and my American bikinis look like bloomers. But we definitely were not giving up those extra inches of cover.

When we got home from the beach, Miss Pommerly made us do our homework, and then it was dinnertime. The usual meal was pasta and bread. Prudence Pommerly loved pasta and bread. And cake. Her maid Gina, who laughed all the time, baked a cake every day. Next to Cornelius the Cat, it was Miss Pommerly's fondest pleasure. And after two weeks of sharing Miss Pommerly's pleasures, Evan and I noticed our bodies had begun to expand. Not good.

Sometimes after a big starchy dinner—before my sister and I started going out at least three nights a week—we would all sit together in the living room. Cornelius would jump into Prudence's lap and knead her large thighs, purring loudly, eyes crinkled in a smile, while she stroked him. Then he would sink his paws into her huge cushiony bosom and rub his head under her chin. "Oh, my Cornie," she would sigh lovingly as we sighed miserably to ourselves.

* * *

In a lucky break, Miss Pommerly went out one night. We were thrilled to have the apartment to ourselves. Evan lay sideways on an overstuffed living room chair, her long hair dangling over one thick arm. I reclined on the sofa, breaking off split ends from my hair. "What size bra do you think old Prudy wears?" Evan asked lazily.

"There's one way to find out," I said.

"Let's go."

We ran to Prudence Pommerly's bedroom. Cornelius the Cat was perched on the bed like a sphinx.

We began searching the dresser drawers. "I think I found it," Evan said. She held up what looked like two baseball mitts sewn together. We started guffawing. It was wicked.

Cornelius watched us, his tail snapping back and forth like a whip. His ears were laid back flat and his black pupils were the size of nickels.

Evan put on the huge bra over her clothes and pirouetted slowly. "How do I look?"

"Stacked," I shrieked. "Like two mountain peaks. Holy shit, I wish I had some of that."

Cornelius paced back and forth on the bed, growling quietly and hissing, his lips curling to show his fangs, long and sharp.

Evan strutted in front of the mirror. "Look at that chest."

"What melons." We giggled hysterically.

Suddenly, a bellowing snarl came from Cornelius's throat and a fifty pound ball of fur flew at Evan with claws out.

"Owwww!" Evan screamed as she dropped the bra. Horrified, she stared at her arm, where thin lines left by the cat's claws turned bright red. The enraged animal jumped to the top of his mistress's dresser and glared into Evan's eyes. A deep growl rumbled in his chest and his tail twitched.

Evan picked up the oversized bra and swiftly stuffed it into a drawer. "Let's get out of here before he attacks again."

We got out of there fast. And never again did we go in that bedroom.

The worst part: old Prudy's bra size was still a mystery.

* * *

As Evan and I grew to rely on each other, we discovered we had more in common than we realized. By early October, we were going out a lot together after dinner. Our curfew was 12:30, even on school nights, which would have outraged our parents had they known, but Miss Pommerly was glad to have us out of the apartment. Her *never-ending* complaints about our high energy sent us running. Evan always wore an Izod shirt, Levis, and Topsiders; I dressed in a peasant blouse with tattered jeans and flip-flops.

Feeling liberated, we quickly adjusted to the city's spirit. We loved to sit at sidewalk cafès, drinking beer and watching life go by. Sometimes after our afternoon swim, we would meet our friends for a brew at Garota de Ipanema, the sidewalk cafè where Vinicius de Moraes wrote "Girl from Ipanema." His lyrics were scrolled along all three walls. We liked to watch the sensuous, oiled creatures he had written about stroll along the beach in their *tangas,* their lean copper bodies glowing in the sun. Some girls weren't so lean, though. And every day, Evan and I grew to look more like them. In spite of our tightening bikinis, we loved to go to the beach, where an army of hawkers, their trays strapped over their shoulders, peddled their products. Some sold oily suntan lotion that tinted the skin red. Others shouted, "Coca. Cocacola, *e agua.*" On weekends, Cariocans—residents of Rio—played volleyball. Nearby, suntanned specimens with an overabundance of testosterone and thick-muscled thighs chased soccer balls through the sand while passersby cheered. Rio seemed like one big sandy playground.

Evan and I fell in love with the city. It throbbed to a Latin beat. It pulsated. It vibrated. And it never stopped.

Enjoying our newfound freedom, we happily gave in to Rio's charms. Partying became primary, school secondary. The notebooks our father had bought us to keep track of expenses read: taxi, bus fare, cigarettes, beer, beer, beer.

* * *

One night Miss Pommerly was having guests for dinner. She made us eat early in our room. When we were finished, we sat on the bed, stuffed, staring at the leftover mini-raviolis on our plates.

"I wonder if this crap will fly?" I said.

"How can they fly?" Evan moaned, holding her stomach. "They're made of cement."

I picked up a ravioli and tossed it out the window. It spun and twirled like a little top all the way to the sidewalk.

"Hey!" Mischief flickered in Evan's eyes. She knew she shouldn't, but . . . She picked one off her plate, held it out the window, grinned at me, and flung it.

I hurled another. Then it was Evan's turn. It grew easier—less guilt with each toss. Soon we were throwing raviolis in a continuous flow, laughing like crazy. We kept the pasta flying until our plates were empty and a spotty ecru sidewalkscape had been created around a small palm tree, where Miss Pommerly's guests would walk on their way in.

"Old Prudy's company'll think she got their dinner off the sidewalk," Evan said. The idea was so hilarious, we lay on our bed and guffawed, holding our sides, until we were exhausted.

The next morning when we stepped out of the building on our way to school, Miss Pommerly gasped loudly. She kept saying, "Ooh. Ooh," as she wrapped her skirt around her big legs and carefully picked her way through the checkerboard of smeared ravioli. "I won't forget this," she said.

It sounded like a declaration of war. Lucky it was two against one. Unless we counted Cornelius.

Chapter 17
Jack

Acquiring a gold license was more difficult than I expected. I made a quick trip to Washington to find out what had delayed the acceptance of the application. A bored official told me I couldn't get a license to trade gold without a record of operation. And I didn't have a record of operation.

That same old story. You can't get a job without experience. And you can't get experience without a job. Maybe Jerry could pull a few strings.

But progress was evident in other areas. By the time Jerry drifted into Greenwich from Miami in mid-October, letters were arriving from Vince Warner's furniture company about purchasing Brazilian gum wood and oak. Two boxes of new letterhead had arrived with the heading: The Meridian Corporation Limited; Post Office Box 86, Road Town, Tortola; British Virgin Islands, West Indies.

We got an estimate of $35,000 to pack our furniture and ship it by barge to Brazil, which easily resolved the question of whether to keep our furniture or sell it.

We felt bad about selling the house, but Jerry reminded us that being a long-distance landlord would mean nothing but trouble. "You're better off making a clean break. When you come back, you'll be able to buy bigger and better." As always, he pronounced the words carefully; they made good sense. Besides, we needed the house proceeds for living expenses.

On the subject of the gold license, I was happy to hear Jerry say, "Don't worry. I'll handle it."

My stomach pains kept coming. The hot vice that often gripped my middle convinced me to see a doctor. He blamed stress and gave me a prescription for a mild tranquilizer with strict orders to take it easy. If the pain continued, he'd do a lower GI series.

While he was in Greenwich, Jerry used our house as his base of operations. He received several phone calls. One day when he was out, I took an excited message about a cattle deal in Argentina. Little by little, he was lifting his veil of secrecy, allowing us to learn more about his enterprises. It seemed the more he grew to know us, the more he grew to trust us.

Meanwhile, a persistent light-headedness forced me to stop taking the tranquilizers. Soon after, Marilyn had to rush me to the hospital, bent over with pain.

Jerry stayed in New York City while I underwent three days of tests. The cause was not found.

After Jerry left for parts unknown, we worked on the house. Fresh paint and a new floor gave the kitchen a needed face-lift. New carpeting brightened the master bathroom. A crumbling plaster wall in Lynne's room was replaced—sending plaster dust everywhere—and plaid wallpaper was hung, with Marilyn's regrets that Lynne wasn't there to enjoy it. When the spruce up was finished, the old dowager coaxed us to stay. It made the Brazilian prospects less attractive and made us wonder why we had waited until the eleventh hour to fix up the rest of the house.

The open house brought a steady stream of enthusiastic real estate brokers. They predicted a speedy sale.

Chapter 18
Jack

One day in late October, I received a phone call. A rich female voice said, "Mr. Kelley, this is Prudence Pommerly."

"Well, hello, Prudence, how are you?" Sensing trouble, I put on a forced cheerfulness.

"Mr. Kelley, after much deliberation, I have finally come to the conclusion that I am *not* cut out to live with two teenage girls."

She might as well have dropped a bomb in my lap. "Have the girls done something wrong? Are they in trouble?"

"It's just that they're so . . . energetic, so . . . spirited. I cannot comprehend it, I cannot appreciate it, I cannot control it, and I *cannot stand it*!" Tears hung at the edge of her voice.

I was stunned. "I thought you were used to teenagers."

"Mr. Kelley. Putting up with a classroom of teenagers all day is one thing. *Living* with two teenage girls, day after day, week after week, is another matter. And I simply can*not* cope with it any longer." Her huge voice shook.

"I can sympathize, Prudence. Believe me, I know what it's like to live with teenagers. Most of the time, it's worse than a poke in the eye with a sharp stick."

"I beg your pardon?"

"Just a little joke, Prudence."

"Mr. Kelley, this is *not* a joking matter!"

"No, it isn't," I said, sympathetic in spite of myself. "Prudence, I'll do my best to find another place for the girls to stay, but please bear with me. It's not that easy." I hadn't the slightest idea where to begin. "You couldn't stand just six more weeks? Just until Christmas vacation?"

A hysterical tune filled my ear.

"Okay, okay. Don't worry. I'll have the girls out of there as soon as I can. All I ask is that you keep them until I can make other arrangements." I couldn't resist another attempt at humor. "Just don't throw them out on the sidewalk."

"Oh, my word. Mr. Kelley, what kind of person do you think I am?"

"I was only kidding, Prudence. It makes life a little easier," I said, hoping she would take the hint. "I'll see what I can do and get back to you as soon as possible."

"I'll be waiting for your call, Mr. Kelley. Good-bye."

Marilyn came into the room. "What was that all about?"

"Oh. The old prude is having a little trouble adjusting to two teenage girls."

"Oh, no." She looked panicked. "What are we going to do?"

"It'll work out." Since Marilyn had a tendency to worry, I often kept a problem to myself until I found a solution.

"Oh, Jack. I wonder if we did the right thing, sending them down there all alone. So young. Maybe we should have kept them at home. Maybe—"

"Let me refresh your memory," I interrupted, feeling a bit guilty myself. "We were concerned about their chances for college. So we decided that an uninterrupted senior year for Lynne and junior year for Evan would be the most beneficial. Remember? All the conversations we had? God!" I started pacing. "And if you recall, we *both* agreed that because the move would be in the middle of the school year, enrolling them in Rio was the best solution. In spite of the pitfalls." I paused to take a breath. "Am I right or what?"

"Well, yes, but . . ." She frowned, suddenly suspicious. "Why are you so defensive?"

"I'm not defensive. We did it and it's done. It's too late to change things now."

Her shoulders sagged. "I guess you're right. I just wish they weren't so far away."

I put an arm around my wife and kissed her forehead. "I'm sorry I'm such a grouch. I guess I'm a little uptight."

She glared at me. "Oh, really. I hadn't noticed." It must have been my sorry expression that prompted her to lean her head on my chest. "But I do understand," she said.

* * *

I didn't know what to do. I could go to Rio and set the girls up in an apartment with a maid. Or they could live in a hotel for six weeks. Was I out of my mind? My two teenage daughters unchaperoned in Rio?

Finally, I called Antonio Battista. He offered his sympathy. "Let me see what I can see, Jack, and I'll get back to you."

"I'm sorry to lay this on you, Antonio. I feel like I've got one hand tied behind me, being so far away. God, it's a helpless feeling!"

I could hear Antonio draw on his cigarette and exhale loudly. "Don't worry, Dad. I understand what you're going through. But as the kids say, 'cool your jets.'" He laughed. "I'll call you as soon as I've found a solution."

* * *

Antonio called the following day. "I have good news, Jack. The perfect solution."

"Well, for God's sake, Antonio, don't keep me in suspense!"

Antonio chuckled. "Your girls are welcome to stay with my wife Cynthia and me until the rest of the Kelley family arrives. How does that sound?"

"That sounds like good news to me, Antonio. The best news I've heard in weeks, as a matter of fact. But come on, do you *really* have any idea what you're getting yourself into?"

"By and large, probably not, never having had kids of our own. But we're used to teenagers. We're with them every day. So it shouldn't be a complete shock."

"I don't know how to thank you. You'll never know what a comfort it is to have Lynne and Evan in such good hands. God, Antonio, I don't know what I would have done without your help. I can't thank you enough!" My relief was so great, I felt light-headed.

"Don't worry about your girls, Jack. Just concentrate on getting the rest of your family down here."

"I'll do that, Antonio. And thank you again. You saved my life."

Now I could tell Marilyn the truth. I found her upstairs in the bedroom.

"Damn it!" she said after I confessed that Prudence Pommerly had more or less kicked the girls out. "I knew it. We shouldn't have sent them down there alone. That was a huge mistake!" She sat on the bed and stared at the floor. "All we thought about was college. We didn't consider their physical and mental well-being. No, of course not. All we cared about was having them get ahead. To satisfy our own egos. Those poor kids. If they survive this, I hope they're not scarred for life." She looked up at me. "I hope they'll forgive us."

I was sympathetic. "Hey, Mare, I honestly believe they'll be okay. In fact, it sounds to me like they've got more spunk than they need. Remember, it was Prudence who cried uncle. And living with Antonio and his wife, they'll have to toe the line. I think it turned out for the best."

"I hope you're right. They're so young. And so far away. But we had no choice, did we?" Then it dawned on her. "Hey! You lied to me, you bum." She gave me a small smile. "Actually, I think I'm grateful."

Chapter 19
Lynne

Evan's and my life *really* changed. And *definitely* not for the better. Our curfew dropped to 10:00, and our social life was reduced to one measly night out during the week. It was lucky we had each other. School took on more importance, which was no great surprise, living with an English teacher and the principal of the Senior School. Talk about discipline! The Battistas had no children, so they were practicing everything they had ever learned from books on us. Their human guinea pigs.

The only good part of living with the Battistas was the short block and a half walk to Leblon beach. Our great escape. Once we had crossed the *avenida* and stepped off the steaming sidewalk, we loved to take off our flip-flops and feel our feet sink into the deep grainy sand as we trudged to our favorite spot to spread out our towels. The beach was exciting. And dangerous. Rolling waves, like a fierce battalion of oncoming soldiers, pounded the sand with roaring force. More awesome, the silent undertow lurked like a shark beneath the surface, a hungry thief. Most Brazilians made the sign of the cross before they got in the water. It was a lesson in respect of the ocean that Evan and I closely followed. We always swam together.

Our American bikinis bulged with an extra twenty-five pounds each after six weeks of Prudence Pommerly's bread, pasta, and cake. Luckily, we had tans, which made our white fat look less ugly.

The November sun was bright that weekend, and the beach was packed. We floated just past the break of the last wave, in the calmer rollers. We admired the mountains as we bobbed up and down like two round corks, enjoying what little was left of our freedom. We still couldn't believe we lived in Rio de Janeiro.

I leaned back in the cool water and let my legs rise to the surface. "Isn't this great?"

Evan didn't answer.

I lifted my head. "Evan?"

She was gone.

"Evan?" I yelled, spinning in the water, looking on all sides. "Evan! Evan!" At last I spotted my sister, thirty yards out to sea, waving like crazy.

"Evan, you come back here this minute!" I yelled. "This isn't funny! I mean it! Get back here!"

In the next instant, I was floating next to Evan. "What the hell's going on?"

Evan's face was full of fear. "The undertow!"

"Oh, my God!" I flailed my arms in the water. "Start swimming hard!"

We tried to do the crawl but didn't get anyplace.

"What are we going do?" cried Evan.

Without warning, I was sucked underwater. It felt like somebody was pulling me down by my heels and I couldn't get away. I'd never been so scared. I thought of my family. What would happen to Evan? It seemed like I was down there for ages until finally I came up, gasping for air. My hair was in my face and I couldn't see or breathe. "Evan?" I called.

"Here," she said.

I started waving my arms and yelling, "Help! Help!"

"They can't understand English!" Evan said, her face so white.

"It doesn't matter. Just get their attention."

"They'll never hear us. They don't even see us. Oh, God, we're gonna drown!" She started to cry. A wave hit her in the face and filled her mouth with salt water. She choked and coughed.

"Evan! Evan!" I yelled. Though I was only sixteen months older, I felt responsible. "Don't cry. Scream! Scream your lungs out! Wave your arms! Don't think about anything else!" I said a silent prayer and began screaming.

We both shrieked until our throats were raw, our voices poor competition against the roar of the ocean. We waved our arms frantically as we drifted farther from shore, sinking and rising like two pieces of wood at the whim of an uncaring sea.

After what seemed like hours, I saw a group of about six men gathered on the beach, pointing in our direction. "Look. Look, Evan." I felt a stab of hope as the men crossed themselves in unison, like a football team leaving the huddle. They appeared small from that distance. I saw them join hands to form a human chain and slowly walk into the ocean. Inch by inch, they made their way through the churning water, fighting the force of each wave.

At last, the undertow grabbed the first man and carried the whole chain toward us. We started swimming hard, straining to reach the men, with little headway. Driven by the will to live, we plowed our arms forward, kicking hard, as we fought the vicious pull of the sea with strength beyond what we believed we had.

The men shouted in Portuguese as they worked to get closer. One minute they were inches away; the next minute, yards. A tug of war, a struggle between life and death, rescuers and victims.

When I had just about given up hope, I felt a hand grab mine. Quickly I turned to reach for my sister, but she had drifted almost ten feet away. Stretching as far as I could without losing my grip, I shouted, "Come on, Evan! Kick! Swim!" Weak from her struggle, Evan feebly moved her arms. The men yelled encouragement in Portuguese as the line fought to reach her.

At last. My fingers touched Evan's and curled tightly around them. A cheer of victory went up. The line changed direction and a new battle began.

Together, we fought the undertow, keeping hold of each other. We struggled to swim across the current. With only our legs to propel us, we had to work twice as hard.

We were all at the point of exhaustion when, in one miraculous moment, the sea became our friend and heaved us ashore with a mighty wave. We dropped each other's hands and scrambled to higher ground. Gulping for breath, we sprawled on the wet sand, drained of energy. We just lay there.

One by one we pulled ourselves to our feet and just stood there, too stunned to speak. Everybody was shivering. Thin rivulets of water trickled down our bodies. Finally, Evan and I shook hands with the men. We said, "*Obrigada! Obrigada! Muito obrigada!*" Never had our "thank yous" been so inadequate or more heartfelt.

The men began talking among themselves, shaking hands, slapping one another on the back. They were lean and tan and muscular. I couldn't see their faces very well without my glasses and my hair was heavy and still stuck to my face.

As the impact hit us, Evan and I hugged each other and cried. Then laughed. Then cried.

"Oh Evan," I said, "if anything ever happened to you, I'd die!"

"I couldn't stand it if I lost you," said Evan.

Salty and caked with sand, our hair snarled masses, we hugged again as we realized a new bond had formed between us.

Months passed before we had the courage to swim again.

Chapter 20
Jack

Before Jerry had left Greenwich for unknown destinations three weeks earlier, he and I had purchased matching miniature audio cassette players so he could send recorded messages to me by mail. Jerry had conceived of this solution for keeping communication open while he was out of phone contact. I, in turn, would send letters or tapes to Jerry's Miami address.

First, a cablegram arrived from Jerry, advising me that his next visit would be delayed. Ten days passed without a word. My stomach ached. Another week passed. The next morning, the first audio tape arrived in the mail.

> *Good morning, Jack,* the tape said. *As I advised you in my telegram cable, I was going to be delayed due to circumstances beyond my control, which I'm sure you understand. I've not received, uh, any letter communication from you, and to tell you the truth, I'm a little worried . . . about your hospital report.*
>
> *I want you to know that should there be anything wrong . . . seriously wrong . . . that you can count on me in any which way. Uh . . . it won't make any difference in our agreement. I just wish that you'd tell me, and should you desire me to keep that a confidential item, you*

know that it will be treated as such . . . from anyone. Please let me know.

As previously stated, due to circumstances beyond my control, I will not be able to pass by New York and visit with you to go over these items with you and just to visit with you. These are not good times, and they're not getting any better so . . . I do hope you understand.

*As far as the business end is concerned, we're doing triple A-1. I have contracted for the delivery of fifteen kilos (*of gold*) per month for sale locally within the areas at an estimated traffic margin less the trip charges. Delivery should start between the ninth and twelfth of December. It will be on a strictly rotating basis. And this date coincides with the nine-day maximum period that I had originally discussed with you. However, it has started, and I think on that particular date that you should be there to see what goes on, just to see what it looks like.*

The aircap boat, uh, the business seems to be larger than I had originally discussed with you and the question of the fiberglass should be ascertained by you during my absence out of the States. Try to find out as much as you can pertaining to the fabrication of fiberglass and the cost and construction of the molds. Just whatever you can pertaining to the business because I think that is what we will do immediately in Brazil.

I've also made commitments for a large ranch in the very north of Brazil which could be utilized for our meat business at a future date, which of course you have the same opportunity to become involved in as we had discussed.

The furniture situation looks excellent. We can do almost anything that, uh, your friend requires for his fabrication. However, we will need, uh, exact samples for, uh, power production. These samples would then be copied exactly and a price given, and a type of wood shown. So please have your friend assemble for you the samples of the chair legs and table legs, whatever pieces that he would require. The frames can also be made there. However, they should be made at a future date. As far as a sample is concerned, it might not be a bad idea to have it sent down at this time and, uh, copied for the future.

Pertaining to your house, we have everything under control. I have paid an additional month, not as a rental, but to hold the house until fully documented and completed. I found this to be necessary since there seems to be a great influx of Americans and Germans into Belèm now. The Pennzoil Company has two large drilling rigs in the north of Brazil, and their executives will live in Belèm. The Japanese Aluminum Company is going to start a rolling mill in the Para area as well as US Steel utilizing a port north of Belèm. This, uh, makes the requirement for sophisticated housing very critical, and, uh, they've seen what we've done. Therefore, not only the price but the availability of homes that could be utilized with the surrounding ground area are getting to be more of a premium than when you were there.

The best thing for you to do at this stage of the game is to clear your own decks and be able to come down and assist. However, it's more important for you to do the clearing of the decks in the United States rather than be down in Brazil and sit, at this present time.

I cannot tell you, uh, where I am at. It is of no importance. However, Alexander Graham Bell would not be suitable. A friend is carrying this into the States and mailing it probably in Miami or San Juan. Should there be a need to reach me, I expect to be in Munich, Germany the thirteenth of this month. You have the telephone number, I'm sure. Other than that, my estimated return into the United States should be at the end of November as we had estimated. Other than that, I'd better close now. I send you and Marilyn and the kids greetings. Speaking about kids, uh, I'm sorry I did not have a chance to go to Rio and visit with your daughters. However, I made a call and at the time I called they were fine, doing well in school and not too many problems other than what would normally be expected for a changeover of this kind. I will advise you from Germany the day of my return.

This is the end of my message. Good luck to you.

Chapter 21
Jack

She was beautiful. Once I had the proceeds from the sale of the house and was making an income from our new business, I would have no trouble meeting the monthly payments. My new green and white Cessna 185 had just arrived at Westchester County Airport from Wichita, Kansas. She seemed to quiver with energy, like a thoroughbred racehorse waiting to show her stuff. I walked around her, taking in every rivet, every detail, touching the rudder, the wings, the prop, amazed that she was mine.

Once I had meticulously ticked off all the items on the preflight checklist, an instructor joined me for the checkout ride. It was the first time I had flown a tail-dragger. I would have the extra pleasure of meeting the challenge in my own plane.

As a surge of power lifted Cessna 2660S off the runway, leaving the terminal behind in seconds, I was smitten.

Chapter 22
Marilyn

Soon after Jack's new plane arrived, Lynne and Evan came home for their summer vacation. I had circled the date on the calendar in red: December 20, 1973. A little thrill went through me as as I watched the charter plane taxi to the gate at Kennedy Airport. *My girls are home.* Soon, a line of smiling American School students and teachers began to descend the stairway. I gasped when Lynne and Evan finally appeared, bearing a slight resemblance to two rosy stuffed sausages. But my joy was unbounded when I embraced my daughters, feeling their vitality and their ample young bodies.

After a boisterous round of laughter and hugs, I stood back to get a better look at them. "Boy, it's good to see you." I hugged them again. "I can't wait to hear about Rio."

Lynne and Evan exchanged a glance. No doubt they had much to tell me. And probably a lot not to tell.

From the corner of my eye, I noticed a beaming couple lingering nearby. When I smiled at them, Antonio Battista approached and introduced himself and his wife.

I warmly shook their hands. "I'm so happy to meet you. And so grateful for all you've done!" While we talked, I scrutinized the couple who had been my daughters' surrogate parents for the last seven weeks and was ashamed to feel a twinge of jealousy.

The Battistas accepted a ride to Bridgeport, giving me a chance to know them and to again express my appreciation. Before we said good-bye, I invited them to dinner on the weekend.

Once they were gone, Evan began her tirade. "Good riddance," she said. "They treated us like guinea pigs. They were always trying out stuff they learned in books, even though school was over and we were at home. How could you make us live with the principal and a teacher? They were unhumanly strict!"

"They treated Cynthia's dog better than us," added Lynne. "It was disgusting. They even made Evan go to school when she was throwing up!"

"Why?" I asked.

"They thought she was hungover."

"Really," I said quietly, and then dared to ask, "Was she?"

"No. She was really sick."

What have they been doing down there? I realized how serene my life had been the past few months without my two oldest teenagers. The Battistas might have stories of their own to tell, I thought. And maybe I didn't want to hear them.

* * *

The familiar teenage chaos had the household buzzing again. Jeff Perillo and Pete Sullivan spent all their free time at our house. They barely seemed to notice the extra pounds on their girls, who wore new clothes I had bought them to fit their new figures. The young sophisticates savored the limelight as they entertained family and friends with tales of their foreign experience.

The days approaching Christmas were more jubilant than usual. Renewed excitement for the Big Move fairly bounced off the walls.

On the night the Battistas came for dinner, Diane and Heather carefully checked out their sisters' other Mom and Dad. Later, they told Jack and me, "They seem nice. But we wouldn't trade. In spite of the stuff you make us do."

Chapter 23
Jack

When dinner with the Battistas was finished, Antonio quietly said to me, "Is there someplace we could talk privately?"

"Of course." With a feeling of dread, I led him upstairs to my den and shut the door. I sat at my desk and Antonio sat opposite me on the couch.

He lit a cigarette, took a deep drag, and exhaled a long deep breath. Finally he spoke. "I have a neighbor in Ipanema. Colonel Eberly. He's the air attachè to the American Consulate in Rio. He also happens to be a close friend of the American Consul in Belèm." He became momentarily absorbed with another attack on his cigarette before he continued. "I mentioned your friend's name to him."

"Jerry Green."

Antonio nodded. "I hate to be the bearer of bad news, Jack, but . . ." He stared at the floor a moment before he went on. "I'm afraid your friend may not be the nice guy he appears to be."

My heart picked up speed. "What have you heard?"

"Eberly tells me that the military have had Jerry Green under surveillance for quite some time. By and large, they're pretty closed mouth about it, but I did learn they suspect him of some kind of fraudulent activities. What they are, I don't know. He's smart. They haven't got any evidence against him yet. But they do believe he's up to no good."

I felt as if I were being cut down in small slices.

Antonio vigorously rubbed his cigarette stub into a pulp in a huge glass ashtray, looking more like the recipient of bad news than the bearer.

His words raced through my mind. *Jerry under surveillance. The military suspects. Not sure. Fraudulent activities. Haven't got evidence.* "Well! That's an alarming but somewhat nebulous bit of information." I laughed drily. "And at the moment, I don't know what to say. Or do."

"I'm really sorry," Antonio said, "but I thought you should know. If the allegations are true, the safety of your girls, and the rest of the family for that matter, may be at risk. This man is powerful and smart, and if he's working the wrong side of the law, he's dangerous as well."

"I'm afraid you're right, Antonio. Thank you for telling me." I tried to smile. "I know it wasn't easy."

Antonio looked grim as he lit another cigarette. "By and large, it's one of the toughest things I've done in a long time."

"You may have saved us a lot of trouble. And I want you to know I appreciate your sticking your neck out like this. Not everybody would have done it."

I held a growing fondness for Antonio Battista, about whom I knew little except that the man had extended himself in friendship more than once. And for no good reason I could think of except that Antonio was simply one of those rare good people.

* * *

I was surprised at how calmly Marilyn accepted Antonio's news. "We'll do what we have to do," she said. "If Jerry turns out to be a crook, we'll shift gears and go in another direction. We haven't passed the point of no return yet." She stared into space. "Of course, I could think of a lot better places to throw forty thousand dollars. And I'd miss living in Brazil. The adventure of it. But." She gave me a weak smile. "We'll survive. Whichever way it turns out."

After I hugged her, she added, "Let's not tell the family about this. We'll celebrate Christmas like it's the last one in this house. We won't say anything until we know for sure."

"Right," I said. "For all we know, Jerry could be okay."

* * *

I left messages at all the phone numbers Jerry had given me, and I sent a telegram to his PO box in Miami. When there was no response, I began to wonder if, by some mysterious means, Jerry had gotten wind of Antonio's disclosure.

Again, I called my friend and attorney, Howard Fox, who immediately began a new investigation into Jerry Green's background.

At the end of the girls' vacation in mid-January, their return to Rio was put on hold. Marilyn and I had too much respect for Jerry Green's power and cunning to jeopardize our daughters' safety.

Lynne and Evan had mixed feelings about remaining in Greenwich. They had learned that after a few months' absence, home was not the same. They said even Jeff and Pete were different. They were confused. And bored. So they focused on losing weight. They hated being teased about being fat. But what they hated most was not knowing what was going to happen.

* * *

Jerry Green's silence had pushed my patience to the limit. It was the not knowing that frustrated me. Would we be going to Brazil? Was Jerry legitimate? Should I start looking for a job? I needed answers. If Jerry wouldn't come to me, I'd go to him. And I'd start my search in Rio.

As soon as I checked into the Trocadero Hotel, I contacted Jerry's acquaintances. Marcos da Matta was an attorney working for the Federal Ministry of Justice, a graduate of Columbia University Law School, and the interpreter for me and the others. Ronaldo Nelson, energetic, in his early thirties, was an eager entrepreneur looking for new opportunities. Pedro de Aquiar, a cousin of Jerry's lawyer Carlos Alberto, appeared to do nothing but hang around.

None of these men had any love for Jerry Green. Out of what seemed to be pure contempt for him, they were eager to befriend me. Pedro, in constant communication with Alberto in Belèm, was happy to deliver information that Green would soon be traveling to Rio from Germany.

On Jerry's scheduled day of arrival, only one flight was due from Germany, and I was there to meet it. When Jerry disembarked and walked to the baggage area, I watched him with satisfaction. *I've caught me a fish!* I went to greet him. "Hi, Jerry. Welcome to Rio."

It took a moment for him to muster a smile. "For Chris' sake, Jack, you surprised the bejesus out of me. What the hell are you doing in Rio?"

"I've been trying to reach you for weeks, Jerry, but you don't answer your messages." I could feel my anger rising. "So, I decided to look for you. We have to talk."

Jerry shrugged, appearing unconcerned. “Fine. Let’s go to the Trocadero. I’ll check in, and we can talk in my room.”

By the time our taxi had reached the Trocadero, my adrenaline was working overtime. I was incensed that Jerry might have bilked me. And I was scared. No telling what Jerry would do to save his neck.

I excused myself for a few minutes, went to my room, and retrieved my .45 from under the false bottom in my carry-on case. The .45 was a bulky, heavy pistol, too cumbersome to tuck in my belt. So, I taped it above my ankle, hoping it wouldn’t bulge. It felt awkward, but I liked the security.

I returned to Jerry’s room. “Sit down,” Jerry said. “Make yourself comfortable.” He was as cool as I was nervous. The scent of his fresh aftershave made me wish I’d splashed some on myself to hide the smell of sweat.

Jerry crossed his legs and leaned back on the couch. “Okay, my friend. What’s on your mind?”

Opting for the upfront approach, I recounted exactly what Antonio had told me.

As the story unfolded, Jerry grew increasingly grim. “Those are serious allegations. Rumors like that could restrict my ability to operate.” He was visibly, yet controllably, angry. “I’ll have that attaché removed from his post before he knows what happened. And believe me, I can do it. I’ve got connections where it counts. Remember?”

He wore a chilling smile as he picked up the phone and placed a call to Washington. Then he hung up to wait for the operator to call back. Fuming silently, he drummed his fingers on the arm of the couch. His mouth was pressed into a barely visible line. His steely restraint heightened my uneasiness.

The phone's bell broke the tension. I listened closely as Jerry related the story to the party at the other end, speaking Colonel Eberly's name in well-enunciated hostile tones.

When he hung up, he was his old unruffled self. His large smile displayed the full size of his teeth. "Very soon our friend, Colonel Eberly, will be receiving his orders to return to the States," he said with unbridled smugness. "I hope it teaches the good colonel that interfering in other people's business can be detrimental to his career.

"In my line of work, it's easy to make enemies," he continued. "You see, once in a while I have to step on somebody's toes and, naturally, they take exception. You may have done me a great favor, my friend. I may have just eliminated one of those enemies. I guess it's our form of office politics."

He faced me squarely. "I hope you won't let this incident upset you. These things happen all the time. But you know that. It's part of doing business.

"What really makes me mad is while I'm out risking my neck for the cause of democracy, people like Colonel Eberly are sitting on their asses behind a desk in some cushy office. The Brazilians know what I've done for them. If it wasn't for my contribution, Che Gueverra would, at this moment, have his men settled all over the north." He stood up. "Colonel Eberly can go to hell!"

He thought for a minute. "I think I know where the story may have come from. There was a USAID representative stationed in northern Brazil while I was acting as an agent to sell Brazilian rice to the Philippines." His proud grin contrasted oddly with his earlier demeanor. "You see, I wear all kinds of hats. Anyway, somewhere along the line somebody got greedy and committed some sort of fraudulent action. Which is not unusual when you're dealing in South America, although they certainly don't have a monopoly on corruption. So this AID representative had to put the blame on somebody, to make it look like he was on top of the situation. Unfortunately for him, he made the mistake of choosing yours truly. Of course, nobody could find any proof because I hadn't done anything wrong." His smile turned sly. "And shortly thereafter, our USAID representative just happened to be recalled from Brazil. As I said before, my friend, it pays to have good connections."

And a strong desire for revenge, I thought.

I could see the evidence now lay in Jerry's favor. Also apparent was the power Jerry wielded through his impressive list of connections: power that he exercised freely and with great pleasure against his enemies.

I stretched my legs, letting some of my tension go.

Jerry's eyes grew wide. "What the hell are you doing?" he asked, staring at the .45 on my ankle.

"Your lack of contact made me suspicious," I said. "I thought you were trying to pull one over on me."

"Stop worrying," Jerry said. "We're okay. Honest."

Noting Jerry's solemn reaction, I thought, *I believe Mr. Green has developed a new respect for me.*

* * *

We remained in Rio a few days more, working to restore our mutual trust. Jerry introduced me to his friends in the SNI (the Brazilian equivalent of the FBI) and to some Brazilian military officers in Rio. For me, it was the final assurance that Antonio Battista's well-intentioned information was, in reality, *mis*information.

"I hope you'll stay with me as we originally planned," Jerry said. "I need somebody in Brazil I can trust to oversee operations while I'm traveling. The gold is just beginning, so that's in a crucial stage. I'd like to get the airboats going. That project looks very promising. The Recife fishing enterprise needs help. Wood for your friend's furniture company is another lucrative enterprise. There's no end to what we can do." He looked at me. "Stay with me, my friend. I need you. And I still think we make a good team."

I could find no reason to disagree. Besides, he had my forty grand.

Antonio Battista, though still harboring doubts, accepted the news and promised to give the girls a home until the Kelleys arrived en masse.

Before I left for the States, I gave Carlos Alberto a $1400 deposit to hold an apartment in Rio for us that belonged to his aunt.

It looked again as though things could move forward. As soon as I returned to Greenwich, I would send Evan and Lynne back to school. They would be there by the end of January, two and a half weeks late for the new term. *Those poor kids,* I thought. *I hope they're as tough as I think they are.*

Chapter 24
Marilyn

With the latest upset behind us and Lynne and Evan back in Rio, Jack and I were free to concentrate on the tag sale of our belongings: a monumental undertaking to dispose of a lifetime's accumulations. We couldn't simply toss things into the *save* box, or the *throw-away* box, or the *sell* box. We had to take time to remember, to smile, to cry. It was difficult not to be deterred by sentiment.

The job took two weeks of fourteen-hour days. Jack hired a professional to do the pricing. Friends and relatives helped organize the hundreds of items. I numbered and catalogued every piece and listed them in a black ledger.

On the first day of the sale, a frigid Valentine's Day 1974, people shivered in the early morning cold as they lined up an hour ahead of starting time, two-deep across the broad front porch. They took turns peering through the living room windows. The line went down the steps and the long driveway all the way to the street. People parked on the lawn, against the stone wall, any place a car would fit. We had to call a policeman to keep traffic moving.

Inside, Jack and I, Jack's mother, sister, nephew, and two friends—seven altogether—made last-minute preparations before manning our stations, forewarned to be on the lookout for little old ladies with big pockets and oversized shopping bags.

Most of the furniture was for sale. The dining room table was loaded with utensils and bric-a-brac of all kinds ("*There's* my barbecue set!" said Mother Kelley); furniture lined the walls; the kitchen displayed a nearly-new refrigerator that dispensed cold water and ice, a double set of ironstone china, and a variety of pots and pans; the butler's pantry offered forgotten and unused china and bar equipment; one bedroom held six rented garment racks jammed with decades of clothing, a virtual treasure for four young girls who liked to play dress up. We had strung ropes across doorways and the third floor stairway to indicate Out of Bounds. Closet doors were tightly shut to keep out nosy bargain hunters. Our two cars were washed and polished: a one-year-old forest green Buick station wagon, beautiful but thirsty, whose appeal was shrinking fast in the midst of the world's first fuel crisis, and a two-year-old white four-door Toyota that was growing more desirable by the minute as gas prices shot to the sky. Lynne's Volkswagen had been sold already to a friend. The three-car garage held trikes, bikes, tools, ladders, a wheelbarrow, a tractor, and a barbecue grill. A Sunfish was set up on the back lawn.

One man's junk was another man's treasure. A shopper would need great restraint to go away empty handed.

On the dot of nine Jack opened the front door and released a surge of humanity that scattered in every direction.

Within minutes a line had formed at my checkout table in the foyer. One of the first buyers was a dealer with a handful of tiny bronze animals and a sterling silver engraved baby cup that had come from a sealed box in a roped-off bedroom. "I'm sorry," I said. "These aren't for sale." I frowned at the man. "That's why they were packed away."

Jack's sister came rushing downstairs. "They're going through all the closets!"

"We'll put up signs," I said.

The signs were no more effective than doors and ropes. "These people are crazy," Jack's sister said. "Invading boxes, looking for bargains. You'd think this was the world's last tag sale." Jack was jubilant when he came up from the basement. "I just sold the old toilet. I was going to take it to the dump." He sold the Buick wagon for one third of what we had paid for it the year before. "We could have been stuck with a gas guzzler," he rationalized. "And they'll let us keep it a few more days."

All day, the front door let in gusts of chilly air, as it constantly opened and closed. Piece by piece, our possessions were carried out. I felt strangely detached, too numb for sadness.

By the end of the third and last day, our remaining crew of four—Jack's mother, our friend Jake, and Jack and me—was reduced to a complete stupor. With the welcome departure of the final shopper, four bone-weary souls plopped onto the last few pieces of furniture in the living room. Mother Kelley held a jelly glass half-full of straight Scotch. Jack, Jake, and I had ours with ice and water. We talked quietly, exchanging favorite anecdotes of our tag-sale experience.

The huge front door was hanging by one hinge. Hundreds of hands had polished its brass doorknob to the shine of a new penny.

I shivered. The house had an eerie feeling, a strange quiet, like after a storm. Our home for eight years, now just a house. I felt a flood of melancholy.

Good-bye, old house. The first pangs of remorse nipped at my heartstrings, and I jumped up. "Let's go eat," I said with forced brightness.

* * *

The bulk of our belongings was gone, but the residue still had to be dealt with. Carloads of clothing and leftover odds and ends would go to a thrift shop. Furniture would go to a consignment shop. A few special pieces would find temporary homes with Jack's family. His brother put an end to the bidding war on the Toyota by buying it himself and letting us keep it until we left.

A man called from Spain to buy the red and gold wing chair and two lamps that went with the bedroom set he had bought earlier.

Slowly things were falling into place. Two huge boxes of newly purchased linens waited to be shipped to Rio. The pile of things to be sorted shrank. The large dining room table went into storage. Each day, the house grew emptier. It, too, would soon be gone. Two families had already come back three times to look at it.

* * *

"How's everything going?" It was Father Durgin calling, a close family friend who often came for coffee after Mass on Sundays.

My body ached with fatigue, and a sore muscle under my rib kept reminding me I had lifted too many boxes. "I had no idea it would be this much work," I said.

Father Durgin laughed. "It's probably a good thing."

"And yet I have the greatest feeling. Ever since we got rid of all our stuff, I feel so unencumbered. So free!"

"It sounds like you're ready to join the clergy. We give up our worldly goods so we can concentrate on doing God's work."

"I can understand why. I never realized how possessed I was by my possessions. Now I can go anywhere in the world and have nothing to worry about but my suitcase."

"It's a great feeling. Possessions do get in the way. And on that note, I'll wish you and your family the best and let you get back to work. If you and Jack have a problem—of *any* kind—remember, I have good contacts. In *this* world, I mean. God be with you now."

* * *

February 19, 1974. Jack's forty-first birthday. Hour-long gas lines had become commonplace because of the fuel crisis, and what would happen next was anyone's guess.

The day was cold and blustery with no sun. At Westchester County Airport, Jack, our daughter Diane, and I shivered in the piercing wind as we loaded the four-seat single-engine Cessna, which looked too small to carry such precious cargo all the way to South America, with much of the trip over water.

Our friend, Tom Ryan, a captain with Pan Am, had agreed to share flying duties with Jack. He appeared with his fourteen-year-old daughter, Vicki, who was Diane's age. Since Tom thought it was safe enough to bring his daughter, I had suggested Diane go too. I figured it would be an unforgettable experience. As it turned out, it was more exciting than anybody had expected.

Tom greeted us all and smiled at Diane. “All set for the big trip?”

“Are you kidding? I’ve been ready for days!” Diane was the envy of her friends, flying to Brazil in a small plane. Though she and Vicki hung in different groups, it would be good for her to have somebody her own age to talk to.

The generous carrying capacity of the Cessna 185 Stationwagon, as it was called, was packed full, but Jack was confident the plane’s 300 horsepower engine would find the extra weight no great challenge.

He and Tom had carefully planned their itinerary. They would head for Florida and then island hop over the Caribbean to the Atlantic.

“The weather report doesn’t sound promising,” said Tom.

“So I heard,” Jack said.

“Really?” I asked, my concern deepening.

Tom put his arm around me. “Don’t worry, Mom, we’ll be careful.”

“I’ve filed the flight plan,” Jack said, “and I’ve done the preflight check.” He looked at me. “So. I guess we’d better get going.”

I said good-bye to the Ryans first. Then I wrapped my arms around Diane’s thin body. Diane, two inches taller than me, squeezed tightly and lifted me off the ground. “G’bye, Mom.” Her voice squeaked with excitement. “See you in Rio.”

“You take it easy, do you hear? Did you bring your diary?”

“Yes, Mom. And don’t worry.” She ran to the plane, huddled against the cold in her light windbreaker, and climbed into the backseat with Vicki.

Jack took me in his arms. "Take good care of yourself and Heather. Pretty soon we'll all be together. And always remember, I love you. Always have, always will." He kissed me, a long, hard kiss, then stood back and gazed at me as if etching my face into his memory.

Did he fear he wouldn't make it? Before I could ask if anything was bothering him, he smiled, turned, and climbed into the plane's left side.

Trying to ignore the dark clouds overhead as 2660S took off on Runway 1-6, I waved furiously from the tarmac as the plane tipped its wings in a final good-bye. It climbed to the right above White Plains, to an intercept point over New Jersey, and then headed south. I didn't feel the frigid air whipping around me until the plane was the size of a fly.

On the drive home, I concentrated on the next two weeks. Heather and I would sleep at our friends' the Warners while I finished closing the house. Then it would be our turn to head south.

At home, my footsteps echoed as I walked through the empty rooms of my beloved house, memorizing the architectural details. The upside-down fleur-de-lis wallpaper, crumbling chimneys, and cracking walls now seemed part of the house's charm. I stopped in the dining room. The red silk moiré draperies were still hanging at the windows; we had no more use for them. Our family would never celebrate another birthday or eat another Christmas dinner in this room. A lump formed in my throat as I remembered the laughter and the fun. I hurried upstairs to pack.

On the empty bedroom floor, our cat Jasmine was curled up in my open suitcase as if to say, "Don't forget me!"

Chapter 25
Jack

Heavy head winds fought us all the way to North Carolina, where we made a rough landing to refuel and file an instrument flight plan—IFR. After we departed, the weather deteriorated. The fully-loaded aircraft bounced through the clouds like a ping-pong ball. To his embarrassment, Tom Ryan was hit with a touch of air sickness. "747s don't bounce like this," he joked.

Tom and I had our work cut out for us. With no autopilot or wing leveler to maintain our heading and altitude, we constantly had to drive the plane. Always on guard. We'd push through one gust and the next one would hit us. The Cessna bucked through the soup at 75 percent cruise power, fighting to keep its capacity load at 8500 feet.

Not a sound came from the girls in the backseat.

At dusk we made a bumpy landing in Charleston, South Carolina. Tom and I were exhausted. After tending to the plane, we checked into a hotel near the airport. Tom went to bed with a severe headache, and I took the girls to dinner. Sometime during the meal, Diane secretly arranged to have a cupcake with a lighted candle brought to the table. I was truly surprised. I had forgotten all about my birthday. The small cake with its single flame symbolized one of my most memorable years.

Chapter 26
Diane

Wow! What a way for my father to spend his forty-first birthday. He and Tom had to switch to instruments because we were flying through one huge black cloud and the visibility got so bad. It poured rain and thundered. Lightning flashed all over the sky. Once in a while we'd hit an air pocket and the plane would suddenly drop. It was like riding on four square wooden wheels. We never knew when it would happen. It was so intense, I thought I would die, but I was calm inside because I trusted Dad. I really appreciated my seat belt. I felt like a rag doll that was tied down.

Then Dad did something that *really* scared me. Without saying a word, he reached his arm around to the backseat and handed me a rosary. His brother Robert had given it to him before we left. It was really special because their mother had given it to Robert when he was a fighter pilot in World War II. He had it with him when he was shot down and held as a prisoner of war in Stalag Luft 1 for fourteen months. And now Dad was giving it to me to hold. What did he think was going to happen?

Vicki and I sat close together. When it was *finally* time to land the plane, we had to descend through rain and darkness. I hoped we wouldn't crash into anything. How hard would we hit the ground? Luckily, the wind was quieter. I couldn't see much until the runway lights made a hazy glow. I was so happy to see those lights. And even more happy to plant my feet on the tarmac.

While airport workers helped tie down our plane, a DC-7 came in for a landing. A strong gust of wind pitched it over onto one wing, and it threw off a trail of sparks along the runway. If our little plane had been a few minutes later, that gust could have flipped us.

What a day! I had spent the longest time of my life with my father. Dad was at work a lot, so I never saw him much. When he was home, he was the big guy who yelled at me when I did something bad. (Which I was good at. Just ask my mom.) But I knew he loved me. He gave us rides in his plane and took us skiing in Vermont and on vacations to St. Croix. But after today, with how he kept us safe, I *really* appreciated and respected him. And the best part? A special bond was growing between us.

Chapter 27
Jack

By morning the rough weather had blown through. We departed for West Palm Beach to pick up a life raft and other survival gear for passage over the Caribbean. Florida's easy climate was a welcome contrast to the popcorn-machine ride of the previous day and the chilling freeze at home.

From West Palm Beach we had a pleasant hop to the Bahamas, where we put down in Georgetown around 4:30 that afternoon. A dark-skinned driver wearing a Yama Bahama straw hat picked us up in an old jeep and took us to the motel. The motel was on the beach, which pleased the girls.

Once we checked in, we took a walk on the beach. The time Tom and I had already spent with our teenage daughters was having a magical effect. Open minds replaced contrary attitudes. And two dads discovered the charm of fourteen-year-old girls. We were in a lighthearted mood at dinner, glad the last two days were behind us, and we looked forward to what lay ahead. Afterwards to prolong the evening, we went to the motel roof to admire the night view of Georgetown. The flawless show of stars in the moonless sky inspired a lesson in celestial navigation, which the girls greatly enjoyed—to our surprise.

We began the morning early, cleared customs, checked the plane for takeoff, and with Tom in the captain's seat, taxied to the fuel area to top off the tank. A towering black man stood in front of the pumps, arms folded. I jumped down and smiled amicably. "Fill 'er up," I said. Smiling broadly, the man shook his head. "How come?" I asked.

"No fuel," said the man, still smiling, arms still folded.

I pulled a twenty-dollar bill out of my pocket and offered it to the handsome giant. "Are you sure?" I asked.

At the suggestion he was open to bribery, the titan glared at me, as if to say, *How dare you?* His voice boomed like thunder. "We have no fuel, sir." He thought for a moment and softened a bit. "The Arabs, you know."

"Yes, I know." I grimly looked around the field. "Is there any place else around here we can get fuel?"

"No, sir. There is no fuel on the island."

I put away my twenty and got back into the plane. "We'll have to refuel in South Caicos. Goliath won't budge." We prepared for takeoff and Tom taxied into position. The airstrip was short and rough—exactly what the Cessna taildragger was made for, and she took it with ease.

Thirty-five minutes later, we refueled at South Caicos with no trouble. "What a relief," Tom said. "St. Croix, here we come."

Except for spotting the Dominican Republic and Puerto Rico in the distance, the trip was over solid ocean. "Hope you girls brought your water wings," I said. Finally, we dropped from our 10,000 foot altitude for the approach to Harry Truman Airport, happy to see St. Croix's brilliant aqua-colored water lapping at its white beaches.

We leased a car at the airport and drove to the condominium we owned with another family, which I had reserved for one night. Other than the time spent there for school vacations, we rented out our unit to cover the mortgage and condo fees. It was in a small complex near Pelican Cove, where everybody swam, snorkeled, and listened to steel band music. We had many fond memories of our stays there.

It was a friendly place. Fellow owners escaping the north's winter weather were happy to see us. The air smelled sweet. The palm trees swayed. Their leaves made a pleasant brushing sound. The four of us relaxed on the patio, surrounded by hibiscus. The music of waves hitting the coral reef on the nearby shore had a calming effect. We spoke of our family's future.

"I still don't like Jerry Green," Diane said, her mouth set in a stubborn line.

"You'll change your mind once you're in Brazil," I said confidently.

"He'll still be a creep," she said.

After a dip in the pool, Tom and I took our daughters downtown to Christiansted. We went to The Reef for dinner and then danced to steel band music. The empty steel drums' high resonance added to the cheerful atmosphere as we tried to move our hips from side to side. "Mom calls this the St. Croix shuffle," I said. "She always laughs when we try to dance like the natives."

"I know," said Diane. "I really wish she was here."

"So do I."

In the morning, we refueled with no problems and headed for Trinidad, following the chain of Lesser Antilles. Then we circled back around St. Kitts, Nevis, Antigua, and Guadeloupe so the girls could take pictures. The vivid green hues of the islands' mountains and their shadows made stunning contrasts against the azure blue water. The girls' cameras clicked like crazy. I called their attention to the crops of tall stalks growing on some of the islands. "I think that's sugar cane."

"Wow," Diane said. "It sure looks different in our sugar bowl."

Next, we flew over a marina. You could tell by all the yachts that this was the height of the season. I was happy to note that most of the islands had a basic airstrip. *Just in case.*

The steady easterly winds over the islands had grown stronger than forecast, prompting Tom to interrupt our sightseeing. "These winds are slowing our progress," he said. "We'll have to make an unscheduled fuel stop."

He communicated with Pan Am island base operations to locate some 100 octane fuel. After transmitting to three different islands, he had three identical answers: *no fuel available.*

Pan Am base ops on Martinique, a French possession, indicated they might be able to help. But when we switched to Martinique approach control, we were bluntly informed that no fuel was available. "Being there is half the battle," I said. "And we need fuel." The tower repeated the statement several times as we descended on our final approach.

After landing, we taxied to operations and were met by three heavily armed French military police, who brusquely put us through a brief inspection and then escorted us to the terminal to fill out a questionnaire.

"Any chance of getting some fuel?" I asked. "We don't have enough to get to Trinidad."

The question immediately shot the level of hospitality from cold to hostile as a dark-skinned captain, at least six foot four and 250 pounds, emerged from operations to berate us for landing after being told no fuel was available. He showed no concern that our alternative was an unscheduled drop in the ocean.

Diane, her face pale, whispered, "The French are our friends, right, Dad?"

"I thought so," I said. Tom and I exchanged a glance.

"Get back in the plane, kids," he instructed. They obeyed without a word.

"No petrol," repeated the irate captain.

"Half a tank," I bargained with a forced smile.

The man glared at me. "No petrol!" He launched into a lengthy tirade, slipping from poor English to rapid French and back again while pointing toward town.

"Got any idea what he's talking about?" I asked Tom.

"I'm not sure," Tom said. "He doesn't seem to want us to leave, but he claims they have no fuel." He said to the man, "Please, *monsieur,* speak more slowly."

As the officer complied, it became clear that the Martinique policy during the fuel crisis was to sell fuel *only* to those who spent a few nights (and, he should have added, a few dollars) at the casino. Otherwise, no fuel.

"No deal!" I glared at the stubborn tyrant.

Tempers flared. Six heavily armed French MPs took their places nearby. The girls sat like statues in the back of the plane.

While I was arguing with the French Caribbeans, Tom walked back to the plane, climbed in, and taxied the short distance to Pan Am operations. He spoke briefly with a mechanic who directed him to the chocks immediately to the left front of a DC-7 cargo plane getting fuel. By the time the Cessna's engine had clicked to a stop, the ladder was up and the hose from the DC-7 had been handed to one of the fuel crew, who was already on the Cessna's wing, removing the fuel caps. Thanks to Tom's Pan Am connection, fifty-five gallons were dispensed before the hose was pushed back into the DC-7.

By this time I had left the soldiers in disgust. I walked over to the Pan Am hangar and paid for the fuel—three American dollars cash per gallon, a high price in 1974, but worth every cent. Then I joined the others in the plane.

We waited while a Pan Am operator called the military to persuade them that, since Tom and I were good guys, we should be allowed to leave. Looking confused, the operator came out to the plane.

"What's the story?" Tom asked.

The operator shook his head. "First they say okay, and in the next breath they say no go. You can't trust these people. They're unpredictable."

Tom and I thanked the man and watched him walk away.

I looked at Tom. "I've had enough of this place. How about you?"

Tom eyed the French militia standing en force near the terminal. "I'm with you." He glanced at the girls. The engine was idling. "Shall we go?"

He and I exchanged a long look. "Let's do it," I said. I turned to the backseat and checked the girls' seat belts. Three armed MPs sat in a jeep, watching from the sidelines.

"Daddy," Vicki asked, "will they shoot at us?"

"Don't worry, honey. We won't give em a chance."

Tom taxied slowly toward the terminal as if going back to see the authorities. I looked upward, left and right, and then upward again to check for incoming traffic. The girls held hands.

"All clear," I said.

Diane yelled, "They're following us."

A jeep was coming after us. Two of the guards stood in the backseat, holding onto a bar, rifles in hand.

"They won't catch us," Tom said firmly. He guided the Cessna to the nearest runway, turned sharply, cracked the flaps, and threw the throttle to the wall. A vibrating roar filled the air. We thundered down the runway, reaching airspeed in twenty seconds. The jeep slowed and then stopped. Tom eased back the wheel to lift the nose, trimmed it up, and then headed for Piarco on the island of Trinidad.

No one spoke until the airport was in miniature behind us. Then Tom burst out laughing, cutting the tension in the cabin. "This is a great little airplane!" he said. "I don't think I've ever had such a fast takeoff."

"With a full load to boot." I patted the dashboard. "Good job, two six six zero Sierra!"

The girls, unnaturally quiet for the past two hours, cheered. "It's a good thing the French aren't our enemies," Diane said.

"Who needs friends like them!" said Vicki.

"It was a surprise," I said. "I never expected that kind of treatment. The folks at Pan Am saved our hides."

A few hours later Tom brought the plane down at the international airport on the island of Trinidad, just above Venezuela, and taxied directly to Pan Am air operations. The base originally had been set up to handle Pan Am activity in Central and South America. It had a luxury motel, three dining rooms, a good kitchen, and a beautiful pool. The walls were covered with pictures of the old flying boat days. Over dinner, Tom and

I exchanged stories with two Pan Am crews, and our two teenagers absorbed it all. The fliers spoke about the banning of the interior skin that used to line the cabins of commercial airliners. It had been desirable because of its light weight and low cost. When it was discovered in the late sixties, however, that passengers who survived a crash could die if the ceiling and wall covering started to burn, causing a discharge of cyanide gas, it was immediately outlawed—much to the fliers' relief. Despite my interest in aviation, I had never heard about the problem.

In the morning, we refueled with no problems. It was my turn at the wheel. We took off and headed for Georgetown, in British Guiana, South America. As we flew closer, we caught sight of Georgetown's airport, almost completely surrounded by jungle. "Take a good look down there, girls," I said, "and see if you can see any Indians. Or snakes. Or crocodiles." But it was impossible to see anything through the dense foliage. I brought the Cessna in over the trees, made a quick drop, and landed smoothly.

The smothering heat and humidity shocked us when we stepped out of the plane. Again, our first concern was fuel. This time, friendly Indians were happy to fill our tank; they offered to sell us knives, tortoiseshell combs, and orange juice as well. To show our gratitude for the fuel, Tom and I bought combs for the girls before going to lunch at the airport. Then, with our tank and our stomachs full, we took off for Paramaribo in Surinam, formerly Dutch Guiana.

That night, an exotic jungle hotel was our haven, surrounded by palms and banana trees. Their dark, heavy leaves were splashed with bright red and yellow flowers. The food was far different from at home. Rice and a tuberous potatolike starch were prevalent, served with beef, chicken, and mysterious tropical fruit. I enjoyed the coffee. The farther south we went, the thicker and stronger it became. Here it was like espresso.

In the morning we started for our final destination. Belèm, Brazil. As we flew over the coast of French Guiana, we could see Devil's Island off to the left. Tom told the girls about the French penal colony, deserted since the fifties after a hundred years of punishing criminals. Almost seventy thousand convicts had died there, mostly from tropical diseases. "Although some were murdered by fellow prisoners," Tom added. "Others went insane after years of solitary confinement."

Diane shuddered. "I'm not surprised." Her Martinique experience had made her an expert on the French.

The girls stared at the small island. "It looks like just a bunch of rocks," Vicki said.

"It's probably haunted," Diane said.

"No doubt," Vicki said.

As we drew closer to Belèm, we crossed the equator at the mouth of the Amazon.

"When is it going to happen?" Diane asked.

"When is what going to happen?" I asked.

"Whatever happens when you fly over the equator."

"You mean zero Gs. No gravity." I checked the girls' seat belts. "Hold onto your hats." I dove to gain air speed, pulled into a climb, and then pushed the nose down to arc over. Suddenly weightless, we were lifted from our seats, straining against our belts. Without gravity, loose objects floated in the cabin. "That's zero Gs," I told them. "If you didn't have your seat belts on, you'd be floating too."

"That's more like it," Vicki said. She grabbed an airborne camera as Diane rescued a small purse.

Continuing on, we flew over the Brazilian island of Marajo, an enormous delta where thousands of cattle were raised. "See if you can see any big snakes crawling around," I said. "The world's largest population of anaconda lives down there."

A chorus of "yuck" and "gross" came from the backseat, and then the girls were quiet while they looked out the windows. "I see some canoes," Diane said.

"The Indians dig those canoes out of tree trunks," I told them. "They live in the shacks built over the river."

A short while later, we landed in Belèm. Courteous and efficient uniformed agents helped us clear customs without a ripple. The international language was English—or some remote facsimile.

Pedro Da Silva, Jerry Green's Belèm gofer, and Pedro de Aguiar, Alberto's cousin whom I had met in Rio, met us at the airport. They waited for Tom and me to tie down the plane and retrieve our luggage, and then drove us to a nearby motel. The four of us, tired but happy after the safe completion of our six-day journey, showered and dressed for a celebration dinner.

The next day Jerry arrived at our motel with Da Silva, in time to meet Tom and Vicki before they left on the afternoon Pan Am flight to New York. After a few minutes of small talk, all six of us crowded into the car, and Da Silva drove everybody to the airport.

He and Jerry waited by the car while Diane and I said good-bye to the Ryans. Diane and Vicki hugged each other. "I'll miss you," Vicki said. "This was the best experience of my life."

"Mine too. So far," said Diane. "I'll miss you too. Say hi to everybody in Greenwich."

Tom shook my hand. "That was quite a trip."

"Thanks for coming," I said. "If it wasn't for you, we'd still be in Martinique."

"I hope it's smooth sailing from here on. I'll call Marilyn when I get home."

I watched them walk away. Diane squeezed my arm. "I'm going to miss them too," she said.

"But we have lots to look forward to." I rested my arm on my daughter's shoulders and led her back to the car. "So let's get started."

Da Silva drove us and Jerry to the Green homestead. Starr was waiting for us, her shapely showgirl legs looking extra long in her short black shorts. Her skin was surprisingly white after all her time in the tropics. She had a hairdo fit for the stage at the Latin Quarter. It seemed out of place with her attire and the locale.

The house that I had remembered as comfortable though sparsely furnished had, in my absence, been filled with ornate, hand carved mahogany and rosewood antiques. A majestic rosewood credenza in the living room grabbed my attention with its intricately carved trim and deep magenta tone. The carved mahogany headboard in the master bedroom was almost as impressive. *I hope to hell it wasn't my money that bought the furniture,* I thought.

Jerry and I soon became immersed in our work. Diane stayed with Starr and the young maids, digesting her first taste of life in Brazil. When a woman came to the house to give her and Starr a shampoo, set, and manicure, she decided she'd like living in Brazil.

On the eve of Ash Wednesday, Jerry took Starr, Diane, and me into Belèm for Carnival, the Brazilian version of Mardi Gras.

Along the way we came upon a large black floppy hat in the middle of the road. As we drew nearer, it began to move. It was a giant tarantula crossing the road.

"You never know what you'll find," said Jerry. "But be careful! Everything isn't as docile as that tarantula." He told us about a truck driver who, while changing a tire, had been killed by two bushmasters, nasty twelve-foot long snakes that go after anything that moves.

"I guess you have to watch out for snakes wherever you are," I said.

Jerry gave me a shrewd smile. "There are all kinds of snakes, my friend. All kinds."

I returned his smile. "As I said . . ."

When we reached Belèm, the Carnival parade had taken over the streets of the city. Dancer's costumes sparkled in the sun. They swayed to the music, spellbound.

"I can feel the samba bands beating in my chest," Diane said.

We watched people of all colors laugh, sing, and clap. Their last blowout before Lent. The whole city was seduced by the magic. It didn't take long for Diane to fall under the spell.

"This is the biggest and best costume party I've ever seen," she said. In all of her fourteen years.

Chapter 28
Evan

Carnival in Rio! It was the wildest party Lynne and I had ever seen.

The city was all charged up. It felt like the whole place was beating in time to the music from the samba schools. Those were the neighborhood clubs that practiced all year long, just for Carnival. The students strutted in their handmade costumes of shiny cloth trimmed with feathers and sequins, parading through the streets and dancing. They even stopped traffic. Car exhaust floated in the air. Whole lines of dancers boarded buses, barely missing a beat. They crowded in with the laughing riders and shook everybody's bones with their loud music. Every year Rio celebrated Carnival. Big time. It was drunken! Happy! Insane!

We heard there were loads of murders—nearly as many during Carnival as in the whole rest of the year—but it didn't stop the partying. Brightly colored decorations waved in the breeze. Hotels were full to the brim with tourists. Partyers from all over the world slept on the beach. Everybody wore costumes. For five crazy days, Rio was one huge wild playground.

Lynne and I were thrilled to be part of it. The Battistas had temporarily relaxed the rules, and, I have to admit, my sister and I threw more energy into Carnival than school would ever see. Since we were each fifteen pounds lighter, we made filmy skirts out of scarves and wore them over our bikinis to copy the half-naked Brazilians. Every night we went out with our school friends to a night club called Monte Libro. Not even a scream could pierce the bands' earsplitting noise. People were jammed to the walls. We could only jump up and down to dance. Our bare flesh rubbed against other people's bare flesh. Sweaty and smelly. There were no strangers.

What a great party! We wished our friends could see us.

Chapter 29
Jack

A week after we arrived in Belèm, Diane and I flew by commercial airliner to Rio. I had chosen to leave the Cessna in Belèm, closer to the Macapà gold mine and the cattle ranches in the north. Besides, I had no desire to make the flight without a copilot. Whether I had flown the 1600-mile straight line over dense jungle or the safer 2200-mile route along the coast, it would have been a long, lonely trip in the small single-engine plane.

Lynne and Evan were so happy to see us, I let them move into the Trocadero Hotel with Diane and me. Together, we called Marilyn at the Warner's.

She had some disturbing news. "Howard Fox called. He was shocked to hear you'd already left."

I felt a stab in my gut. "What did he say?"

"Nothing specific. But he sounded concerned that you had left before he got back to you."

"I assumed no news was good news. He didn't tell you anything?"

"No. He was just very upset about your leaving."

"Well, it's too late now. What do you want to do?"

"Well, this is how I see it. We're straddling the river, with too much forward momentum to turn around. Howard's call scared me. But he didn't have a good reason to change the plan. We're this far. I think we should keep going."

"I think so too. So. We'll meet you at the airport. I can't wait to see you."

The girls started yelling, "Love you, Mom. Hurry up and get down here."

I gave each of them a turn on the phone before I said good-bye. Pretty soon we all would be together. At least *that* was a sure thing.

Chapter 30
Marilyn

I tried to find a comfortable position in the small aisle seat on Pan Am's night flight to Rio. The pulled muscle under my ribs kept reminding me of all the boxes I had lifted. That, and thoughts of what I might have forgotten, plus excitement at seeing my family, made it impossible to sleep. Twelve-year-old Heather, sitting next to the window, would doze and wake, look around and say, "I can't believe we're finally going to Rio." Our poodle, Pom Pom, was the calmest of all. Under the influence of a tranquilizer, she sat peacefully in the middle seat, facing forward and erect like a regular passenger. Jasmine, also under sedation, rode in a box in the hold.

After we landed, Heather, Pom Pom, and I waited in line to have our passports and immunization certificates checked. Rio's humidity felt thick and heavy after New York's cutting March winds. The flood of foreign words and signs confused me, and I was struck with a sudden compassion for immigrants. I felt a new camaraderie with people who had migrated to new countries, their heads buzzing with dreams, their chests pounding with fear. These newcomers—infringers to some—arrived in alien territory, out of tune with everything they knew, totally at the mercy of strangers. Now I was one of them.

My strongest worry was about Pom Pom. "Let her hair grow shaggy," Jerry had advised, "so she'll look like a mutt. If she looks valuable, the authorities will confiscate her and sell her."

"Mommy," Heather cried, "there's Jasmine!" She pointed to a dark, thin man in a khaki uniform who stood on a box, holding up a calico cat, his hands under her front legs. Her long body hung limply, as if she were trying to make herself thin enough to slip away.

"Oh my God!" I said. "Hold the dog." I gave Heather the leash and pushed my way through the noisy, sweaty crowd, excusing myself in English. When I reached the man, I shouted above the din, "That's my cat."

The man stared blankly at me. I pointed to myself, then pointed to the droopy animal. "My cat. My cat."

"Ah!" He smiled, spoke foreign gibberish, and handed me the cat and her box. In her panic, Jasmine twisted and clawed at me, trying to get away. I struggled to keep my grip as I worked my way back in line, where Heather, the great animal communicator, coaxed our frightened cat back into the box.

"Let's make sure the latch is secure this time," I said.

It seemed to take forever for officials to sanction our collection of human and animal papers. When at last Heather and I carried our pets to the waiting room, we were grabbed by three exuberant teenagers and one happy daddy. Our family was together again.

* * *

We settled temporarily at the Trocadero Hotel. For two days, Jasmine's tranquilizer kept her weaving, legs spread, eyes crossed. I took a plastic-lined drawer from a bedside table and filled it with newspapers and sand from the beach to make a litter box. Unfortunately, a litter box wouldn't work for the dog. We had to sneak her down the service elevator, hoping we wouldn't get caught. Our clandestine talents, however, were lacking. On the third day, the dreaded call came from the manager. The animals had to go to a kennel.

* * *

On March 8, my birthday, we had a wonderful family dinner at the restaurant in the Trocadero. Afterwards, Carlos Alberto, Jerry's soft-spoken lawyer from Belèm with amazingly long eyelashes, invited Jack and me and our two oldest daughters out to celebrate. Somehow he managed to communicate that Diane and Heather were too young to go. "It's not fair," Diane complained. "We always miss the fun."

"You're only fourteen. Your sister's twelve," Jack explained. "Don't worry. We have plenty of time for fun in Rio with the whole family." We hugged them and promised to be back soon.

Alberto led us to a nearby night club ("ni-chee clew-bee") called LeRoi. We joined six others at a long table. Alberto's cousin, de Aquiar, sat next to a jolly man called Brasil, whose black wavy hair glistened with pomade. Next to him was another of Alberto's cousins, Ronaldo Nelson. His companion, a pretty woman called Tanya, was obviously attracted to his stocky build, short brown hair, and yellow-green eyes. Next to her sat Silveira, a tall fidgety man with a crew cut, and his conservatively dressed wife, Maria. Nobody spoke English.

A bottle of whiskey with measuring lines on it was placed at each end of the table next to a bowl of ice cubes. Each person received an empty glass.

I looked at Jack. "That's it?"

He shrugged. "Guess so."

"What about the girls?"

"Oh come on, Mom," Lynne and Evan coaxed. "It's a special occasion."

I was in a festive mood. "Well, maybe just one. But sip it slowly!" I warned.

The girls looked at each other and giggled. *With our mother's permission,* I knew they were thinking.

Ronaldo caught my attention. He pointed to the gold wedding band on his left hand and then at Tanya, and shook his head in the negative, a boastful smile on his face. His yellow-green eyes sparked with a touch of devilment as he put his finger to his lips to signify a secret.

Then he left the table and disappeared. A few minutes later he returned with a basket of roses and placed them in front of me. The room darkened suddenly and a cupcake with a lit candle was brought to the table. Everyone in the "ni-chee clew-bee" sang "*Feliz Aniversario Natalicio.*"

I was warmed by the Brazilian friendliness. I thought it was a good omen.

After we returned to the Trocadero, the manager called. In halting English, he politely requested that our daughters refrain—*por favor!—from* dropping pigeon eggs out the window. People on the sidewalk were complaining that something from above was hitting them on their heads. "You guys went partying without us," Diane said, "so we had to make our own fun." The tiny hard-boiled eggs were left over from breakfast.

* * *

On Sunday we all walked to a Catholic church a mile away. A woman greeted us inside. She beckoned Jack and I to sit down and then led the four girls away.

"Where is she taking them?" I asked.

"Maybe she'll sell 'em."

"Jack, this isn't funny!"

"Come on. We're in church."

"We're also in Brazil! It's different here, in case you hadn't noticed."

"Just keep your shirt on and say your prayers."

"Hmmmph. I don't like it." Still, I knelt beside him. Looking around, I was surprised to see so few men, considering the majority of Brazil's population was Catholic.

When Diane and Heather appeared later to carry the bread and wine to the altar, Jack gloated. "They're back." Then they were gone again.

At communion time, Lynne and Evan led Jack and the other men down the aisle to receive communion. The women waited at the back of the church for their turn, one of many signs of their secondary status.

From then on we went to a church on the other side of Rio that catered to Americans. It was a small, wooden contemporary structure full of friendly people who spoke English, and where we all could sit together. It took two Volkswagen taxis to carry the six of us, but nobody complained. The church was a haven, a link with the familiar.

* * *

The cost of taxis and buses was low—the equivalent of seven cents for a bus ride, though inflation would double the price in two months. Eating out was another bargain, but service was slow.

Living at the Trocadero Hotel in Copacabana was a gentle way to ease into a foreign lifestyle. Each morning the girls gathered in our sitting room where room service set up a breakfast of cheese, hard-boiled pigeon eggs, crusty rolls, cereal, lush tropical fruit we didn't recognize, fresh squeezed juices, milk, tea, and coffee.

Outside, an army of orange-uniformed men lined the beaches and sidewalks to rake up the previous day's debris, ankle deep in spots. Brazilians, proud of their bodies, took their morning jog on the mosaic sidewalks skirting the beaches, while others worked out on the sand in their *tangas.*

After the girls left for school, Jack and I would walk across the boulevard to the beach to watch fishermen in large wooden rowboats drag their nets ashore. Their women, sun-dried and beaten by the wind, waited on the beach, shouting over the thundering waves like proverbial fishwives. When the boats were close enough, they waded into the churning surf, their wet skirts and aprons pressed against their legs, to grab the huge nets and begin the laborious process of hauling them in. The largest catch usually was garbage—white plastic foam cups, empty bottles, and food wrappers. Here and there, a colorful flopping fish danced his last samba.

Often, Jack and I walked along the half-moon beaches of Leme, Copacabana, Ipanema, and Leblon on Avenida Atlantica, the boulevard for rich tourists. Sterns and other elegant jewelry stores decorated their windows with eye-catching displays of magnificent rings, necklaces, and bracelets draped around huge uncut hunks of topaz, amethyst, crystal, and quartz, some over a foot high, all mined in Brazil. The jewelry cast a vivid rainbow of colors: aquamarine, in shades that ranged from deep turquoise to pale, almost clear, aqua; topaz like yellow sun; soft purple stones of amethyst; rich blue sapphires; blood red rubies; and warm green emeralds and tourmalines. Jack remarked that compared to New York, these prices were a steal. Then he told me about a runway Jerry had described. It was made of pure amethyst.

Outdoor cafés spotted the sidewalks. Everyone—except the waiters—seemed to be in a hurry, driven by some mysterious inner force. *Cafèzinho?* Frustrated drivers, unable to find parking places, left their cars on the sidewalk, where policemen plastered large signs across their windshields with glue that only Coca Cola could dissolve. And always in the background, the continuous hollow echo of the ocean's roar and the traffic's din.

Sometimes, Jack and I walked inland, away from the ocean. One day, we came to a body lying on the sidewalk. "Maybe he's just sleeping," I said. Just then a man came along and nudged the body with his foot. It turned slightly, and one arm flopped open and lay stiff. The man continued to roll the body with his foot until it fell off the curb into the street.

"Oh God," I said. "That poor soul. I wonder if they'll just sweep him up and throw him in the garbage?" I said a silent prayer for the man. "They don't seem to have much respect for human life. Or death."

"Come on, kid." Jack's voice was soft. He put his arm around me, and we quietly walked away.

* * *

By some strange mystery, the apartment for which Jack had given a $1400 deposit to Jerry's lawyer, Carlos Alberto, never materialized, nor was the money returned, and Alberto was conveniently out of touch in Belèm. We had a feeling the money was gone for good, but our greater concern was finding our family a home.

Our new friends, who had been introduced to Jack by Jerry, came to the rescue. Marcos da Matta, in his fifties, was an attorney for the Federal Ministry of Justice.

Since he was bilingual, he was the interpreter. Ronaldo Nelson, a young entrepreneur always looking for a deal, was the philanderer who had arranged for my birthday cupcake. And Silveira, tall and fidgety, had also been at my party. He knew one phrase in English: "I loave you." Each day they brought a newspaper to the hotel and pored through the real estate ads with Jack and me.

Finally, a place was found. Silveira's landlady had an *apartamente* for the Americans just around the corner from Silveira. "*Muito grande,*" Silveira said, his arms shaping a huge circle. Jack and I agreed when we saw it. The bright, airy furnished apartment on the thirteenth floor of 1260 Avenida Atlantica overlooked Copacabana Beach and was very grand.

Moving day was March 16, a sunny Saturday. Jack and I and the four girls, plus Ronaldo, Silveira, and two young men he had hired, formed an assembly line to pass suitcases and boxes from the hotel to a relay of Volkswagen taxis. Everyone but Marcos da Matta, the lawyer, helped.

While the rest of us labored, da Matta, a tall, thin man, with skin an unhealthy beige color, watery brown eyes, and thinning gray hair, sat at the Trocadero's sidewalk bar, enjoying his favorite pastime of sipping whiskey, while he cheerfully dispensed words of encouragement—some Portuguese, some English—to the passing parade of movers. People walking by glanced, curious, and continued on, while cars raced past, the constant roar of the ocean beyond.

I paid no attention to a brief, piercing twist that cut through my sore muscle as I hoisted a box into a waiting taxi.

After the move was finished, Jack paid the two boys and made a circle with his thumb and forefinger to declare their work A-OK. To his surprise, the gesture unleashed a chorus of loud, unrestrained Portuguese. Though he understood not a word, Jack could tell they were not singing his praises. After Silveira had calmed them, he explained to Jack—in vivid body language—that his gesture meant "fuck you." The signal Jack should have used was a thumbs-up.

The apartment was more than we could have hoped for. Released from a tiny elevator, the six of us crowded into a small tile-walled foyer that led to a broad hall. The girls pushed one another for the best spot to gaze through a large arch that opened to a huge living-dining room with sliding glass picture windows overlooking the ocean.

"Hey, Mom, not too shabby, huh?" said Evan.

"It's beautiful," I agreed.

"Let's go see the bedrooms," Diane yelled as she ran to the end of the hall and turned left, her three sisters close behind. Their shoes thumped a drum roll on the bare wooden floor.

"Hey, look at these funny bathrooms," Heather called. "They have two toilets."

The girls crowded around me while I tried to explain the purpose of a bidet, accompanied by a chorus of snickers.

I quickly changed the subject. "And look at these white marble walls and floors. Aren't they something? The most elegant bathrooms we've ever had."

The girls acted impressed, but then ran off to claim their rooms.

Lynne yelled, "Evan and I have dibs on the front bedroom. Next to the sunporch."

"They always get the best one," Diane complained. "It's not fair."

"They're the oldest," I said, "so they get first choice."

"Rats." Diane ran down the hall. "Come on, Heather, let's go see our room."

After inspecting the front bedroom, everybody assembled in the back bedroom.

"This room is bigger than the front room," Diane said. She gave her two older sisters a satisfied smirk. "And Mom, you and Dad can have the middle room with the double bed."

"And that settles that," I said.

Satisfied with the sleeping arrangements, each went off on her own to explore. I walked toward the front, past Lynne and Evan's new room, to see the sun-porch, a long, narrow room surrounded by windows. Unfortunately, anybody who sat on the slipcovered couch would miss the view of the ocean. "This is a good place for homework," I told Heather, who had followed me. "No distractions."

A door at one side led to the main room, but I returned to the archway in the front hall to enjoy the full picture. On the left, the dining area held a large Sheraton table, ten matching chairs, and a broad china cabinet; on the right, the living area was furnished with a long sofa and two side chairs upholstered in red and white embossed taffeta, with occasional tables and a TV set. The highly polished parquet floor displayed a variety of Brazilian woods, with an intricate light-toned design set around a handsome dark medallion in the center. As I admired the beautiful rooms and the fine furniture, I couldn't help think that our good fortune was a sign that things would go well. I turned around to the kitchen across the hall. It was large with a mosaic tile floor, a marble counter and sink along one wall, an enamel table in the center, and two refrigerators that looked well past their prime. I walked through a small room with two laundry tubs, but no washing machine. Beyond was a plain tiled bathroom and a small bedroom with a bed, chest, and lamp. Even room for a maid.

I returned to the grand room and stood to one side of the center medallion. It was too beautiful to stand on. Looking around, I smiled and took a deep breath. A salty sea essence blew through the open windows where thin white curtains billowed. From below, the blended cadence of ocean and traffic broadcast a steady flow of soft background music. This, now, was home.

* * *

That night, Ronaldo Nelson, the young entrepreneur with a mistress, invited all of us to his apartment to have dinner with his wife, two little daughters, and his parents. Three maids served us. The pretty, young Mrs. Nelson—unable to converse with her guests—quickly grew bored. She sighed forlornly throughout the evening and spent a great deal of time studying her well-manicured nails. Still, it was a compliment to foreigners to be invited into a Brazilian's home, a promising beginning to life in Rio.

Chapter 31
Marilyn

Sunday morning, the smell of incinerator smoke woke me and set me coughing. A stabbing pain lodged in my ribs and refused to budge. It twisted like a knife with every move. "It hurts to breathe," I said as I bent forward, my arms crossed over my chest.

Jack thought of the fastest way to get help. "Silveira lives around the corner," he said. "Maybe his doctor would see us." His hand trembled as he dialed Silveira's number.

Within minutes, Silveira stormed into the apartment, raving like a madman. His towering physique added to his commanding presence as he flailed his arms and ranted, his short brown hair standing on end, his pale green eyes blazing.

We all watched, dumbfounded, momentarily forgetting my problem. Jack had no way of calming Silveira. He asked Diane to call her Brazilian-American friend from school. "Ask him to come *pronto* to help us translate." Then he pantomimed to Silveira that someone would come to explain his problem to us. Silveira stopped his outburst to watch Jack's odd gesticulations. Finally, he shook his head and started pacing the room, talking to himself, his eyes still sparking. The girls huddled close to me as they watched him.

When the buzzer rang, Jack ran to the door to meet Richie, Diane's classmate. He rushed the boy into the living room. The fourteen-year-old's brown eyes, tanned face, and curly blond hair broadcast his dual heritage. Silveira immediately launched into his booming harangue, gesturing wildly, rekindling his anger. When at last he finished, he waited in silence, still breathing hard, while Richie, his dark eyes wide, explained that Silveira was angry because we had gone to Ronaldo's for dinner. "I think he's jealous," he concluded. By feeding Jack's fawning words of conciliation to Silveira, he managed to bring him to a level of rationality where he could grasp my predicament.

His grievance forgotten, Silveira promptly called his doctor and his wife. The doctor was on a Sunday holiday; his wife appeared in three minutes.

Silveira explained his next call to Richie, who explained it to us. "He's called the Federal Hospital and asked them to send a doctor. The Federal Hospital is for everyone, but it's used mostly by the poor. He's sorry, but with his doctor away, he didn't know what else to do."

Soon two men in white rang the bell and came into the living room, where we and our guests were seated—except for Silveira, who paced nervously while Richie explained my malady to the men. One of the attendants grabbed my shirt and raised it over my head, exposing my bra to everyone. His eyes focused on my left rib, which had protruded abnormally since birth. "The rib is broken," he proclaimed through Richie. "She will have to go in the ambulance to the hospital."

I looked at Jack. "If you don't come with me, I may never see you again."

Jack smiled gently. "I'm with ya, kid." After we said good-bye to everybody, I shuffled out the door with Jack holding my arm.

Outside, a white van with painted windows waited on the sidewalk with a crowd around it. Without offering to help, the attendants gestured for me to get in the back. I got down on all fours, wincing and grunting, and crawled in with Jack's help, muttering "Ouch" through clenched teeth. When we got inside, Jack perched on his knees to help me onto the stretcher, and then sat beside me on a small jump seat. The attendants closed the doors.

"Just like Greenwich," I said hoarsely.

As the ambulance started to move, Jack rolled down the window.

"Tell me what you see," I said, trying to ignore the pain.

"We're driving through the park. On the sidewalk."

"On the sidewalk?" I bit the insides of my cheek to keep from laughing.

The siren burped a series of low, short warnings.

Jack launched into a play-by-play. "We're going at a good clip. People are running in all directions."

"Ha ha. Ow!" I held my side.

The siren blasted into a full wail as we lurched forward and down with a thud.

"Ouch!"

"We just went off the curb. We're in the street. Going like a bat. Cars are scrambling. Trying to get out of the way."

"Ouch! No more! Please!" I tried to stifle my laughter. "I can't stand it."

At last, the ambulance rolled to a stop and the doors opened. Both attendants waited, miserably bored, while I groped my way out with Jack carefully trying to help. Finally I rolled over on all fours and crawled out backward, modestly trying to keep my skirt from creeping up. I eased myself into an upright position and walked delicately to the nearest open doorway. A man in white wearing a stethoscope waited for me.

"Wot ees your name?" he asked.

"Marilyn Kelley."

He searched his pockets unsuccessfully for a piece of paper and then, shrugging, gave me a pen and held up his hand. "Write here."

Incredulous, I pointed to the man's palm. "There?"

He nodded.

I signed the man's palm, unable to stifle a grin.

Afterward, the man took me into a small room, where flies buzzed in and out of two screenless windows. He motioned for me to lie down on a black examination table. One end was littered with small piles of sand from previous patients' shoes. I lay there, watching the flies, wondering whether we should have stayed in Connecticut. While the doctor examined me, he managed to impart—with bad English and tedious repetition—that he was engaged to an American girl he had met while attending medical school in the States. How did he get through an English-speaking medical school? I wondered as he probed my ribs. More important, How much did he learn?

When he was finished, a woman in white came in to help me undress for an X-ray. The old machine hummed loudly while it took pictures of my chest.

By the time I was dressed again, the doctor had read the X-rays and reached his diagnosis. "You have pay-nay-mon-aya," he announced.

It took several repetitions before I realized he was trying to tell me I had pneumonia. "Oh, I really don't think so," I said.

He shrugged. "Well, maybe lung disease." He eased me toward the door. "Now you go woo-mon's bee-yul-ding."

Jack was waiting outside. "Jack, if I have a lung disease, I'll be on the next plane to Greenwich. This place is like the dark ages!"

"Don't worry, we'll see a private doctor before we do anything," he assured me.

We walked across a barren dirt courtyard, past a hospital compound of one-story structures, and entered the women's building. Straight ahead was a long ward with at least ten beds on each side, almost all filled. The usual antiseptic hospital smell was missing.

I was led into an examining room, with no regard for the dignity of a heavy black woman who was bending over to receive an injection. Her skirt was up around her shoulders and one large bare cheek could be seen hanging like a thick lace ruffle over a dimpled thigh. The room was in complete disarray. Bloody gauze pads cluttered the floor. An archway to the hall had been blocked off with a louvered folding screen. A head kept bobbing up over the top, trying to peek in.

After the black woman left, I was joined by a doctor. He was obviously embarrassed. "I want to apologize for the conditions," he said in halting English. The head bounced above the screen. A woman in the hall shouted angrily. The doctor said, "Brasil is not a rich country like the United States."

As I eyed the filthy surroundings, my pain was briefly overcome by a desire to help, even if only to sweep the floor.

The shouting in the hall had reached a decibel that made conversation impossible. The enraged woman screamed at the peeper as she tried to remove him from the premises. His vigorous response made it obvious he didn't want to leave. His voice sounded vaguely familiar.

The doctor looked sheepish and shrugged.

I gave him a weak smile, then it came to me. The voice was Silveira's.

It grew fainter as he was escorted from the building in a clamor of footsteps and shouting.

In the ensuing quiet, the doctor examined me and asked questions about the pain. Eventually, he determined that I had inhaled too much incinerator smoke and had strained a muscle from coughing. "Someone will be in to give you a shot for pain," he said. His voice was consoling. He left.

The nurse returned and selected a needle from an open tray. *Here comes hepatitis*, I thought. As I bent over, skirt hiked up like the elderly heavy woman, the needle jabbed me. It felt not only square but rusty, and my fears were reinforced.

When I was finished, I shuffled outside, now sore in two places. Jack, Silveira, his wife, Diane, and Richie were waiting for me. "What a ride we had!" Diane said. "Speeding over the sidewalks, blowing the horn. It felt like we were going ninety! I think he's crazy." A playful smile tweaked her face as her opinion of Silveira's mental state sneaked past him in English.

Richie's eyes were big as quarters. "Yeah!"

The six of us crammed into Silveira's sports car for the ride home. With me aboard, he drove like he was hauling a crate of eggs. The other passengers, prepared for another hair-raising ride, gratefully leaned back and relaxed.

When we reached our building, Silveira parked on the sidewalk, as close to the door as he could get. I clenched my teeth against the pain as everybody pushed and tugged to help me climb out. We thanked Silveira for his help, said good-bye to him and his wife, and went upstairs. I rested while the shot took effect. Jack did laundry by hand and Lynne made dinner. The younger girls sat with Richie in the living room. He appeared reluctant to leave, perhaps afraid he'd miss whatever happened next.

* * *

The following afternoon, our landlady, Eva, who shared the thirteenth floor with us, came for a visit. She and I sat in the living room. My hip where I'd gotten the shot hurt more than my rib, convincing me I had merely reinjured the muscle I had pulled while packing in Greenwich. Dense clouds floated by the window while Eva and I passed my Portuguese-English dictionary back and forth, reading the foreign words to each other. Our pronunciation was so abominable, however, we ended up sitting elbow to elbow, pointing to the words. A tedious half hour later, I understood that a maid would come the next day to clean the apartment and take me to the market.

Sure enough, the next afternoon, Adichi, a very heavy, very dark older woman appeared at the door. With a ready smile showing beautiful white teeth, she shuffled in on her elephantine legs and got right to work. First she set about cleaning the apartment in steady slo-o-o-ow motion. When she finished, she and I went to market, communicating in sign language.

The market, an open double storefront, was full of interesting wares. In the cases were all sorts of mystery meats with foreign labels. My main goal was to avoid goat, an unheard of dish at home. Since chicken was easily identifiable—with head and feet attached or, if desired, live—that would be what we ate most. Another dish that would never grace our table was the dried, filleted white fish densely covered with moving black scales that, I realized with a closer look, were flies. Adichi selected okra and lettuce from a strange assortment of vegetables, while I chose some delectable-looking giant fruit. When we got home, Adichi immediately plunged the fresh produce into a sink full of bleach and water. As da Matta later explained, this was to kill the bacteria from the human fertilizer farmers used.

While Adichi made dinner, the girls did their homework, except for Evan, who was playing in a tennis tournament. I worked on my needlepoint and Jack paced the living room, worrying aloud. Jerry had not made contact in over two weeks.

The sound of the buzzer grabbed everybody's attention. Adichi motioned for us to stay seated and shuffled in her sandals to the door. A moment later, Silveira walked into the living room. He had come to see how I was doing, and he had brought a translator, Danny, the shoeshine boy from the Leme Palace Hotel.

Silveira happily accepted Jack's offer for a drink—whiskey, of course, as they called their Scotch. Danny, a tall, lean dark-skinned young man, too jumpy to sit still, declined, opting instead to walk back and forth in long rapid strides while he translated.

Each time he relayed Silveira's message, he added a few words of his own. "This guy's crazy." "He doesn't know what he's talking about." "He's in another world." "What an idiot!" Oddly, Danny's English had no trace of an accent.

When dinner was ready, and since Silveira showed no signs of leaving, we invited him and Danny to stay for dinner, suggesting Silveira call his wife and invite her as well. Maria appeared almost immediately, and Adichi added three more places to the long table.

Danny refused to join us. "Blacks don't eat with whites," he said. "I'll eat in the kitchen with the help." No amount of coaxing would change his mind. He disappeared when the whites sat down at the table.

There was no doubt that Danny had Silveira pegged correctly. Silveira acted erratically, refusing to sit down. "No eat!" he said. "No eat!" He went around the table and pretended to vomit on each plate—much to everyone's revulsion—to illustrate what would happen if he ate.

Heather screwed up her face. "Yuck! I'm not going to eat this food after he spit on it!"

"He didn't spit on it," said Diane. "He puked on it."

"Girls, that's enough." I was growing anxious. "Try to ignore him and maybe he'll stop."

Jack's face mirrored my concern.

Silveira disappeared into the kitchen and returned with a full glass of Scotch. Danny was at his heels shouting, "No more booze." He grabbed the drink from Silveira, strode to the open window, made a motion to pour it out, and then changed his mind. Instead, he lifted it to his mouth in one grand swoop, tilted his head back, and downed the whole glassful in a huge gulp. Then he gestured toward the table. "Go sit down," he croaked. He returned to the kitchen to finish his dinner.

Silveira came back to the table and began declaring his love for Jack. "Kel-lay, I loave you," he repeated again and again. He grabbed a table knife and mimed cutting his wrist. "Blood brothers, Kel-lay."

"Sit down, Silveira." Jack's voice was stone cold.

The girls watched, motionless. They knew their father was close to the boiling point.

"But Kel-lay, I loave you." Silveira approached Jack with the knife. "Blood brothers. I loave you."

Without a word, Jack stood up and stormed out of the room.

Maria burst into tears.

"He's going for his gun!" Lynne shouted. I ran after him with the three girls, yelling, "No, no!"

We found him leaning on his dresser, his head resting on his arms. "I had to get away from the sonofabitch."

"He's crazy," I said.

"We thought you were going to get your gun and shoot him," Diane said.

Jack stared at her. In a dull monotone, he said, "Don't worry, honey, I'm not going to shoot anybody."

In the living room, Danny and Maria were engaged in a raucous shouting match with Silveira. As we filed out of the bedroom, Evan stood in the hall in her tennis whites, looking befuddled. "If anybody cares," she yelled over the clamor, "I lost."

"That's too bad, dear," I said as I marched back to the table, ignoring the commotion on the other side of the room. "Come and have dinner."

"You should have been here," Lynne told her.

"Yeah! You really missed it," Diane said.

By the time we were seated at the table again, our guests were on their way out, without dinner.

"Good riddance," Heather said.

We had already given Evan a replay of events and had nearly finished eating when we heard loud voices drifting up from the street in what sounded like an argument between Silveira, Danny, and the doorman. A few minutes later the buzzer rang.

"I'll get it," Jack said, his voice tense. Everybody got up and followed him. Danny and Silveira stood in the vestibule. Silveira was holding a plate with a piece of cake and a candle.

Danny looked at us, gathered around the door. "He says it's his birthday. I tried to keep him away but he insisted on bringing the cake."

Silveira thrust the cake at me. "*Para mew aniversario natalicio.*"

Without warning, Danny grabbed the plate from my hands. "Don't eat that!" he yelled. "It's got drugs in it."

"Drugs!" I said, feeling a sudden chill.

"Get that bastard out of here!" Jack shouted.

Danny shoved Silveira into the elevator and pushed the button. The door closed and their voices grew fainter.

"Oh God," I said. "He was in here with the kids!"

Ten minutes later the buzzer rang again. It was Danny. Alone.

Jack's patience was gone. "What do you want?"

"I'd like to speak to you."

"You've got sixty seconds."

Danny was nervous, close to twitching. "Silveira . . . he's a crazy man."

"Tell me something I don't know."

Danny flinched under Jack's icy stare. He was thin and wiry, no match for Jack. "Tonight . . . uh, could've been trouble." He let out a nervous giggle.

"Really?" Jack glared.

"I thought . . . uh, maybe you'd like to give me something . . . You know . . ." Danny gave him an endearing smile. "For all my trouble."

Jack stared at him, incredulous. "I think you'd better leave," he said, his voice quiet and then rising, "before I do something we'll both regret!" He grabbed Danny's arm, lifted him out the door, and slammed it shut. We could hear the elevator door open and close, followed by the high-pitched hum of its descent.

Evan sighed. "I'd love a dull day."

Adichi had joined us in the hall, the whites of her eyes rotating like two strobe lights. She wore a faint smile that seemed to say, "This place is crazy, but I think I like it."

"By the way," I said to Lynne, who was doing well with Portuguese, "would you ask Adichi what time she's leaving?"

After a brief conversation, Lynne reported, "She said she's not leaving. She's going to live with us!"

"Oh God." My hand went to my head. "I must have missed something in the translation."

Chapter 32
Marilyn

Jasmine purred vigorously, rubbing against every leg in sight—human, chair, table—while Pom Pom bounced from room to room, investigating all the corners of her new home. Unfortunately, each had come from the kennel with her own colony of ticks. Diane and Heather found the tiny blood suckers a few days later, climbing their pale green bedroom walls. Their screams brought everybody scrambling to watch, horrified, as the gray bloated bodies moved in a muted, slow-changing design. They were everywhere, in the girls' beds, their clothing, even on the closet walls. Heather, the great animal lover, quickly recovered to observe the engorged ticks, fascinated, while her sisters expressed their disgust. Diane did a little dance of repulsion, wagging her arms and yelling, "Gross! I'm going to throw up." Jack immediately ran out and bought something to fumigate the room, plus a special powder to rub on the animals.

For the next week, Diane and Heather slept on the sunporch. I feared the little critters would find the landlady on one of her frequent visits, though as far as I know, they never did.

To the girls' delight, Jasmine had another surprise. She was pregnant.

Chapter 33
Jack

I couldn't sleep. Why didn't Jerry call? Where was he? And where was the promised income from the gold? Had Jerry deceived me after all? I refused to believe it. A con man would have bolted after he got the money. Jerry had stuck with us. Why, then, was he playing hard to get?

At last, I heard from Ronaldo—who had heard from his cousin, Alberto, Jerry's lawyer—that Jerry was arriving in Rio on the afternoon flight from Belèm. I made a special trip to the airport for a surprise welcome. But Jerry never arrived.

For lack of something to do, I spent most mornings at Ronaldo's office. Years of soccer on the beach had given Ronaldo thick thighs and a tanned, healthy look. When he sat behind his desk talking on the phone, he bounced with energy in his chair.

Sometimes Brasil was at the office. A paunchy, middle-aged man with pomaded wavy black hair, he had renamed himself Deus Mar Brasil—God, sea, and country. His occupation was never discussed, though he acted important.

Sometimes Marcos da Matta was there, arousing my curiosity about his work schedule at the Federal Ministry of Justice. He always dressed the part of a government lawyer, in a suit and tie, unlike his friends who wore short-sleeved sport shirts and slacks. His hands always shook slightly, no doubt the residual of the previous night's imbibing.

Occasionally, one or more of Ronaldo's cousins made an appearance, seeming to have nothing to do but hang around.

Often during their talk of business matters, the men would discuss clever ways of squeezing extra profit from their deals. Ronaldo bragged about his scheme to cheat the phone company of his long distance calls. "The phone company will never miss it," he said. "They are big. I am small." Brasil praised him for his cunning. Da Matta, the lawyer, acted like this was the normal way of doing business as he translated for me. Ronaldo ran a pen back and forth through his fingers, grinning as he listened to the English version of his scam. I merely smiled and shook my head. Ronaldo gloated. "Like Watergate."

One day it was just the regulars in the office—Brasil, da Matta, and Ronaldo. After their routine business discussion, Ronaldo turned to me. Before he spoke English—a slow process—he always hummed first, as if to prime his motor. "Hmm," he began, "Kel-lay, we see . . . *quatias filias* . . . go *Escola Americana* . . ." He rubbed his thumb back and forth over his fingers to impart that it took money. "We see . . . big *apartamente* . . . *Avenida Atlantica.*" Again he rubbed his thumb over his fingers. "We see . . . big money . . . go out." (Money was one English word he'd learned quickly.) "We see . . . no money . . . come in." He leaned back, folded his arms, and smiled slyly. "Kel-lay," he purred. "You bigga magnata?"

Jack Kelley? Business magnate? Why not? I nodded in the affirmative.

A cunning laugh rolled from Ronaldo, happily joined by Brasil and da Matta. "That's what we thought," Ronaldo said.

Maybe it was the reason Ronaldo and Brasil made so many evening visits to our apartment. They were a jovial pair, entertaining the girls with card tricks and making conversation, of a sort. They surprised us by throwing their trash out the window. Empty cigarette packs. Fruit pits. Half-eaten ice cream cones.

The Brazilians had been shocked to learn that none of us had *carteiros de identidades.* Brasil looked grave. "En Brasil, mon . . . woomon . . . cheeldren . . ." He shook his head. "No *carteiro*? Ha! Arrest. No reason."

Ronaldo added, "Sit in park at night?" He looked through the Portuguese-English dictionary. "Es . . . loiter. No *identidade*? Arrest."

The girls listened, wide-eyed.

Slightly alarmed, Marilyn said, "I'd better keep moving when I walk the dog after dinner."

Of course, a payoff would fix everything. Evan told about a friend who had been sitting on the beach with her boyfriend. "The police came up and said, 'You're under arrest. Give us your Levi's'"

"Did she take off her pants in front of her boyfriend?" Diane asked. There was mischief in her voice.

"No-o-o." Evan glared at her. "They gave the police all their money, and the police went away."

Brasil nodded in agreement. "*Brasil es muito corrupto! Nao es Estadas Unidas! Es Brasil—una militar ditadura* . . . ah, ah, deek-tay-torrr-sheep. If arrested, *prisao . . . adeus.*" He said it forcefully, as he said most things.

I grew more anxious as I listened to the pitfalls of living in a military dictatorship.

The dictionary made the rounds.

Ronaldo expanded on Brasil's declaration. "If go to . . . pree-zone, good-bye. If no like, take to beach. Shoot!"

"No trial?" I asked.

"Trial?" Ronaldo snorted. "They no like, they shoot. Es trial."

I gestured to Brasil for the dictionary. "*Pelotao de morte*," I read. Squad of death.

"*Sim.* Yes." Ronaldo and Brasil smiled without humor.

Marilyn looked as troubled as I felt.

With youth on his side, Ronaldo was learning English with impressive speed. He told us that he and his friends believed Jerry was playing a heartless game with us. "Hmm," he revved, "to hurt family—Kel-lay, May-ra-leen, and *filias*—es cru-elle. Jerry Green no es good mon. We no trust!"

Ronaldo's words were like a blow to the stomach, giving substance to my fears.

If these men were right, Jerry was corrupt and so was Brazil. Marilyn and I were ignorant of Brazilian ways, unable to speak the language. What chance did we have with so much against us?

We wondered if we could afford to stay in Rio. As Ronaldo had said, big money was going out, no money was coming in. In 1974, US $1300 a month for rent was big money. And a major cause for concern. The profit from the sale of our house would shrink fast.

Chapter 34
Marilyn

Our adjustment to a South American country did offer distractions from our precarious situation. Our new kitchen lacked a toaster, dishwasher, clothes washer, and dryer, and the brittle rubber molding on the two antiquated refrigerators was a great passageway for cockroaches. When someone opened the door of the small pantry, hundreds of them scurried for cover. Eventually, we came to accept them as an unpleasant part of living in the tropics. I'd watch them disappear, give a little shudder, brush off the cookie bag, and take a cookie. After all, these bugs were small compared to the three-inch variety I saw in the incinerator and the five-inch creatures on the sidewalks. I couldn't help think that perhaps the biggest roach of all, the one to be most feared, was Jerry Green. Yet, I still allowed myself to hope otherwise.

Also in the kitchen, an old water filter stood on the marble counter. It was supposed to make tap water potable, though our Brazilian friends advised us to drink bottled water. Milk came in floppy plastic bags meant to stand—which they did not—in small plastic pitchers with one corner snipped for pouring: a messy process.

The one modern appliance, a television set in the living room, was nearly useless because of the language difference. Even Yogi Bear spoke Portuguese, being smarter than the average bear. Soap operas were the most popular nighttime fare.

Every Thursday morning, the *feira* came to our neighborhood, where fishermen and farmers set up their wares on a block closed to traffic. Adichi always took me to shop among the inviting piles of incredibly inexpensive fresh shrimp and strange-looking fish displayed on chopped ice in makeshift wooden booths. Mounds of fancy fruits and vegetables, many unfamiliar, gleamed in the scorching sun. It was always crowded, the shoppers elbowing each other to make their purchases. Together, the two of us would fill our shopping bag, pointing at something, and then grinning or frowning. Adichi always insisted on carrying the bag home, where she would, as always, immediately soak the produce in a sinkful of bleach and water.

On Sundays our family often walked to Ipanema's General Osorio Square, a small park where the grass had been worn away by foot traffic. Local artisans displayed their crafts in the shade of tall tropical trees and Jack and I temporarily forgot our worries as we walked past tables of hand-tooled leather pocketbooks and belts, paintings of local scenes, and pottery. Sometimes we took the girls to Jardim Botanica to see samples of Brazil's plush flora. Towering royal palms lined the paths leading to lush gardens and small ponds. Greenhouses displayed bromeliads, orchids, and cacti. The carnivorous plants fascinated the girls. "Would one bite me if I touched it?" "How do they chew?" They were relieved to hear the plants only devoured bugs. After their tour, the girls would be ready to go out for lunch.

Though a welcome distraction, the process of adjustment was no match for the cold truth. If Jerry Green didn't call soon, we would have to go back to the States.

* * *

Jack was loaded with guilt. One morning after the girls had left for school and Adichi had cleared away the breakfast dishes, he paced the living room. "I was too eager," he said. "I believed Jerry. I bought his crazy ideas, moved my family to this godforsaken place, and ruined everybody's lives." The playful spark in his light blue eyes was gone. "I ought to be strung up like the big fish that I am. Hook, line, and sinker. I swallowed it all!" He stopped pacing and stared out of the picture window, his hands buried in his pockets.

"Stop it, Jack,." I said. "You're forgetting one important fact. You and I made this decision together. We both knew it was a gamble, and we were willing to take the risk." I rose from the couch and joined him at the window. "I believed in you then, and I still do. *You* didn't let us down, Jerry did. He lied to us and he was good at it. We *both* trusted him and now we're in this mess." I sighed. "We just have to find a way out of it."

I failed to add that I thought living in Brazil was dangerous and our only friends had dubious backgrounds. I was scared and I longed to be home where it was safe. But I hid my feelings, knowing Jack needed me to be strong.

I watched the waves run to the beach one after the other—so steady, so predictable, so unlike our lives. "I admit," I said, "I thought we'd be here longer than a few months, but if we have to go home, so be it. As far as the kids are concerned, switching schools was tough, but on the other hand, how many kids have the opportunity to live in a foreign country—and I do mean foreign! It's taken our lives from the ordinary and made them unique. Besides, kids are more resilient than you think.

So, believe me, if we went home tomorrow, it wouldn't be a total loss." I smiled at him. "Look at us. You and I are closer than we've been in a long time. The whole family is."

"Thanks to adversity." His tone was bleak, his handsome face sad.

"It's a small price to pay."

"Come here." He drew me close for a quiet embrace. "I love you, Mare. I don't know what I'd do without you."

I wrapped my arms around him and lifted my face to his. "That goes both ways. And remember, we're in this together."

When the girls heard they might be going home, their reaction—or lack thereof—was a surprise. But a slow, subtle change in their behavior evolved: a new consideration for their parents and for each other, fewer arguments and better manners. They seemed to sense our fears and dejection and were trying to make life easier for us.

Magnifying our somber mood, angry tropical storms would race through Rio without warning, leaving the city in darkness. Foamy white caps danced crazily on a black ocean, while towering waves pounded the blowing sand and kept on rolling, dangerously close to the street. Twice during power failures, the dog and I were trapped in the stuffy dark service elevator. In the grip of claustrophobia, I would frantically yell for help until a voice sounded in the hall, shouting Portuguese. Somebody would come and pry open the doors, and I would climb out, carrying Pom Pom under my arm while I gulped air and gratefully repeated *Obrigada!* Then the dog and I would walk up the last several flights to home. On the thirteenth floor, the building swayed and shuddered in the wind. Doors slammed; glass shattered. Adichi would huddle in her room and pray. As suddenly as it had started, all would be quiet.

* * *

When failure seemed imminent, and Jack and I believed we would never see Jerry again, he appeared. The easygoing charmer we used to know was gone, replaced by a solemn stranger with a gray ominous look, void of the omnipresent tombstone smile. Still, he didn't sweat. Still cool as a reptile.

He talked with us all morning and on through Adichi's three-course lunch, reassuring us that remuneration was forthcoming. There had been unforeseen delays in the gold mine operation, he said. New projects would begin. Taiwan was ready to buy a huge order of shrimp from his friends in Recife. He would include Jack in the deal to tide him over. And he was negotiating prices on lumber for hardwood frames for Vince Warner's furniture company. These deals took time. Just be patient, he said.

We wanted to believe him. Oh, how we wanted to believe him. But our hope had grown fragile.

And yet . . . maybe the plan *would* work. Jerry *had* come to see us.

* * *

March dragged by at the pace of a three-toed sloth. Jack spent many mornings in Ronaldo's office discussing new businesses that could keep us in Brazil. Da Matta would interpret until he grew tired. He'd hold his head in both hands and beg, "No more. Please. No more. My brain is ex*haus*ted. It is time for a drink!" With da Matta, it was always time for a drink.

* * *

Not used to being idle, I tried to find a routine. After morning exercises on the living room floor—with Adichi rolling her eyes and clucking—I wrote letters at the dining room table, where I could see freighters and cruise ships go by. When I finished, Pom Pom and I would walk the letters to the post office, five blocks away. One day as I sat on a bench to have a smoke, two boys about twelve years old asked if they could shine my sneakers for a cigarette. Having not yet heard the Surgeon General's warning, I gave them each one for their excellent English but refused the shine, since my shoes were cloth. Every day, Adichi prepared a formal full-course lunch for me, the table set for a queen—a bored and lonely one. After lunch I would nap, play solitaire, read, work crossword puzzles, and do needlepoint, anything to get through the waiting and worrying. Three cigarettes a day grew to a pack of Brazilian Hollywoods. If I attempted to dust or sweep, anything to quiet my restlessness, Adichi would shake her head, roll her big eyes, and cluck her tongue, offended.

Adichi rose at dawn each day to make breakfast and set the table. Around seven, while the girls dressed for school, Jack or I walked Pom Pom two blocks to the bakery for hard rolls and pastries, since we had no toaster. Every day, the same clerk would ask, "*Que es a nome dea cachorro*?" "Pom Pom," we would answer. Then he would tell the other clerks the dog's name, and they would laugh their heads off. Every morning it was the same routine. Jack and I were too engrossed in our worries to ask what Pom Pom meant. When we got home from the bakery, breakfast would be on the table, complete with a platter of fried eggs sitting in puddles of animal fat.

Adichi kept the household going without instruction. She washed all the dishes and laundry by hand—including heavy towels and sheets—cleaned, cooked, and served three full meals a day. One of her specialties was *feijoada,* spicy Brazilian black beans. Another was fresh okra—nobody's favorite. Whenever she made pot roast, she threw a cork in the pot. Nobody knew why. Five and a half days a week, she dragged her heavy old body around from dawn until 9 p.m., and ended by washing the kitchen floor. Then she retired to her room and, unable to read, simply sat in the dark and prayed. She used newspaper for toilet paper. And though she was very poor, she didn't steal—an extraordinary trait in a maid, we were told.

For all her hard work she received three dollars a day, plus room and board. I appeased my guilt with my landlady's verification that it was the norm, and if I gave her extra, it would only cause trouble with the other maids. Besides, I rationalized, Adichi told Lynne she liked working for Americans. They were less demanding and ate dinner earlier than Brazilians, who ate at 10 p.m. She said she would go anywhere with our family except *Estadas Unidas.*

* * *

One morning as Jack was leaving for Ronaldo's, I stopped him. "If you don't take me with you, *I am going to lose my frigging mind!*"

He looked at me. "Well, why not?" he said after a moment. "Get your hat and let's go."

The men were astounded to see me. "Hmm . . . Kel-lay! Kel-lay!" Ronaldo protested. "En Braseel . . . *nunca* wu-mon come to bee-uze-ness! And wi-fee? No ho hoooo! *Nunca! Nunca!*" A sly smile appeared. "Meestress? Eh." His hand undulated in a gesture of doubt. "M*aay*be meestress."

I was outraged. The dignity of all womanhood was being maligned. "In the States," I said, "women are treated with respect. Including wives!" I folded my arms and glared at the three men. "I am Kelley's wife. I go *with* him."

Ronaldo, Brasil, and da Matta looked at Jack for confirmation. He suppressed a smile, appearing pleasantly surprised at my adamant response. "This is true," he said.

So, for the sake of harmony, the men adapted to the crazy Americans' ways. Unsure of how to act with a woman present, they simply treated me like "one of the guys," even telling slightly off-color jokes and listening with surprise when I told a few of my own. I loved jokes. Unfortunately, the pause after each sentence for da Matta to translate took out the punch, though both sides laughed politely at the end.

At least three mornings a week, Jack and I went to Ronaldo's office. I was an enigma, to be sure, but the men treated me with respect—something they neglected to do with their own women.

Usually after business we went out for drinks, especially if da Matta was there. And I, the young Greenwich matron, learned to drink like the best of them—with a glass, a bowl of ice, and a bottle of whiskey. When I would ask, on the sly, for some *agua mineral*, the men would turn away and smile.

They often spoke of Jerry Green, gesturing emphatically. "Jerry Green is no good," they would say, their deep voices rumbling. "To pull a family up by the roots?" Fists pulled up imaginary roots. "For no reason? Aaaaah!" They shook their heads in disgust. "The man has no heart."

Jack said he understood why Jerry had urged him to avoid these men. He was beginning to believe they knew more about Jerry than he did.

Chapter 35
Jack

How Marcos da Matta kept his job at the Federal Ministry of Justice was a mystery, since he was seldom there. In his early fifties, he had a young family from his second marriage and worried about supporting them. He always seemed to be short of funds and rarely able to contribute to the bar and restaurant bills. Though he was always quick to suggest going.

He loved Bing Crosby and sang dirty jingles in his best Crosby imitation. "She was only the stableman's daughter, b-b-b-boom, but all the horse men-nu-er."

Often, after a few drinks, he would ask the question that seemed to weigh heavily on his mind: "Do you know anybody who wants to buy a warehouse full of powdered milk?"

"Where did you get the powdered milk?" Marilyn or I would ask.

"Well you see, it's like this. When Kennedy was president, your country gave a shipload of powdered milk to Brasil to feed the poor. But Brasil is very corrupt, you know, and the poor never got the milk. It is still sitting in a warehouse, waiting for the highest bidder to fill the bureaucrats' pockets."

"But that was over ten years ago!"

Da Matta would nod his head and smile sadly. "Yes, I know." Then he would hum a little Crosby and say, "And now it is time for another drink."

In spite of da Matta's lust for whiskey, he was bright and engaging. But his most attractive feature was his command of English. Marilyn and I wanted badly to share a conversation in complete sentences with someone besides our family, and Marcos da Matta, with all his faults, was the only person we knew with whom that simple, previously unappreciated pleasure was possible. It led us to spend more time in bars and pick up more bar bills than we ordinarily would have done.

* * *

Days passed with no word from Jerry. And no money. My unreturned phone messages were beginning to pile up.

One day, to my surprise, Jerry returned my call.

By then, I was incensed. "I've had enough of your bullshit," I told him. "I don't believe you ever intended to do business with me. This was all just a fancy ploy to get my money. But what I can't understand is how you could do this to Marilyn and the kids after all the time you spent with us. You were involved with our move. You helped find a school for the girls. You watched us turn our lives upside down! What the hell kind of man are you?"

Jerry spoke soothingly. "I can understand how you feel, Jack. But you're wrong. These things take time. You have to be patient. We'll be seeing income from the gold any day. So relax, my friend. Keep your Irish down. Everything will work out fine, just the way we planned."

"Bullshit! I don't buy your pretty story anymore. I want my money back. Now. And if I don't get it, you'll be very sorry you ever met me. Got that, pal?"

Silence.

When Jerry finally spoke, he sounded offended, hurt. "Jack, in a few more days, you'll forget—or wish—that we'd never had this conversation. I'll talk to you then." He hung up.

What now? I wondered. What should we do? How would we get our money back? How would we find Jerry? The constant traveler. Probably on the run.

Totally frustrated, my mood dropped even lower. "Green screwed us," I said to Marilyn. "And look what I've done to you and the kids." My optimism was gone.

When I was forced to wire the Greenwich bank for additional funds, I gave the US dollars to Ronaldo to exchange on the black market for six cruzieros each, rather than the four the Rio banks were paying. Why not? This was Brazil.

Like corruption, inflation was out of control. The government couldn't print new bills fast enough, so they had simply devalued the one-thousand and ten-thousand cruziero notes down to one hundred cruzieros each. Luckily, with the strong value of the dollar, we didn't notice too much of a change in our cash outflow. Without an income, however, any amount was draining our reserve.

* * *

Ronaldo came to our apartment a few days later. His youthful exuberance fairly leaped from his eyes. He had exciting information from his cousin: Jerry Green and Pedro Da Silva were trying to use my plane to carry drugs across the border.

"Oh, my God!" Marilyn said. "We haven't finished paying for it yet. And it's registered in your name, Jack. You could get in trouble."

I laughed bitterly. "Finally. The truth is out. Jerry's a drug dealer."

"We're partners with a criminal," Marilyn said. "He stayed at our house. Our whole family has been in danger all this time. Now what do we do?"

I had no quick answer.

"You need a lawyer," da Matta told us. "I'll introduce you to my partner."

When we were alone, Marilyn asked, "Do you think da Matta's partner takes his work more seriously than da Matta does?"

"Let's reserve judgment till after we meet him," I said. "We don't have a lot of time to find somebody else."

* * *

The next afternoon we met da Matta at the Federal Ministry of Justice and took a cab to a small, old stone building. Da Matta led us to a private office in the back. His partner sat behind a mahogany desk, his back to a large window facing a tall modern edifice. Two walls lined with cases of books added to the man's appearance of a modestly successful lawyer. He rose when we came in and da Matta introduced us. His partner motioned for us to sit down. He was a soft-spoken gentleman with gray hair, dark eyes, and a stocky build. He listened carefully while da Matta told our story in a long Portuguese discourse. His broad hand moved back and forth across a sheet of paper as he took notes, his thick fingers working the pen. He conducted himself in a businesslike manner and appeared sufficiently competent to instill confidence. When da Matta finished, the two lawyers drew up a preliminary request for an official investigation to determine the criminal responsibility of Jerry Green.

After Marilyn and I had signed the necessary papers, we went with da Matta to the Barman's Club to have a drink. And another, and another. While da Matta sang his dirty jingles in top Crosby style, Marilyn quietly asked me, "Can we trust that lawyer? He's the partner of a drunk."

"He seems to know what he's doing. Let's give him a chance." I shrugged. "Who else do we know?"

She shook her head, defeated. We sat back and drank, letting the liquor tranquilize our troubles away.

It was dark by the time we took a taxi to our apartment. The three of us weaved our way through the park, stepping carefully around a woman and her children who were sleeping on a bed of newspapers laid out on the hard sidewalk. When we reached the corner of our building, da Matta—Columbia Law School graduate, attorney for the Brazilian Ministry of Justice—unzipped his fly and urinated on the wall. It fit the occasion. *Piss on everything!* I thought.

The girls were in a near panic by the time we arrived. We had missed dinner without so much as a phone call! "I'm so sorry." I felt lower than a worm. It was obvious we were slightly intoxicated. "We didn't mean to make you worry. I'm so sorry." Again, I had let our family down.

We were standing in the hall when I suddenly doubled over in pain.

"Oh my God, he's having a heart attack!" Marilyn cried. She put her arm around me. "Come on. Let's go sit down. Or maybe you should lie down on the couch."

I shook my head. "I'll be okay in a minute."

Da Matta, instantly sober, grabbed the phone and called for an ambulance, his hand trembling uncontrollably. Then he left.

"It's stress, only stress," I whispered, hugging my chest.

"Oh, Jack." Marilyn's eyes filled with tears. The girls were quiet.

The pain passed as quickly as it had begun. Marilyn persuaded me to lie down on the bed. It had to be stress. It couldn't be a heart attack. I couldn't leave Marilyn in a foreign country alone with four children and a dwindling bank account.

By the time the ambulance arrived, I was in a deep sleep.

Chapter 36
Jack

April Fool's Day. They ought to call it Jack Kelley's Day, I thought, for the biggest fool of the century.

Marilyn and I sat in the back of a Volkswagen taxi. My legs were crammed into the space behind the front seat. We were on our way to the Federal Ministry of Justice to meet da Matta.

While we waited at a traffic light, I watched a commonplace scene on the sidewalk: a woman decked in gold and diamonds scowling at a shabby, shoeless beggar who pressed her face close in an aggressive solicitation. By now such scenes no longer bothered me.

"Come on, Jack," Marilyn said, "don't be so hard on yourself."

"You sure hooked a loser when you got me!"

"You caught me, remember?"

"Well, either way, you got a raw deal, you poor kid."

No matter what she said, I felt as low as I'd ever been.

When we arrived in the stark offices of the Justice Department, we found da Matta at his desk in a highly disturbed state—or perhaps merely entertaining a severe case of the day-after-the-night-before tremors. "Oh, Kelley. May-ra-leen." he said. "This is very serious. Jerry Green is a dangerous man. I worry for my children."

His children, ha! He's worried about his own behind.

"Take it easy, da Matta," I said. "I'm the one who should worry, not you."

"But I am your lawyer. I am involved."

"Are you trying to tell me you want out?"

"No, God help me. I need the money." Da Matta put his hands on his desk and folded them to stop their shaking.

His phone rang and he jumped. His conversation with the caller further agitated him. He hung up and looked from one of us to the other. His face twitched and he shifted in his chair. "This is it! That was Ronaldo. He says Jerry Green is leaving the country. Today!"

I rose. "I'm going to the American Embassy."

"Great idea, Kelley." Da Matta sounded relieved. "In the meantime, I will tell my partner to speed up the Request for Investigation. Then we'll meet at St. Tropez for lunch."

"Tell your partner we need that paper today," I said.

As we left da Matta's desk, Marilyn whispered, "He forgot to mention drinks with lunch. On your American Express card."

"That's the least of my worries," I said. I took her elbow as we walked from the elevator to a waiting cab.

Ten minutes later, we arrived at a modern office building where the American Embassy was located. We rushed to the fifth floor and were quickly taken to a small office, where a tall, fair-haired representative in his early forties met us. He listened closely while we spoke, his eyes growing bigger as the story progressed. "Umm, yes, well, I can notify the authorities in the States, and I'll need a copy of the Request for Investigation." He scratched his well-combed hair, unable to stifle a smile. "This is incredible. Of course, we'll do all we can."

He rose and shook hands with us. "Please, keep me informed."

"That was a waste of time," I said as we left the building. "Jerry will be long gone before anything happens there."

Da Matta was waiting for us at St. Tropez, sipping a whiskey.

Within minutes, Brasil joined us. There seemed to be no secrets in the tightly-knit group.

We were nearly finished eating when Brasil was called to the phone. A minute later he returned, red-faced and excited. He blurted out the news in Portuguese, his voice projecting to the far corners of the restaurant. People turned from their lunches.

"Oh, God!" Da Matta ran his trembling fingers through what was left of his graying hair. "Kelley. This is it. Jerry Green is flying to Munich at 11 o'clock tonight! Ronaldo said you must go to Belèm immediately. He will meet you at the airport."

Brasil jumped up, knocking over his chair. He said he had a car and chauffer waiting. "*Vamos!*"

"Good luck, Kelley," said da Matta.

I grabbed his arm. I was an inch taller than da Matta's six feet, twenty pounds heavier, and at least twelve years younger. "What do you mean, good luck? You're coming too, you bastard. You're my lawyer."

"But the papers aren't ready. There is no reason for me to go," da Matta whined. "Oh, God, Kelley. I fear for the life of my children."

"You don't have time to be afraid, da Matta." I let go of him and worked to keep my voice under control. "Just go speed up the process and bring the papers on a later flight."

Da Matta thought for a moment. "Oh, God. It is impossible."

"*Now* what's the problem?"

"My partner has to be paid. I have no money for a ticket."

Impatiently, I pulled out a wad of bills. "Here's three thousand cruzieros. I'll pay you the rest in Belèm."

Da Matta's normally dusky face had paled to a sickly yellow. "But Kelley. The life of my children!"

I could feel my own face get red. "Da Matta," I said, my voice rising, "your children better worry about their *father's* life if you *don't* go to Belèm tonight."

"Oh, God." Da Matta took a gulp of whiskey.

I paid the bill, and Marilyn and I ran to catch up with Brasil, who was waiting at the curb with the car.

Brasil nodded toward the driver and struck the pose of a strong man. "Bo-dy-guard," he said. He got in beside the man, and Marilyn and I got in the back.

I gave Marilyn instructions: "Pack a few shirts and underwear in my small aluminum case and get it to da Matta before he leaves."

"What about your gun?"

"I can't risk it on a commercial flight."

"Be careful, Jack. I wouldn't put anything past Jerry Green and those Brazilians. You don't know what you're getting into, and it's not worth getting killed for."

I gave her a cold smile.

"Goddamn it, Jack! If you dare get yourself killed and leave me stranded in this fricking country with four kids, I swear, I'll never forgive you, you sonofabitch."

In spite of myself, I laughed at her uncharacteristic outburst, glad to see the fight in her so close to the surface. I put my arm around her. "Don't worry, my love. I promise to come back in an upright position."

Ronaldo was waiting for us at the airport, looking solemn. "I have pee-stol." It made him smile. "And mees-tress." His smile broadened as he held out his arm and Tanya appeared.

Tanya's presence made me wonder if this trip was just a lark. The pistol made me think otherwise. "Ronaldo," I said, "you can't take a pistol on an airliner. You'll get in big trouble."

"No trouble. Have *documentos.*" He winked. "*Ilegal!*"

Typical, I thought.

I barely had time to buy a ticket and give Marilyn a quick hug and a kiss.

Her last words were, "Be careful, damnit!"

Chapter 37
Marilyn

Brasil and I watched the plane take off. For some reason, knowing a woman was with them gave me a bizarre sense of security.

The "chauffeur" was waiting for us in the car. To my relief, Brasil got in front with him. As we pulled away from the airport, it occurred to me that Brasil was a virtual stranger. On his evening visits when he played cards with the girls, he showed an agreeable disposition and flaunted his enormous ego, but what was beneath the surface? Now here I was, alone with him and his driver—*the bodyguard.* For all I knew, we could be on our way to Chile!

I relaxed when the car turned onto Avenida Atlantica and stopped in front of the apartment. The driver left the motor running while Brasil struggled with his Portuguese-English dictionary to convey the message that in *una hora* he would pick up Kelley's suitcase and deliver it to da Matta.

While I was packing, da Matta called. "May-ra-leen," he whined, "I must talk to you."

"I'll come with Brasil to bring the suitcase," I replied.

Da Matta let us in. His wife and two young sons were out. He led me into a small study and shut the door. Brasil waited in the living room. "Sit down, sit down." His hands quivered. I feared he was going to back out. "This is it, May-ra-leen! I am afraid for the life of my children. Those men are very dangerous. You don't know. I am very frightened."

I braced myself for an argument. "Da Matta, you can't quit now. Kelley needs you! All you have to do is deliver the papers and give him some legal advice."

His hands fumbled through his thin, oily hair. "May-ra-leen." He looked at me imploringly. "I need money. I have bills to pay."

I glared at him. "Are you asking me for a bribe, da Matta?"

"Oh, no, no, *noooo*, May-ra-leen. It costs money to go to Belèm, you know. And I don't have any."

"Da Matta, you forget. I was there when Kelley gave you three thousand cruzeiros. That's enough to get you to Belèm and pay for part of your services."

Da Matta's watery brown eyes darted from side to side, as though he were rummaging his mind for memory of the money. "I don't have it."

"You don't have that money? What did you do with it?"

"I had to pay some bills," he said feebly.

I inhaled deeply and slowly let it out. "Da Matta, if you think you've got problems now, you haven't seen anything yet. Because if you don't show up in Belèm, you'll have to face Kelley's Irish temper, and believe me, when that temper gets rolling, it's big enough to start World War III. You won't even have time to say your prayers."

"Oh, God!" Da Matta held his head in his hands and muttered in Portuguese. After some thought, he said hopefully, "Maybe I can get the money from my partner."

"You do that, da Matta." I stood up. "Just make sure you're on that plane tonight. If you want to stay in one piece."

"Jesus, Mary, and Joseph!"

"Good-bye, da Matta." I left the room, putting an end to further discussion.

Brasil rose as I came into the living room.

"*Vamos,*" I said, and kept on walking. Brasil and da Matta exchanged a few quick sentences, and then Brasil followed me out.

I relished my small triumph. It was irrelevant that da Matta was a malleable, sniveling coward and that I had exaggerated the size of Jack's temper. What mattered was, da Matta was going to Belèm.

Chapter 38
Jack

Ronaldo, Tanya, and I were pushing our way through the crowd at the Belèm airport when Ronaldo spotted Jerry and Starr in line for an outgoing flight.

Ronaldo drew his gun and ran toward Jerry, bellowing like a wild man. Six local police appeared from nowhere and swiftly surrounded Jerry. With cold-blooded roughness, they cuffed his hands behind him and clamped a chain around his neck. I was surprised at the police's dramatic response and wondered what the story was. The real story. They brutally jerked Jerry's neck chain as they dragged him through the noisy mob, which had edged closer to get a better look. Starr followed, appearing lost.

The temperature was at least 105 degrees, and the stagnant, rancid air clung to everything like a wet blanket. People yelled and shoved. Nausea rose in my throat at the strong smell of sweat. My soaked shirt stuck to my body. I could feel the dampness on my forehead.

Jerry was drenched too. It was the first time I had seen him sweat. As I watched the police escort him from the airport, I noted with a touch of malice how a neck chain humbled a man, in spite of his manicured nails, Rolex watch, and Gucci shoes.

Ronaldo told Tanya to go to the motel at the airport, and then he and I followed the police car in a taxi.

At headquarters the police stood Jerry on a table, stripped him naked, and searched him. Jerry looked at me, bewildered. "I thought we were friends," he said.

"So did I." I watched coolly as the police brutally threw my fallen partner in jail.

"You'll pay for this, Jack. You and your family." Jerry's voice was heavy with the lust for revenge. Nobody treated him this way and got away with it.

I felt a coldness in my chest as I walked away from him.

Ronaldo and I spoke to the police chief. The chief, a large, handsome blue-eyed blond of German descent with a sufficient command of English to convey his sentiments, sadly shook his head. "I am afraid this has ruined everything," he said. "We have been observing Jerry Green for months. We think he is running drugs. I doubt now that we will get him on that offense." He looked dejected. "We have spent so much time! It is too bad your young friend got excited."

"I'm so sorry," I said. "I had heard Jerry was under surveillance, but when I confronted him about it, he did a good job of proving the report was a mistake." I remembered the day in the Trocadero hotel room when Jerry had called Washington. Apparently, Antonio Battista's information had been legitimate after all.

"Oh, well," the chief said. "I am happy to arrest the bastard on any count."

After I made a formal complaint, Ronaldo and I went to the motel. I hoped the police were honest and sharp enough to keep Jerry behind bars for a while. Jerry's freedom would put my family in jeopardy.

Soon after, I received a call from Carlos Alberto, Jerry's lawyer. Alberto told me Jerry would return my money within a few days.

Though it was 2:30 a.m., I called Marilyn, knowing she'd be awake anyway, wondering what was happening.

"Now that Jerry knows you mean business," she said, "maybe we'll see our money again."

"I'm too tired to talk about it," I said. "I just wanted to bring you up to date." I asked about the girls.

"They're fine. I'm fine. Adichi's fine. We all miss you." She warned me to take care of myself and we said good-bye.

* * *

During the night, da Matta arrived in Belèm with the finalized Request for Investigation to Determine the Criminal Responsibility of Jerry Green, addressed to the Police Delegate. It stated that Jerry Green, "by fraudulent means and tricks, obtained an unlawful advantage and appropriated the high sum of US$40,000.00 to the detriment of the Plaintiff." A brief summary of the Kelley/Green story followed.

The next morning, da Matta and I met with Alberto and Jerry at the jail. Carlos Alberto was all business, his soft voice and long eyelashes conveying the virtuous determination of a law-abiding attorney. My attorney, Marcos da Matta, fidgeted and twitched, his voice loud and high-pitched. Fear personified. Jerry's eyes were like pistols, pummeling me with bullets of hatred. I tried to appear calm to camouflage the storm in my gut.

With the promise to repay me within twenty-four hours, Jerry Green was released.

"I don't trust them," da Matta told me. "Alberto is not a lawyer. He is disbarred. He is as crooked as they come!"

* * *

A slow twenty-four hours ticked by. No contact. No money. Da Matta and I went to the police station to notify the authorities. The chief's sharp blue eyes danced with pleasure as he sent a van to Jerry's house to arrest him. "We'll get the bastard one way or another!"

Da Matta and I waited at the station for them to return. The heat was heavy with humidity and apprehension. I paced restlessly, smoking cigarette after cigarette, trickles of sweat rolling down the inside of my shirt. Da Matta, in a gray suit and black tie, sang his dirty ditties and spoke to God under his breath while he fidgeted with his papers with trembling hands.

Finally, Jerry Green and an entourage of police paraded in. Jerry wore handcuffs and a neck chain again. His hair was mussed, and his shirt was dirty from lying on the van floor. His entire body exuded hatred, and his dark eyes glared like lasers when he saw me. "I'll get you," he growled in a steely voice. "Nobody treats me like this and gets away with it. Starr's under sedation."

"Well, Jerry, you wouldn't play by the rules. All you had to do was pay me."

A guard ended our conversation by yanking Jerry's neck chain and dragging him away.

"Oh, God!" da Matta said.

Chapter 39
Jack

As I now saw it, Belèm was a tropical frontier town crawling with unsavory creatures that crept out from under their rocks whenever they smelled potential.

One colony of *contrabandistas* was squirming around *me.* It seemed we shared a common interest: they also hated Jerry Green. Jerry had committed the unforgivable act of betrayal. He had violated the "code of honor among thieves."

The bandits, who were definitely capable of more than just carrying stolen goods across the border, swapped stories about Green at a dark corner table in their favorite café, a plain, dingy open storefront with white tile walls and a gritty black and white mosaic floor. I listened to them boast about their exploits. Sly smiles twisting across their tanned faces. Mouths pinched on cigarettes. Eyes squinting against the smoke. Stopping now and then for da Matta to translate. Each crook tried to outdo the other. Some tales rose to the level of *Ripley's Believe It or Not.*

As I listened to one story after another, I was surprised to feel a kinship with these barbarians. Other times, I found myself wondering what the hell I was doing in a mangy café in a South American border town, an American family man, surrounded by a crafty pack of thieves, swapping stories about a common adversary.

One night after an evening with my new "friends," I lay in my motel bed staring at the cheap draperies that covered the sliding glass doors. It suddenly dawned on me that the bed's location made me a perfect target. The outlaws knew where I was staying. I had a strong feeling their alliance could change at the shake of a *cruzeiro.*

Bullets penetrate glass!

I jumped out of bed and grabbed the mattress, sheets and all. Dragging it to the bathroom, I threw it into the tub. When I climbed in and lay down, I got pinned in the middle. Tail down, legs up. To keep the blood from draining from my feet, I wedged them against the corners of the tub, knees pressed together. That was how I slept. I figured it was better to wake up *stiff* than to wake up *as* a stiff. Every night I dragged the mattress to the tub and slept with my knees under my chin. And every morning, bent like the hunchback of Notre Dame, I dragged the mattress back to its proper resting place and tucked in the sheets so nobody would be the wiser.

On Friday, April 5, my fainthearted lawyer returned to Rio, overjoyed to be getting out of Belèm in one piece. Da Matta left me in the hands of two Belèm lawyers. A hearing was scheduled at 10 a.m. on Monday, a week after I had arrived in Belèm.

Ronaldo remained in Belèm with me. His cousin Carlos Alberto—Green's disbarred lawyer—kept passing "confidential" news to him about Green's plans. Ronaldo immediately passed the news to me and my new *amigos.* Not that it seemed to do any good.

The waiting became intolerable. Too much time for my mind to play games. I went to inspect the Cessna. I was concerned about the rumors that Jerry and his flunky, Pedro Da Silva, had tried to steal it. For a change, luck was on my side. Everything seemed to be intact. No harm done. Still, I planned to check my plane often.

Seeking help anywhere I could think of, I visited the commandant of the State of Para. Para was run by the army, as was all of Brazil, and the commandant had the rank of colonel. The colonel was a hospitable man. He took me on a sightseeing tour of a large warehouse filled with hundreds of cases of Queen Anne Scotch, cigarettes, Levi's. All confiscated contraband. "It is the problem of a border town," he said. He was aware of Jerry Green yet offered nothing but sympathy.

With idle time on my hands, my imagination took over, feeding my fears of Jerry, the revengeful thieves, even Ronaldo. My calls to Marilyn were full of self-recriminations, complaints about boredom or about making a long-distance call, which was always complicated by language difficulties, tropical inertness, and faulty connections. Nothing was easy.

* * *

On Monday April 8, at 10 a.m., Jerry Green was ushered into court. The room, embellished with beautiful Brazilian woods, had an aura of dignity in spite of the smell of sweat. The empty jury box had finely hand-carved polished benches and a commanding rosewood rail. A gate separated spectators from participants. Judging from their worn, faded clothing, most of those present that day came from the poor majority. Many had Indian features. Jerry's proud attitude set him apart from the other defendants, who appeared humble and afraid, though his swarthy coloring resembled theirs. With my height and pale complexion, I felt out of place in the crowded room.

Jerry told the judge his story—surprisingly similar to mine—emphasizing that I had been a willing participant, and that he had stressed the disadvantage of my inability to speak Portuguese, adding that it would be necessary for me to come to Brazil to see local working conditions for myself. He accurately described the money transaction, calling it a simple loan. To my amazement, he admitted using the money for his own personal profit—twenty thousand dollars to furnish his house in Belèm with antiques, as I'd feared. He recognized his debt to me. He said he never had been arrested or prosecuted. This was the first time he had been involved in a case of this nature. That was all he had to say.

Then he was released.

I wondered what would happen next. Would the bastard just walk? My faith in justice was on a downward slide. But I wasn't ready to quit.

Disappointed at the news, the *contrabandistas* took it upon themselves to punish Green in their own way. They sipped *cafèzinho* with Ronaldo and me at their favorite table in their favorite cafè while they worked on a plan. We would band together and "get" Green. Everyone would be satisfied.They would get their revenge. I would get my money.

Of course, to carry out this dangerous mission would be *muito dificil* and would involve giving out many favors. And therefore, though they hated to bring up such a delicate matter, it would be necessary for me to contribute funds to ensure the success of this very important task.

At hearing this from Ronaldo, my new and totally inadequate translator, I said, "Tell them they will get their money *after* the mission is accomplished. Not before!" Ronaldo looked baffled. He was no da Matta. I tried again. "No Green, no *dinheiro.*" I grabbed Ronaldo's arm to act out *caught.* Then I said, "Get Green . . ." I rubbed my fingers together and nodded. "*Sim dinheiro.*"

They got the message.

The crooks heard—I suspected from Alberto—that Green was staying at Alberto's house in town. It was time to act. They would pick me up at the motel that night at nine. We would get Green.

* * *

The night was brutally hot. At 9:00, I walked through the damp clinging air left by an evening storm and climbed into the back of an old black Brazilian Ford. The short trip from my room had raised a mustache of sweat. I recognized the driver from the café downtown, but the other man in front was a stranger. They grunted *boa noite,* good evening.

The car headed toward the main road. It felt like a hundred and twenty degrees inside and reeked of sweat. I moved to open a window, and the stranger turned to watch me. His eyes were cold and opaque, like a dead animal's. My chest vibrated in time with my heart. I grinned stupidly at the man. "Hot night."

"Heh, heh, heh." The man's laugh was like a truck on a bumpy road.

I slowly opened the window and leaned back in my seat. The burly thug turned back around. He and the driver had a brief conversation that ended with the kind of laughter that follows a dirty joke.

It occurred to me that this might be my last ride. Allegiances in this part of the world—especially in this circle of humanity—were as fragile as straws in the wind. I wished earnestly that I had my .45. If we turned right at the end of the road, toward town, I could keep on breathing. If we turned left, toward the jungle, I'd better say my prayers. My shirt was soaked.

In what seemed like slow motion, the car turned right. I released a slow, silent whistle. Nobody spoke.

The air from the open window was as hot as the inside air. I mopped my forehead with my handkerchief. I looked at my watch and wondered if it had stopped. The fifteen-minute ride to town seemed endless.

We came to an unfamiliar section of Belèm. The dilapidated shacks and warehouses with broken windows did nothing to calm my fear. A man lay motionless on the sidewalk. I couldn't tell if he was alive or dead. The car slowed as it approached a set of iron gates next to a small wooden booth. Nearby, clumps of weeds wound through a rusty barbed wire fence. A sign with an official emblem hung over the gate. It said *Prisao do Brasil.* Federal prison.

The driver honked the horn, turned off the motor, and lit a cigarette. The other man leaned back and put a foot on the dashboard. I thought seriously of bolting, but this neighborhood looked savage. Long minutes ticked by. Finally, two men built like wrestlers, wearing filthy prison-orange shirts and pants, sauntered through the gate. The driver started the engine. The men got in the backseat, one on each side of me. The stench of dirty hair and unwashed bodies fouled the stagnant air. I breathed in short gulps. The gorillas' massive limbs pressed against me from both sides. Hard as watermelons. Hot as fire. *This must be hell.*

My new friend in the front seat turned around and raised one side of his mouth in an evil smile. He pointed to one of the convicts. "*Homicidio,*" he said smugly. He pointed to the other brute and held up two fingers. "*Dos homicidios.*"

My fear expanded. *Murderers? Two stinking murderers? I must have been fucking insane to team up with these bastards!*

The double murderer had an irritating habit of noisily clearing his throat and spitting huge, thick mucous balls out the window. Every time he leaned and took aim, his sweaty leg pressed harder against mine.

The jailbirds acted as if they were on a joyride, talking and laughing with the men in front. I guessed they were discussing how they would use me to amuse themselves. Would I see dawn?

After about fifteen minutes, we came to Alberto's town house, and the mood changed. I felt the convicts' ham hocks turn rigid. The car rolled down the hill, engine off, and stopped behind another car full of men, out of sight of the armed guards patrolling Alberto's grounds.

Everybody got out. Nobody spoke. I recognized some of the men in the other car from the cafè. Ronaldo was there, looking grave and anxious. Our driver opened the trunk to reveal a small arsenal: pistols, Uzis, and two Browning 12-gauge automatic shotguns. Quietly, he handed a weapon to each man. I got a .38 automatic revolver. I held it in my hands and stared at it. It was a substantial piece of metal. Dread filled my limbs.

The hot silence was broken by the cold metallic claps of shotguns cracking open and shells loaded, barrels spinning in revolvers, and clips ramming into Uzis' receivers. Dogs in the neighborhood started barking. The men scattered, taking cover behind trees, cars, and bushes as they ran toward Alberto's house. I looked for a place to hide. My legs worked in jerky robotic motions.

Silently, the men surrounded the yard. Some took shelter near the thick stucco-coated walls that circled the property. If and when Green appeared, he'd be at their mercy. I pressed myself against a tree.

We waited, each at our station, in tomblike silence. The shooting could start any second. The men were wired so tightly, one shot would set them all off. Bullets would fly from all directions. I crouched lower behind the tree. My chest felt too tight for me to breathe. Sweat poured down my face, chest, back, sides, legs. My shirt stuck to me. These criminals were good at stakeouts. But me . . . I had strayed so far from my own arena, I might as well have been on Jupiter. A thought came to my mind about Taylor & Company. Compared to my present position—squatting behind a tree, in cahoots with a grubby band of thieves and murderers, liable to be shot any minute—it seemed a safe and pleasant place. A goddamn haven, for Chris' sake! A fucking kindergarten! If I had used these tactics on Schultz and scared the living bejesus out of him I might still be working there.

Still no sound. My heart beat in my ears. God, I wished this was over. Where was Jerry anyhow? Why didn't the sonofabitch show his ugly face? Let these trigger-happy bastards blast his head off and then take *me,* Jack Kelley, Displaced American, back to the motel. Or better yet, to the airport. To hell with the money!

A hand pressed my shoulder.

I sprang up and spun around, pistol cocked and ready.

"Kel-lay, Kel-lay! No shoot! Es Ronaldo!"

"Je-zus Christ, Ronaldo. You scared the shit out of me." My heart jackhammered in my chest.

"Green no here. Alberto say. He know we come. He go *pronto.*" With his hands, Ronaldo mimed Green going as we were coming.

I felt as though somebody had just let all the air out of me. "Shit!"

Ronaldo laid a consoling hand on my shoulder.

Slowly the men returned to the cars. We removed the bullets from the weapons and tossed them into the trunk, guns clanking noisily. Everybody got in as before. Me in the backseat. Squeezed between two murderers.

Our first stop was the federal prison. The two felons got out and headed for the gate, back to jail. "*Obrigado,*" I yelled after them. Now I knew what the *contrabandistas* had meant by *favors.* I wondered how much it cost to rent a murderer.

On the ride back to the motel, I was chilled by a piercing fear: the two thugs in the front seat might still plan to finish me off. As part of the job. Or just for the hell of it. Maybe they were frustrated. They hadn't shot anybody that night. As far as I knew.

When the car finally pulled up in front of the motel, I climbed out, as drenched as if I'd been in a tropical rainstorm. "*Obrigado,*" I said. If I'd known how, I would have added, "And thanks for a pleasant evening." Instead I said "*Adeus,*" and left fast.

Once inside my room, I skimmed off my soggy clothes and took a long cool shower. I put on dry boxers and dropped dejectedly onto the bed. It occurred to me that Ronaldo himself might have leaked the plan to his cousin Alberto. The family grapevine must work both ways. I wondered what would happen next.

I didn't have long to wait. Fifteen minutes later, Ronaldo pounded on the door. "Green go!" he shouted. "*Aeroporto. Vamos!*"

I threw on khakis, Topsiders, a shirt, and ran after Ronaldo. A different car and driver waited. During the short ride Ronaldo fidgeted with his gun. My exhausted body tensed again, ready to spring into action.

When we reached the airport, Ronaldo jumped out of the car before it stopped. He ran inside, pistol drawn. I was close behind. We shoved through the crowd waiting to board the night flight to Paramaribo.

We spotted Jerry at the same time. He was in line, his hand cupping Starr's elbow. When he saw Ronaldo and me rushing toward him, his mouth spread in the old familiar smile with the gravestone teeth. "Well, well," he said. "Sorry to leave you, gentlemen, but somehow I feel I must."

Ronaldo summoned a policeman standing nearby.

Jerry said, "Don't waste your time, my friends. I have the required documents." A deep chuckle rose from his throat. "You can't stop me. In fact, I've already passed inspection." He erupted into full laughter, attracting stares. "And by the way, Jack, thanks for the forty grand. Oh!" His voice dropped to a confidential tone. "A word of advice. Watch your family. It would be a shame if they had an accident. *Adeus.*" He moved along in line, still smiling.

A chill traveled down my spine.

Ronaldo's conversation with the cop confirmed Jerry's information. "Green can go," he said. His shoulders drooped.

Powerless, we watched Jerry Green move closer to the plane. Closer to freedom.

As I watched Jerry Green walk out of my life, I felt the vitality and hope drain out of me. I remembered my first visit to Belèm, when the sight of the jungle had filled my head with glorious visions. The visions grew fainter with every step Jerry took. By the time Jerry passed through the gate, there was nothing left. Except fear.

* * *

As soon as Ronaldo dropped me at the motel, I called Marilyn. Gently, so as not to frighten her even more, I warned her to be extra careful. Jerry was on the loose.

The Belèm police chief alerted Interpol. It was small comfort. Our dreams had been smashed. Our lives were in danger. Nothing could change that.

* * *

Later, Ronaldo explained how Jerry was able to flee the country. *"Ilegal documentos,"* he said. "Judge get," he added, as though it happened every day. "Big payoff. Father-in-law of Alberto es judge."

It all had been a sham.

Chapter 40
Jack

I spent a restless night going over the trip ahead, making mental notes. My route in the Cessna would be from Belèm to Porto Nacional, then to Brasilia, and finally to Rio.

I left my motel room at 5 a.m. First, I double checked my gear. Then I had my favorite Brazilian breakfast: stiff-as-a-plank coffee with milk, yogurt, cheese, papayas, and just-baked rolls with plenty of butter and honey.

When I got to the airport, I stared for a moment at what had been my first view of the Brazilian jungle almost a year ago. It seemed a lifetime ago. I went inside to the Brazilian Ministry of Aviation to file a flight plan to Porto Nacional. Owing to both the plane's and my foreign registration, I had to fill out half a dozen forms in triplicate. Each copy had to be rubber stamped. Afterward, the middle-aged official who was to approve my clearance and flight plan adamantly stressed that there would be no VFR (visual flight rules) either one hour before sunup or one hour after sundown. He took great pains to explain the hazards of flying over the jungle, something I already knew but didn't mind hearing again.

The official found some coffee somewhere, and we took it to a meeting room where a twenty-foot wall was covered by a map of the upper Amazon region. This chart started from the Guianas, went down the Atlantic coast covering Fortaleza and Recife, west toward Manaus for a thousand miles, and south to Brasilia. The vastness of the jungle was humbling.

The chart contained hundreds of colored pinheads, many representing the last known locations of lost planes. Some were for World War II Army Air Corps ferry pilots—men *and* women—whose job had been to fly bombers, fighters, and transports from the United States to Recife for their last refueling before heading to Dakar, Africa. In the jungle, the likelihood of their recovery or survival was extremely remote.

The official spoke in a heavy accent. His tone was solemn. He said the Big Top had a way of swallowing airplanes and people. It was like a tent, where trees had to grow seventy-five to one hundred and twenty-five feet tall to compete for the sun. They blossomed on top. What was underneath was hidden. So if a plane landed on the Big Top, it still could fall to the bottom, out of sight from search and rescue aircraft. If one survived.

With that harsh lesson as a backdrop, my flight plan to Porto Nacional with a fuel stop at Carolina was accepted. My estimated time of takeoff was 7:30 a.m.

I was concerned about the plane. It had been dormant since I tied it down with Tom Ryan nearly six weeks earlier. Hard to believe my whole family had been in Rio for only four weeks. As I approached the green and white bird, it looked dirty and neglected. But when I put the key in the door and opened it up, released the control lock and started my walkaround, things seemed to be in decent order. I was worried about the fuel, but each of the sumps on all four tanks contained little, if any, water. The condition of the fuel seemed excellent. I checked the cowl for birds and other unwanted vagrants looking for shelter, but there were none. I lowered the cowl flaps, and they were all intact: no animals, birds, nests, snakes, or large insects. I loaded my duffle, a jug of water, a bag of fresh fruit, another cup of coffee, and then primed the engine.

After cranking it half a dozen times, it finally caught, filling my senses with an exhilarating sound and smell. Nothing could compare to the aroma of aviation fuel and exhaust when an engine first cranked up. The instruments moved quickly into the green. Oil pressure good. Temperature normal. I turned on all the avionics. I carried two ADFs (automatic direction finders), two VHFs (radio bands), radar, and transponder. Everybody seemed to be happy. I flipped to the ground frequency and put the second radio on tower. For ten minutes I sat without communicating and listened to the engine, revving it several times to check the mags. Mags fine. The strobe worked. Everything seemed to be in good order. I contacted ground control and was directed to the active runway to the east.

It felt good. My adrenaline was high. It was a gorgeous morning. The sun had sneaked up and, before it was visible, had set everything aglow in pinks and reds. Cumulus clouds, formed by the abundant moisture, drifted by. The trees with their incredible heights gave a silhouette of the jungle.

I taxied to the active runway, put in ten degrees of flaps, and let her go. The plane acted extremely well. The light load helped. I kept it ten feet above the runway until I was three-quarters of the way to the end, then I pulled it up as I raised the flaps. Reducing my takeoff power, I pulled the prop back. With a lift from the thick, humid air, the Cessna bolted up and away.

Conforming to the directives from the tower, I climbed to 2000 and made a right-hand turn for my first checkpoint, the Tocantins River.

The Cessna ate up Belèm in a hurry. I took my last look at the major port city near the mouth of the Amazon, with its red tile roofs, a few tall buildings, and a mixed bag of memories. After ten minutes over the sprawling population, I reached the Big Top. By then my altitude was 9500.

I could see the Amazon River and its tributaries and was struck by their immensity. Their colors varied from pale brown to dark, depending on the mud and sand content.

Marajo, the delta island at the mouth of the Amazon, was to my left.

All systems checked out well. I cut back to cruising speed.

My first stop would be Carolina, approximately 450 nautical miles away. Meandering miles. I'd stay close to the Tocantins River for an occasional touch of civilization. The primary source of navigation from Belèm was low-frequency non-directional radio beacons, which was why the airplane was equipped with two ADFs: one for primary and one as a backup. Between Belèm and Carolina were two of these radio beacons, each with a range of only fifteen miles. The trick was to hit them on the nose: pick one off my tail and the other as I approached it downriver. They left much to be desired. Especially when there were only empty spaces below.

A haze over the river and part of the jungle subdued the tans and greens and made a beautiful picture.

For the first two hours, I saw no sign of civilization except for an occasional hut by the riverbank. When I finally spotted a dugout canoe carrying two Indians, I dropped low to get a better look.

The expected time to Carolina was four hours, which left me with two hours of fuel to spare. During the second and third hours, large cumulus clouds began building to the southwest, at first barely discernible. As they grew closer, their immensity grew as well. It was a typical occurrence over the jungle: the intense heat of the sun working on the humidity and the moisture, causing the cumes to build. As they grew higher, they reached the colder air, and by afternoon, the rain would come down.

The buildup was growing between me and Carolina. Too broad to go around. Too high to fly over without oxygen. When I was close enough, I tried to penetrate the initial "feathers." It was impossible. I dropped my altitude and found the weather below undesirable as well. Visibility was quickly shrinking to no more than a mile, definite instrument flight rules conditions. But the plane was not fully equipped for IFR.

As the weather closed in, and my palms started to sweat, I decided to go back to basics: When in doubt, do a 180 degree turn.

I implemented my turn and headed back up the river, toward what earlier had appeared to be some sort of airstrip. At the same time, I called the Carolina radio to inform them of the change in my flight plan.

"Cessna two six six zero Sierra calling Carolina approach. How do you read?"

No answer.

I tried again.

No response.

If I failed to reach the airport, I hoped a plane in the vicinity would hear me, so at least my whereabouts would be known. Landing in the middle of the jungle with nobody's knowledge? I might never be found.

"Cessna two six six zero Sierra calling Carolina approach. How do you read?" Still no reply. The silence was exceedingly lonely. I surmised that my failed attempts were due to my low altitude, distance, or both.

Within fifteen minutes, I came to what I had thought, or had hoped, was a crude airstrip. At closer look, it was nothing more than a large sandbar. But its height offered hope that its surface would be hard.

With the Cessna's oversize tires, specifically built for rough-terrain landings, I opted to put down on the sandbar and wait out the bad weather, rather than to return to Belèm, which I knew was doable.

I made two passes before attempting to land. On the third pass I bounced the wheels. The terrain seemed good and hard. Just to be sure, I circled back to look at the indent the tires had made. The surface appeared firm.

I put in twenty degrees of flaps and started my approach. This was going to be the super all-time soft field landing. I kept the nose high, at near stalling speed, and laid the Cessna down as lightly as a feather landing on a baby's behind. The plane acted exactly as it was supposed to. The terra firma cooperated. The sandbar was like a tennis court.

I taxied back to the inland side, put the plane in position for takeoff, and shut it down. Then I opened the door, took a big breath of fresh air, and settled in to wait out the storm.

Again I called Carolina radio, with no response. The fact that nobody knew my location filled my mind with possibilities—all bad. I remembered the warnings: "It is better to take the long way and follow the coast. If you go down in the jungle, you may never be seen again." As my imagination rambled, my growing anxiety was suddenly interrupted by a loud squawking.

"Varig three five seven calling Cessna two six six zero Sierra. How do you read?" The words were barely discernible through a heavy Brazilian accent, but extremely welcome nonetheless.

"This is two six six zero Sierra. I read you loud and clear. Over."

"Six zero Sierra, switch to frequency one twenty-three point four," requested the Varig Airline pilot. It was a frequency reserved for plane-to-plane communication.

"One twenty-three point four," I said. I switched channels, then said, "Varig three five seven, this is Cessna two six six zero Sierra. How do you read?"

"Six zero Sierra, five by five. How can we help?"

"Three five seven, please inform Carolina radio that I have landed." I gave my location. "I'm waiting for this storm to pass. I'll resume the flight as soon as it breaks. Over."

"Roger on the relay, six zero Sierra. Stand by." After two or three minutes, the airline pilot came back. "Cessna six zero Sierra, this is Varig three five seven. Carolina radio acknowledges. They request your intentions as soon as you are airborne. Are you certain of your location? Over."

"Three five seven, this is six zero Sierra. Many thanks for the relay. My position, as best I can tell, is about a hundred and thirty miles north, northwest of Carolina." I configured my time from the last nondirectional radio beacon down to my approximate location, which corroborated with my topographical map, and gave it to the Varig pilot.

"Cessna six zero Sierra, Varig three five seven. We will descend and come south, southwest down the river to verify. Please acknowledge when you see us. Over."

"Six zero Sierra."

After a span of silence, I heard a rumbling coming down the river. The sound was steady, growing louder by the second. All at once, deafening thunder exploded in the clearing, rattling my bones. The Varig 727 was screaming overhead at 1500 feet, dragging at landing speed, its slats and flaps extended.

I shouted into the radio. "Varig three five seven, this is six zero Sierra. I have you in sight. Look to your left for a green and white machine on a sandbar. Over."

Moments later, "Six zero Sierra, I have you. Location confirmed. Over."

"Varig three five seven, six zero Sierra. A *muito grande obrigado*! I appreciate your passing by. I hope your passengers didn't mind the detour. Over."

"Six zero Sierra, I am happy to do it. When I am in the States, I assume you will do it for me."

"With great pleasure, Varig three five seven. With great pleasure." It was the most gracious gesture of Brazilian hospitality I could ever experience.

As the airliner's engines grew fainter, I got out to stretch my legs and have a drink of water, feeling smug about figuring my location correctly. And then the rains came smashing down. I hurried back inside the plane and shut the door.

A rainstorm in the jungle was unlike anywhere else. The enormous drops came down so hard, they seemed to merge. For twenty minutes I felt like the plane was at the bottom of the ocean. Finally, the powerful deluge tapered into a steady rain. As I watched from the cabin, I noticed, with a feeling of foreboding, streams of water rushing toward me from higher ground. I wondered how fast and how high the river would grow and, more importantly, if the sandbar would soon be submerged. I entertained the idea of taking off prematurely, but before I could make a decision, the rain stopped as suddenly as it had begun.

I opened the door and the humidity wrapped itself around me like a wet wool sweater. A murky hush filled my ears. A scattering of bird calls. I sat motionless, feeling the jungle and listening to its heartbeat. "By God," I announced to the river and the trees and the birds, "I've gone from one jungle to another!" I paused to consider this great revelation. I had gotten out of New York, away from the rats and the snakes, and here I was in Brazil with a new pack of predators nipping at my heels. I had to chuckle. The more I thought about it, the funnier it became. My laughter broke the stillness.

I let it roll, it felt so good, until a distant noise, foreign to the jungle, rudely interrupted my great catharsis. It sounded like an automobile engine. Definitely without a muffler. More like a tractor. Out of the bushes from the south came a battered World War II Willys jeep, put-putting and smoking like crazy. Two dark-skinned occupants were aboard and headed in my direction.

An image passed through my mind of an old cartoon I had once seen in *The New Yorker*: a group of Indians gathered around a bonfire in a jungle clearing, watching a huge bubbling cauldron that held a white man wearing a safari hat and an "Oh shit!" expression. I reached behind the front seat to unzip my duffle and take out the .44 Ronaldo had loaned me. I made sure there was a clip in it and then hid it under my leg. If they wanted me in their soup, they'd have to fight for me.

The jeep parked near the plane and the two young men got out. Their tawny skin, black silky hair cut in the shape of a pumpkin, broad faces and noses spelled Indian. They stayed their distance and stared curiously at me. I kept my eyes glued on them, hoping that somehow it would keep them from separating.

After a short conference, the Indians began a conversation. Of sorts. They spoke a Brazilian dialect. I spoke anything I could think of through the open door of the plane, mostly sign language. As the Indians inched closer, I was able to read the lingo on their T-shirts. One said Disneyland. The other said God Bless Woolworth's. I relaxed. With luck, the last night of my life wouldn't be spent on this lonely part of the planet.

By trial, error, and a series of gestures, the Indians understood that the plane was from the United States. and that I was American. They asked if I would like food or drink. To buy time, I gave an affirmative answer. I handed them fifteen *cruzieros*, and they got in their jeep and drove away. I didn't know if I would see them again.

They returned soon, carrying a small canned ham and a Coke. Evidence that I was close to some kind of civilization. Perhaps a mining camp. I thanked them, and they went on their way. Unsure of Brazilian canning methods, I chose not to eat the ham.

By now the air had grown clear and cooler and the sandbar appeared dry. I fired up the engine and made a quick takeoff over the river.

This time I easily reached Carolina radio. The airport was easy to find, cut out in the middle of the jungle on the side of a river. I landed without a problem, taxied to the lone fuel pump, turned off the engine, and stepped out of the plane. Seven or eight Indians, none taller than four and a half feet, had gathered nearby, their faces lit with excitement at the sight of the Cessna. They kept their distance as I walked the twenty yards to a modest concrete block structure with a rusty corrugated metal roof. I took a last look at my plane, hoping it would be safe, and entered the stale coolness to check in with air control. An official with coffee-colored skin in a white shirt sat behind the operations counter. He frowned at me. "Two six six zero Sierra?"

"Yes, sir," I said. "Happy to be here." I hoped my smile would soften the man's obvious displeasure.

"You are late," the man said. "You delay flight plan. You break rules. No is good." Fortunately, English was the universal language in air control.

"Privilege of the pilot-in-command," I said, my elation at arriving intact quickly deflating. "First consideration is safety of the plane, pilot, and passengers."

The man spoke solemnly. "You broke flight plan."

"Did you receive the message from Varig three five seven?"

The man nodded. Then he grinned, a dark gap beaming in place of a missing tooth, all signs of disapproval suddenly gone. "Yes. You very wise. We know location. We no worry."

"Well, thank you," I said, feeling slightly vindicated. "Varig was a big help." Then my curiosity moved in. "By the way," I said, "those men outside. What are they doing?"

The official's black eyebrows arched over dark smiling eyes. "Indians. Love airplanes. Big mystery. How fly like bird." He tilted his head in fond tolerance.

"I love airplanes too," I said.

"No many planes here. Men come. Wait long time. See you."

"Guess there's not much going on in the jungle."

The man's brows tightened in a puzzled frown.

Even if I explained my little joke, the man probably would not understand. "Can I get some fuel?" I asked.

He nodded eagerly. "Yes, yes." He came from behind the counter and walked outside to work the pump. The Indians inched closer, stopping about ten feet away. Most wore only shorts or loincloths; a few had T-shirts. All were barefoot. When I waved, they giggled and chattered like schoolgirls.

After the plane was refueled, I paid my bill in *cruzieros*, filled my water jug, waved once more, and took off. The Tocantins River was a helpful navigational guide. Though the afternoon flight was uneventful, the jungle was never dull, exhibiting its complex personality and vividly colored winged inhabitants along the way.

It was 4:30 p.m. when I landed at Porto Nationale. I had flown nearly 650 nautical miles, constantly on the wheel and the gauges. Checking radio frequencies, looking for navigational aids, monitoring airline traffic, whatever it took to keep my tentacles connected with the outside world. Next time around, I promised myself, I would have automatic pilot. I was tired, but in a satisfying way. That night, I had no trouble sleeping.

* * *

In the morning, I filed my flight plan and left for Brasilia, a 350 mile trip almost due south, precisely at one eight nine degrees.

The jungle opened for a while, and beneath me shadows of passing clouds raced across vast plains and valleys of vivid greens. Beauty untouched by civilization. Three-quarters of the way to Brasilia, the jungle floor began to rise and hills appeared, with some peaks reaching 4500 feet.

I picked up Brasilia radio and was directed toward the airport by approach control. I was descending from 11,000 feet.

When it first appeared on the horizon, Brasilia looked like a mirage from the Buck Rogers era. The Brazilians had built it as their new seat of government, believing that Rio was going into decline. They purposely chose an inland location to encourage the development of the interior agriculturally and industrially, hoping to force the population away from the coast. Brasilia, the city of the future, was meant to attract and excite the Brazilians.

Instead, an incredible lack of foresight had created an inaccessible, unusable "island." There were no decent roads to the middle of the jungle. Nor had anyone considered living quarters for the gardeners, maids, mechanics, and garbage collectors. As an afterthought, shanties had been quickly erected behind a brick wall.

The approach to the airport was difficult. My eyes kept straying to Brasilia's stunning skyline. The composite of glass, aluminum, shiny mirrors, reflecting ponds, shooting fountains, parks, and esplanades was a spectacle of silver and green rising from the middle of nowhere.

After I had landed and tied down the Cessna, a federal agent took me inside to close my flight plan. Everybody in the airport was friendly.

I met an American pilot in operations who had the lonely job of delivering a Cessna 172 from the factory in Wichita, Kansas, to the Falkland Islands. The two of us checked into the hotel, had a few beers and a hamburger together, and retired early. The next day I would fly the final leg to Rio to the safety of home. Such as it was.

* * *

It was a gorgeous morning. I was eager to get going. I took a taxi to the Brasilia Airport, an expansive empty space that made my small plane look like a tiny bird standing in the middle of a desert.

After I filed my flight plan—with visual flight rules, as usual—I performed my ground inspection. Gasoline topped off. Oil good. I cranked it up, turned on the radios, taxied to the runway—there was no wait—and I was on my way. The flight to Rio was approximately 500 nautical miles. My altitude was 9500 feet. Visibility was impeccable and the wind cooperated, giving me another thirty knots on the tail, which made for a quick ride. I looked down on open, beautiful country. Mountains would spring up suddenly and, just as quickly, would fade into the great openness. My two ADFs came in perfectly, and I had the benefit of my omni—the very high frequency omnidirectional range, or VOR—for about the first sixty miles out of Brasilia.

When I had finished my coffee, I climbed higher to take better advantage of the tailwind. I was enjoying the view when I became aware of a strange sensation. The back of my neck felt as though it were on fire, like a giant heat rash had crept up my backbone. Simultaneously, my vision became restricted. I could still see the instruments, but I was losing my distance vision. I felt a rush of panic. There was no one to hand the controls to.

My mind was in a fog. I fought to keep my wits. It was hot. Everything was closing in. I didn't know what was happening. I tried to think. Finally, with great effort, I identified the problem. Lack of oxygen. I checked the altimeter. 15,500 feet. Far above safety limitations. I rapidly dropped to 11,000 feet and my senses began to return. Once I knew I was okay, I sank back in my seat and took the time—appreciating the luxury of being able to do so—to reflect on the lesson I had just learned. Then I began to shake. A few more minutes and I would have lost my ability to think or react. It would have been a bad day!

* * *

I spotted Belo Horizante off my left wing and made a gentle turn farther south toward Rio. Cloud cover increased dramatically. I communicated with Santos Dumont, the main airport in Rio, regarding my position and anticipated time of arrival. Later I picked up their VOR and ADF and knew I would have had no problem if I had had to fly above the cumulus clouds. I could descend with visual flight rules after I was past the town of Petropolis, if the need arose.

As I zigged and zagged around the huge gathering of cumulus clouds to retain my VFR on the approach to Rio, I was startled by the sudden appearance of Jesus Christ standing in a swirling mist, his arms open, looking directly at me. It gave me the strange feeling that I had arrived in heaven, a concept causing alarm as well as relief. As the clouds parted, the full view of Corcovado, as the huge statue was called, was revealed.

Stirred by my sudden meeting with the Lord, I took a slight detour. When I reached the ocean, I dropped my altitude to 2,000 feet. Ipanema was on my left. As I approached Copacabana, I moved closer to shore and descended to 500 feet.

Chapter 41
Marilyn

Jack didn't say much about Belèm in his phone calls, except that he had some amazing stories and that he was fine. The night before, I had been relieved to hear his voice when he called from Brasilia and gave me his estimated time of arrival at Jacarapagua Airport outside of Rio. He'd been lucky so far, but something could still happen. I trusted Jack's flying skills, but some things were beyond his control, like tropical storms, engine trouble, illness. To quiet my thoughts while I waited for Brasil and Ronaldo to pick me up and take me to the airport, I stared out the living room window at the crashing waves, the Saturday crowd on the beach, people jogging on the sidewalk.

The girls were in their rooms, unconcerned with my worrying, since it was a frequent pastime of mine. Adichi was in the kitchen cutting vegetables. She had changed her day off to be there for Jack's homecoming. When the men finally came around eleven o'clock, Adichi and the girls walked us to the elevator.

Ronaldo drove, his mood somber, and Brasil was quiet, his jolly demeanor subdued. Did they know something I didn't? I sat alone in the backseat, tense all over.

When we got to the airport, we walked in silence to the entrance. Wind gusts played with my paisley wraparound skirt. Inside, we passed two men in uniform sitting behind the operations counter as we made our way to the small waiting room. Brasil and I stood at the picture window, smoking, while Ronaldo paced, jiggling coins in his pockets, sliding his fingers through his hair, occasionally stopping to glance at the empty runway. After forty-five minutes of watching and pacing, Ronaldo spoke to the men at the counter and came back with discouraging news.

"They no hear where is Jack. When he comes?" He shrugged.

My stomach tightened. I went to the counter. "Two six six zero Sierra?" I asked hopefully. The two men looked at me with somber faces and shook their heads. I wondered what had caused the delay. Bad weather? Engine trouble? But no report had come in yet. Ronaldo and Brasil were talking quietly, their hands in their pockets, obviously ready to leave. Knowing as little as we did, I could think of no good reason to stay.

My heart was in my throat as the three of us walked to the car. Back at the apartment, I thanked the men and said good-bye. We promised to call each other if we heard anything.

The girls and Adichi were waiting at the elevator door. Their welcoming smiles changed to looks of confusion when I walked in alone.

"There's no word at the airport," I said. "We'll just have to wait." I tried to smile. "I'm sure he's fine."

I went to the living room, picked up my needlepoint, and sat down. The girls stood near me, asking questions, looking out the window. Adichi went back to her laundry.

Diane suddenly yelled, "There's Dad. He just flew past our apartment."

We all rushed to the window. "Let's see. Let's see." "Omigosh, it's him."

Adichi scurried in, still holding a piece of laundry.

By the time the plane had reached Leme and turned around, we were all hanging out the living room window, waving furiously and yelling. Adichi waved Jack's boxers as she yelled with us, her deep voice adding a Portuguese flavor. I was so relieved to see that little green and white airplane, I could barely get my voice past the lump in my throat. Jack tipped his wings and we waved even harder. I gripped Heather's shirt to keep her from toppling out the window. Jack tipped his wings one last time, and then lifted the nose and climbed, flying west down the beach toward Guanabara to land at Jacarapagua.

Jacarapagua, a military airfield slightly west of Rio, was a single strip used for training.

Jack had got permission from the *Federales* to land there when he cleared his flight plan out of Brasilia.

I rushed to the phone to call Ronaldo. After eleven *very* long days, our family would be together again.

Chapter 42
Marilyn

The reality of being stranded in a foreign country with no income quickly replaced my happiness over Jack's safe return.

"We sold our house," he said as he paced the living room. "We have four kids to feed, clothe, and shelter. And our funds are dwindling." He stopped pacing and faced me. "So. What do we do now? Do we stay in Brazil and find a way to make a living? Or do we pack up the kids and the animals and retreat to Greenwich, defeated?"

I stood by the window, studying him. His whole body sagged. He looked old, drained of energy. Returning in defeat would crush him. "I don't think we should leave," I said. "After all the trouble we went through to get here, we can't give up now. There must be something we could do." I thought for a minute. "Jerry may have failed us, but he was right about one thing. Brazil does have potential."

"I failed us too."

"If you failed, I failed. I wanted to come to Brazil as badly as you did." I added an upbeat observation to bolster Jack's spirits: "As my mother always says, 'Nothing ventured, nothing gained.'"

Jack laughed, a bitter rumble. "Everything ventured, everything lost."

"We did lose," I admitted. "Money. Time. Pride. You name it." I fought the old sinking feeling.

"And plenty of it."

"We'll make it up somehow. We're still young. We have time. Okay, so we made a mistake. Everybody hits the wall at least once in their life." And Jack had tried so hard to make things right. "But," I added, putting on a smile, "if we hadn't come to Brazil, we'd probably be divorced by now." I truly believed this. "From my viewpoint, it was worth the price."

"I did my homework," he said, heedless of my attempt to comfort him. "I checked Jerry out every way I knew how, and it still wasn't enough." He dropped his large frame onto the taffeta embossed couch, stretched out his long legs, and stared into space, his blue eyes opaque.

"Maybe we were too eager," I said. "Maybe we needed a change so badly it tainted our judgment."

"I could see it all working."

"I could too. It could have worked with a different partner." Frustrated, I sat down next to Jack. "So. Here we are. What do we do now?"

"We don't have time to waste."

"I know. But since we're here, shouldn't we at least try to stay?"

He straightened up and faced me. "Aren't you scared? We're burning money like paper and we don't know what to do next."

"Sure I'm scared. But, God, we went to so much trouble to get here. Can't we spend just a little more time looking around?" Stubborn, perhaps to a fault, I wasn't ready to give up. Jack's face filled with love. "Whatever you want," he said, but there was no optimism in his voice.

Chapter 43
Jack

Our Brazilian friends, Ronaldo especially, were full of ideas for money-making ventures. Most were far-fetched, such as selling eggs. The Brazilians' motive was obvious—to remain involved with us. Though I was reluctant to go into business with these particular Brazilians, I discussed prospects with them only because they might come up with a workable concept or a decent contact. Also, I was desperate. One plan I had pursued with Jerry, still worth considering, was selling hardwood to our friend Vince Warner for his furniture company back in the States. Ronaldo contacted a friend in the lumber business and asked for prices. Another idea was to lease tankers from a Greek shipping line, owned by a neighbor in Greenwich, to the national oil company, Petrobras, whose growth was hindered by a lack of ships. The consummation of a deal would give me and the Brazilians a finder's fee. Our neighbor was willing. But despite Ronaldo's and da Matta's braggadocio, they were unable to make the right connection at Petrobas.

One change that would have to take place immediately was to move to a smaller apartment to curb the rapid outflow of funds.

The grapevine was working in all directions. Eva, the landlady, knew all about our problems. Marilyn and I wondered if Adichi could understand English. Had Eva planted her there to spy on *The Americans*? Or maybe Silveira, who lived around the corner, had told Eva after he heard it from Ronaldo or Brasil. No matter how she had heard about our problems, she was willing to help. In fact, she gave us a tour of her less expensive apartments. All disappointments after Avenida Atlantica's luxury.

Even Silveira, who had stayed out of sight since the "blood brother" night, invited us to go apartment hunting. By then, we were willing to accept help from anybody. The stench of rotten garbage, however, in one apartment full of dirty laundry and food-caked dishes reminded me of my first instinct. Don't get mixed up with this guy.

Brasil and Ronaldo tried to discourage us from seeing Silveira again. "Silveira is a pimp," they told Marilyn and me. "And his 'wife' Maria is the whore!"

We took the news as if they were reporting the weather. Nothing surprised us about these clowns.

Again, we visited the American Embassy. This time, I was struck by the overall austerity of the place. No palace, no ornate fence, no uniformed sentries on parade. Only offices on an upper floor of a tall, nondescript building. Did it mean Brazil wasn't important to the United States? Or vice versa? Or was it a cost-cutting measure?

On the eighteenth floor, a well-dressed thirtyish representative met us at the reception desk and led us to a small, plain office. He placed himself behind a large desk. Marilyn and I faced him in two visitor's chairs. I watched him grow bug-eyed as I gave a recap of my adventures with the *contrabandistas*. When I had finished, he shook his head and sent us upstairs to the US consulate.

The consul bore a close resemblance to his embassy counterpart with his clean-cut American look.

Our conversation quickly evolved to how, after all the trouble we went through to move to Rio, we could find an equitable way to stay. A job in the television industry would be next to impossible without a command of Portuguese. The consul was equally unenthusiastic about our chances of succeeding as foreign entrepreneurs. He gave us an American pamphlet on doing business in Brazil, which bluntly stated that success could be achieved *only* with a Brazilian partner. But, it went on to say, it was nearly impossible to find a Brazilian who could be trusted.

We already knew that from our Brazilian friends—a reliable source on the subject. "Brazil is very corrupt. It iss way of life." To us that was a gross understatement.

From the consulate, Marilyn and I went to *Escola Americana* to bring Antonio Battista up to date. He was the good man who had given Lynne and Evan a temporary home, and at Christmastime in Greenwich had imparted the first news of Jerry's connection to the law's dark side. News Jerry had deceitfully disproved with a phone call to Washington, DC, while he and I waited in his room at the Trocadero. Now, as Antonio sat at the headmaster's desk, drawing on the ever-present cigarette as he listened to our story, he seemed genuinely sorry to have been right. True to form, he offered his help and wished us well. In whatever we decided to do.

Afterward, Marilyn and I stopped for lunch at a sidewalk café on Avenida Atlantica. We ordered a Brahma Chopp beer, fish salad, and fruit. The traffic's din was there, as always. The fumes mixed with the ocean's salty aroma. A man walked by with an anteater on a leash and people at the cafè laughed. The little fellow was a mottled khaki color, the size of a small dog, not counting his long pointed tail. He shuffled along as though he enjoyed city life.

"No telling what you'll see next," Marilyn said.

Once our meal came and we started eating, three young beggars swarmed our table like flies. "Can I have your breadsticks?" "Do you want your fruit?" "I will eat your leftovers for you." The boys, ranging between seven and twelve, spoke in perfect memorized phrases. I believe that was the extent of their English.

Aside from the disruption, the boys' ages bothered Marilyn. "What a way to live," she said. "I'm beginning to wonder about Rio. Maybe it's not so great. Everywhere you look there's poverty." She recalled a shabby old woman carrying a child, who begged for her half-eaten ice cream cone. Our Brazilian friends had warned us about beggars borrowing children to appear more needy.

"The filth piles up," Marilyn went on. "The noise never stops." She looked at me. "Maybe I was wrong. Why *do* we want to stay?"

"To follow our plan." I wasn't fully ready to give up. "As you said, there's a lot of potential. *If* we can work through the drawbacks. Also . . . to save face. Besides, we can't yank the kids out of school with five weeks to go. Especially Lynne, at the end of her senior year." I looked around. "You're right about the city. But if we got some kind of business going, we wouldn't have to stay here. We could live on the outskirts."

"That might be better. If it's safe."

"Who knows?" My shallow well of enthusiasm on the subject dried up and I switched gears. "How about a nice pork roast for dinner?"

"Fine," Marilyn said as she rescued her beer from a boy who looked to be about ten. "Except I wouldn't know a pork roast if I saw one, the way they butcher meat."

"Leave it to me. I found a new butcher shop." I paid the bill and we left, letting the boys move in until the waiter chased them away.

Three blocks later, I led Marilyn into a small shop. We stood in front of a glass case of chipped ice and fresh-looking meat. When it was our turn to order, I cleared my throat, let out a snort, gave a few "oink oink," and snorted again. The butcher stared at me, his face blank. Then he laughed. "You don't mean pork, do ya, buddy?"

For one sweet moment, it felt like home.

* * *

A few days later, I persuaded Eva to reduce the rent from 8,000 cruzeiros a month to 5,000 by paying her in advance. At the black market rate of six cruzeiros to the dollar, it would mean going from $1335 to $835. At the lower bank rate of four cruzeiros per dollar, it would drop from $2000 to $1250. Since we had exchanged our dollars for both black market and bank cruzeiros, we would save an average of $500 a month. A definite help to slow the cash drain.

Chapter 44
Marilyn

All four girls faced their uncertain future with remarkable composure. "I hate to leave Brazil," Lynne said. "Or I should say, I hate having *you* leave Brazil. I want to come back here on school vacations." She would be going to the University of Rochester in New York in the fall. "But I'll understand if you decide to go."

"I wouldn't mind graduating from *Escola Americana* next year," Evan said. "But Greenwich High is okay too." She wanted us to know either choice was fine. She really wasn't sure which would be better.

"I think I want to go home," Diane said. "I miss gymnastics. But the kids are nice here. And it's really different."

"I miss riding," Heather said. "But I don't care if we stay."

What trust they have, I thought. *I hope we don't let them down again.*

"We sure had fun here." Lynne gave Evan a secret smile, and Evan giggled. "I'm definitely coming back on my own."

"I'll come with you," Evan said. She and Lynne hooked arms and skipped in a circle, singing a Brazilian tune.

They were best friends now. Nine months ago, who would have believed it? This venture hadn't been a total loss.

I was grateful for our daughters' youthful spirit, their flexibility. I was counting on it to get them through whatever lay ahead.

Jasmine voted to stay in Rio by having her kittens: two blacks, a black and white, and a gray calico like her.

* * *

One afternoon a few weeks later, Jack stood at the open living room window while I worked on my needlepoint. The kittens were riding the thin white curtains that billowed like parachutes in the sea breeze. Jack spotted Lynne and Evan coming home from school, just as a man drove onto the sidewalk and parked his car next to the beach. The man got out, leaned against the car, and stared at our building. It was the second time since Jack had returned from Belèm that he'd noticed someone watching the apartment. When the girls came in, he asked them if anybody had followed them home.

"No," they answered.

"Well, somebody's watching us."

"Let's see. Let's see!" The girls ran to the window.

"Get back!" their father yelled. "Don't let him see you."

They moved back and watched from the shadows, and Jack asked if they had ever seen that man before.

"No," they said. "Never." Lynne was caught up in the intrigue. "I'll go take his picture."

"I'll go with her," said Evan. "We can pretend we're taking each other's picture, and he'll be in the background."

"Good idea," Jack said. "He may have a connection with Jerry."

"Jack," I said, alarmed, "are you out of your mind?"

"It's okay. I'll watch from here."

"A lot of good that'll do if he grabs them and takes off!" I couldn't believe he'd put the girls in danger.

"He won't grab them. They'll be okay."

"Jack!" I protested.

"Oh, Mom. You're such a worrywart. Evan and I can handle him."

"They're right, you know," Jack said.

Did I worry too much? Was I overly cautious? I wasn't sure anymore. "Oh, all right," I finally said. "Just run like crazy if he comes toward you."

Jack gave them instructions. "Don't get too close. If he starts to approach, run like hell. But I really don't think he'll chase you. He's just watching."

While we watched from behind the curtains, Evan and Lynne strolled across Avenida Atlantica, arm in arm, pointing at the sights like two tourists, the camera around Lynne's neck. When they reached the sidewalk, they stopped about ten yards from the man. He was so intent on watching the building, he didn't notice them. Evan turned her back to him and struck a Hollywood pose. Lynne stood far enough away to fit the man, his car, and the license plate in the lens. Evan put on a big smile and Lynne snapped her picture.

They traded places and Lynne posed.

It was then that the "spy" became aware of the girls and their camera. He jumped into his car and sped away, burning rubber.

Buoyant with success, the girls gave Jack and me a thumbs-up.

We waved and I breathed a sigh of relief. Jack scratched his head. "This is a hell of a way to live," he said.

That night a cunning laugh rolled from Deus Mar Brasil's throat when we told him about the man. "No *preocupado!*" he reassured us. "Es bodyguard. I hire."

Chapter 45
Marilyn

Sunday was Adichi's day off. Usually we rented a car and drove to Jacarapagua Airport to visit the Cessna. Sometimes we washed it, and sometimes all six of us piled in for a short ride along the coast after Jack did an intensive pre-flight check. Our main objective was to make sure the plane was still in good working order, that someone hadn't pulled a wire, disturbed the ailerons, or polluted the fuel. We trusted no one.

Sometimes we brought a picnic lunch and ate on the beach in Barra, where only the bravest surfers pitted themselves against the gigantic waves and potent undertow, more dangerous even than in Rio. Lynne and Evan sat with their backs to the ocean, the memories of their own experience still raw.

One Sunday we took a ride on a country road that wound through green velvet mountains. Along the way, we stopped at a roadside stand to buy small paper cups of sugar cane juice, a thin whitish-gray liquid, pungently bittersweet. Heather screwed up her face and shuddered, her ponytails shaking. "This doesn't taste like sugar," she said. "It's awful." We were all surprised; we had expected something delectably sweet. After our ride, we returned to the city, dropped off the car, and then walked home through the park next to our apartment.

Every Sunday evening a samba band played under our windows. The music was contagious, and the crowd moved together as one. We would always join them, feeling the music, swaying in rhythm, the sound tickling our bones. Young children danced on a small wooden stage, the beat in their blood. A common spirit held everyone in its hands until the music stopped.

On Monday mornings Adichi would come back from the farm where her family lived, always with a bagful of shiny giant avocadoes on her arm. She would put them in the blender with milk and sugar and make delicious avocado milkshakes, a flavor we'd never tasted before.

A long month of indecision and frustration passed, a month interlaced with depression and hopelessness.

Adichi, aware of our problems, told Lynne that she would move anywhere with us, except *Las Estadas Unidas.* It was too far away. She said she liked working for Americans. They treated her well, and their early dinner hour ended her day at nine instead of midnight.

To help us, Adichi turned to her religion, macumba. On certain Friday nights after dark, patches of candles flickered in the breeze on Copacabana Beach. These were macumba nights. The worshippers set up altars of gifts for their deceased relatives, whose spirits came by sea to receive them. A small circle of stones or flowers, with several candles to light the way, surrounded the offering. The gift could be a dead chicken, a bottle of beer, coins, or trinkets. After a solemn ceremony, the worshippers left their offerings, the candles blinking in the night, until the wind or the sea or the spirits snuffed them out. In return for the gifts, the worshippers hoped that the spirits would grant them their wishes. If any living soul touched the gifts, a macumba curse would be upon them. Usually the sea carried the gifts away.

One night when Adichi came back from macumba worship, her feet caked with sand, she told Lynne that she had offered her gifts so the evil spirits would leave our apartment.

Her efforts were in vain.

Chapter 46
Jack

Ronaldo, another cousin, and *his* associates from Belèm offered me all kinds of illegal—they made no secret of it—opportunities to improve our finances. Selling contraband jewelry. Liquor. Black market Levi's.

In the meantime, I tried to get formal proceedings against Jerry, hoping to recoup part of our loss by confiscating Jerry's furniture. I had paid for it. Our lion-hearted lawyer, da Matta, invariably in the throes of either hangover, drink, or fear, and therefore useless, prompted us to hire a new lawyer. Naturally, it caused a delay. And though people moved fast—too much coffee?—processes moved slowly. No doubt due to tropical lethargy and Brazilian red tape. In our case, red tape meant papers ending up in deadends created by crooked Belèm officials.

At the US Consulate, I gave a rundown of my experiences. I returned several times to report crimes of the *contrabandistas.* I topped it off with the illegal business opportunities offered by our friends in Rio and their Belèm associates. And a list of names.

The consul thought the Federal Ministry of Justice would be interested in my information. He made an appointment for me with the Minister of Justice. Finally. Maybe I might finally stir up some action.

The consul representative also arranged a meeting with a successful businessman who owned two distributorships in Brazil: one for Coca Cola and the other for

DeHaviland, a British manufacturer of turbo prop commuter planes as well as bush planes. An American, he had come to Brazil in the early fifties and had married a wealthy blonde blue-eyed Brazilian woman of German descent. He invited the whole family to dinner at his elegant home. Compared to our other acquaintances, the man was a prince. Unfortunately, his suggestions for business pursuits required more time and money than we could afford.

With our cash going fast and no hope in sight to generate an income, circumstances dictated our decision. We would leave Rio as soon as school was out and Lynne had graduated.

Rather than go through the trial of flying the Cessna home alone, a challenge I did not relish, I attempted to sell the plane in Brazil. I investigated numerous possibilities, including inquiries at the airport and the consulate, all of which proved fruitless. But Ronaldo, on the lookout for deals like a lion for raw meat, came up with two buyers from Belèm: Carlos Alberto and a man called Francese.

Marilyn was incredulous. "How could you even *think* of doing business with those crooks? How could you even *look* at Alberto after all he's done?"

"If they want to buy my plane, for my price, and save me the trouble of flying it home, they can have it. Believe me, I know who I'm dealing with. If Tom Ryan were here with his Pan Am card, it would be another story. But flying solo to New York is a long goddamn ride. Most of it over water. If I have to sell the plane to the devil himself, I will."

"I don't trust Alberto," Marilyn said. "He's a rotten, lying SOB." But after considering it, she weakened. "On the other hand, I don't want you flying home alone.

I hate to even think about it." Finally she agreed. "It would be a great relief to sell it. As long as you watch their every move!"

With Ronaldo acting as agent, a price was agreed upon.

Later the same week, I visited Ronaldo in his office. As soon as Ronaldo saw me he started to hum, as always, revving up to speak English. Eventually, the words came. "Kel-lay. Bad news. Aeroplane. No deal."

I frowned. "What do you mean, no deal? *Porque*?"

"Alberto. Francese. Have check to buy aeroplane." He shook his head, his yellow eyes dark. "Check no good."

My hopes collapsed. I'd have to fly home alone. But at the same time, I realized Ronaldo had saved me from another con. In retrospect, I couldn't believe I had considered it. "How did you find out?" I asked.

Ronaldo leaned back, rested his feet on his desk and smiled, an all-knowing smile. "They tell me."

I couldn't help but laugh. It seemed the only thing our Brazilian friends were honest about was their dishonesty. One thing I couldn't figure was where, exactly, Ronaldo's loyalty lay. Why would Ronaldo side with me against his own flesh and blood? What was in it for him?

* * *

At the Federal Ministry of Justice, Marcos da Matta and I sat in the office of da Matta's boss, the Minister of Justice, Leonel Panelo. Mr. Panelo had a face lined like graph paper, sallow skin, and thinning gray hair. Looked a bit like da Matta himself, except for the abundance of wrinkles. I told him my story, pausing between paragraphs while da Matta translated. I began with meeting Jerry Green on a plane to Florida and I ended with the present. Gave him names of everyone I had met in Rio and Belèm. The arrest and phony release of Jerry. The rental of murderers. And the illegal business opportunities offered me since Jerry's escape.

Leonel Panelo listened quietly, cigarette after cigarette burning in his smoke-stained fingers. He nodded knowingly, eyes narrowed, a bitter half smile coming and going. At times, his breath quickened and he made notes, grunting with satisfaction. Occasionally, he interrupted to ask a question or have a detail repeated.

Da Matta shifted nervously in his chair as he described the illegal activities of his associates.

After I finished my report, Panelo's dark eyes sparked in his gaunt face, and his words rushed out like a string of firecrackers, periodically punctuated by passionate reiterations of cherry bomb caliber.

Da Matta was visibly distressed as he translated. His face was gray. "He says these Brazilians and Americans are involved in international crime of extreme proportions." Da Matta's trembling hand raked his thin, oily hair. "Oh, God, Kelley. My children! It sounds like the Mafia!" Which was a suspicion da Matta had always rejected after every drink we had bought him. "You better watch your ass."

"*He* said that?" I asked.

"*I* said that. *He* said you should be very careful. *He* said these men are very dangerous." Da Matta folded his hands in his lap to stop their shaking. "Oh God, Kelley, these men are killers!"

I was not surprised.

Later, thinking about Leonel Panelo's information, I was overcome by an urge for justice. In a letter to Senator Lowell Weicker of Connecticut, I sought help and advice. Then I wrote to a friend who worked in

Washington and had access to President Nixon. Nothing would hinder my effort, fast becoming an obsession, to make Jerry Green pay for his crime against the Kelley family.

I wrote a three-page letter to President Geisel of Brazil to apprise him of the case, and included copies of my two letters to the States. Citing the immense growth potential in Brazil, I expressed a desire, as yet unfulfilled, to participate. As a result of my plan's failure, I said, my low finances gave me no alternative but to return to the United States when my children finished school. *In the meantime,* I wrote, *I'm primarily concerned about our personal safety because I know too much and could not be bought by the Mafia, who continue to offer me all kinds of illegal opportunities to improve my low capital.*

May I ask that you help us, Mr. President, since I have been totally frustrated in every way.

Respectfully yours, Jack Kelley.

Whether or not my letter ever reached the president's desk, translated or in its original form, I never knew.

On Friday night, May 17, as a last resort, I left for New York to give the wheels of justice a push.

Chapter 47
Jack

There was a time—and not so long ago—when I had thought of JFK International Airport as the gate to insanity. Now as I walked through the airport, with its crowds moving in orderly fashion, it felt more like a gate to serenity. Amazing how fast one's point of view could do a one-eighty.

I caught the Connecticut limo to Greenwich. Vince and Jane Warner had offered their home as my base of operation while I was in the States.

Two days of unproductive phone calls, however, convinced me I could accomplish more in person. I scheduled a meeting with our Connecticut senator and left for Washington.

* * *

A cab ride through the capital at the peak of cherry blossom time made me wonder why Brazil had been so appealing.

In his office, Senator Lowell Weicker listened to my story and then made appointments for me with the FBI and the Brazilian consulate. If things kept running this smoothly, it would be only a matter of time before I had Jerry in the palm of my hand. I called to give Marilyn the good news.

* * *

For nearly three hours, two FBI agents listened to my story. Their faces revealed nothing. They made a quick note now and then. Offered an occasional humph or an ironic smile. A big difference to the reaction of da Matta's boss at the Federal Ministry of Justice. Finally, one of them went to a file drawer, pulled out a black and white 5 x 7 photograph, and held it up for me to see. "Is this Jerry Green?"

I stared at the photo. It was Jerry all right. A full-face, unsmiling, no-frills shot of the bastard. I pictured Jerry fleeing Belèm and rage rose in my chest. I could still hear his laugh as he passed through the gate. To freedom. It pierced me like a knife, as sharp as the day it happened. "It's him," I said.

The agent returned the photo to the drawer. "We'll look into the matter," he said.

I stared at the man. I don't know which was stronger, my disbelief or my disappointment. I'd wasted my breath for the last three hours.

He gave me a grim smile. "Sorry, pal, that's the best we can do." He might just as well have punched me in the stomach.

Nor did the Brazilian consulate give me any satisfaction. Jerry Green was, after all, an American citizen, and the crime had originated in the United States and was therefore out of their jurisdiction. They were sorry, but there was nothing they could do.

I returned to Greenwich in low spirits. I found a house to rent near the heart of town and far from grand. Face it, it was a step down. But it had four bedrooms and the rent was reasonable, which, with an unresolved future, was an important consideration. At any rate, I hoped to have us out of there and into something better in no time.

Now, after a three-week absence, I would return to Rio to prepare for the trip home. Which involved, among other distasteful items, going through masses of paperwork in reverse, undoing all we had done. And shoving humble pie down my throat.

Chapter 48
Marilyn

Ronaldo called. "Hmm . . . May-ra-leen. Mon in Belèm. Has samples of wood. For fur-ni-ture *de amigo.* En *acidente.* Auto. Verry bad. Verry bad! En haas-pee-tal *vinte dias.* No samples *para vinte dias.*"

A likely story. I spoke in a halting monotone. "That is too bad, Ronaldo. I am very sorry. I guess we will have to wait. Twenty days." I couldn't help smiling. It was the usual stall. "Thanks for calling."

* * *

Brasil had appointed himself nighttime bodyguard for the girls and me. He was faithful with his evening visits and often brought gifts of candy or rosemilk lotion. He was like a jolly uncle, making fun of his attempts at conversation as he flipped crazily through the pages of his Portuguese-English dictionary. He imparted that he had hired a daytime bodyguard to watch the girls go to and from school, a piece of information that both comforted and frightened me.

In his jovial manner, he taught us to play poker. Once, during our evening poker game, Lynne implored me, "Mom, we *have* to do our homework."

Having no wish to be alone with this funny little man, I said sternly, "Don't you girls *dare* leave this table. You stay right here and play poker." Wasn't I a great mother!

When Brasil finally did leave each evening, he and I followed the same routine. I would stand at the door while he waited for the elevator in the tiny private vestibule. Centered on one white ceramic tile wall was a blue image of Jesus Christ. With great reverence, Brasil would gaze at it and say, "Hay-zuus Chrree-stay, a ver-ry gude mon!" Then he would turn to the mirror on the opposite wall and gaze at himself. He'd puff up his chest, put on a grand smile, and say, "Clerk Gobblay!"

Clerk Gobblay?

After rapid consideration of possibilities, I concluded that the paunchy little man with pomaded black hair was comparing himself to Clark Gable. My laughter was part of the nightly farewell ritual.

* * *

Afternoons, while the girls were at school, I often went to the beach. First I'd build a headrest in the sand with my feet and then cover it with my towel, like the Brazilians did. One day, as I lay in the sun reading a back issue of *Time*, I noticed an attractive dark-haired man in a brief bathing suit that left nothing to the imagination was staring at me.

Finally, he came over and knelt beside me in the sand. "You are American, are you not?" he asked. His accent was different from the Brazilians.

"How did you know?" I asked, surprised, trying to keep my eyes above his waist.

He gestured with his head. "*Time* magazine." He smiled, charming, his perfect teeth bright against a tanned face. "And your bathing suit."

I looked down at my American bikini. "What's the matter with my bathing suit?"

His keen eyes traveled slowly up and down my body, making me wish I hadn't asked. Finally he answered, "There is so much of it."

Quickly I asked, "Are you Brazilian?"

"Argentinean. Here on business." He ogled me shamelessly. "Have coffee with me this afternoon."

His aggressiveness flustered me. I thought I had adjusted to South American ways. "I . . . I'm sorry," I stammered. "I can't."

My refusal astonished him. "Really?" he asked. "Why not?"

"My husband wouldn't like it."

Unfazed, he laughed. "We won't tell your husband," he said, as though one would never even consider such a thing.

My old jousting skills were rusty. "Uh . . . uh . . . my children," I said, thinking fast. "They wouldn't like it. *All* of them."

He smiled, confident, aware of his good looks. "How many do you have?"

"Oh, many!" I gave him a wide-eyed look. "Eight, I think."

"Eight?" His smile disappeared as though a storm cloud had covered the sun. He stood up. "*Adios*," he said, and walked away.

I smiled behind my magazine. It was the highlight of another lonely day.

Now that returning to Greenwich was a reality, I allowed my true feelings to surface. I couldn't wait to get back to the United States. It was the greatest country in the world.

Chapter 49
Evan

Brazil seemed scary compared to the United States, but some American families actually came to Sao Paulo and Rio to be safe. The fathers were big executives in Argentina, Venezuela, and Chili, and they had to escape from the kidnappers and murderers who were after them. So sometimes we'd get a new kid at *La Escola Americana.*

That's how Rachel ended up in my class. Her family came from Argentina, and her dad worked for General Electric. They helped him escape.

Rachel and I became friends. One night she invited me to dinner at her family's apartment in Ipanema. Her parents had gone out and it was the maid's night off, so we were on our own. Whoopee! We went to a small market two blocks away to buy some chopped meat that we hoped wasn't goat. When we got back to the apartment, Rachel quickly locked the door and leaned against it.

"What's the matter?" I asked.

"I don't mean to scare you," she said, "but somebody was following us."

"Oh my gosh."

"Can you think of any reason you'd be followed?"

"Yes," I said. "What about you?"

Rachel nodded. "I wonder which one of us they're following."

We looked at each other and started to giggle. It wasn't funny, but it made me feel better. "This is really sad," I said. "It could be either one of us."

We stopped giggling, and Rachel took her shopping bag to the kitchen. "We're not going to let it spoil our fun," she said. She was used to being afraid.

While we ate dinner, we could hardly talk about anything besides the man Rachel saw. Just when we finished eating, the lights went out.

"He must be in the building," she whispered. She got up and groped her way to the buffet for candles, then blindly set them in holders and lit them. "I'd better call my parents." She picked up the phone, jiggled the receiver, and looked at me. "It's dead."

"Oh, God," I said. "Where is he? What does he want?" I rushed to the window and peered out.

"My father thought we'd be safe here," Rachel said as she put the phone back.

I stared out the window, not speaking.

"What is it?" Rachel asked.

"It's dark out there!"

"Of course it's dark. It's eight-thirty at night."

"I mean, *really* dark." I pointed. "C'mere and look. No lights. Anyplace!"

Rachel ran to my side and stared into the thick blackness. She gave a little laugh. "It's a power failure," she said. "It's not just *us*." We hugged each other and then carried the candles to the living room and sat down. "I don't think you should leave until the lights go on," Rachel said.

"You couldn't drag me out of here. I only wish I could call my mom and tell her I'm okay. She worries so much."

"God! I don't blame her, after what you guys have been through."

"Well, your family hasn't exactly been having fun," I said.

Around nine o'clock the lights came on, and we decided it was safe for me to go home. "I'm sure he's long gone," Rachel said. "He probably thinks you're spending the night."

We hugged good-bye, and I set out on the three-block walk to the bus stop, turning every few steps to look behind me. I wondered if it was my imagination that made the same man stop walking every time I turned around. My heart pounded hard when I saw him get in line at the bus stop. Finally a bus came and I made a motion to get on. So did he. I jumped off right before the bus left. He did too.

When the next bus came, I got on. He got on behind me. There were lots of stops during the fifteen minute ride to Copacabana. At every stop I watched, hoping he would get off, but he stayed in his seat, staring straight ahead. He had no distinguishing features, but I still knew I had never seen him before. Twice I stood up to get off, and twice he did the same. My hands started to shake.

Did he want to kidnap me? Kill me?

I formed a quick plan. When my stop came, I would get off at the last possible second and run through the park to my building as fast as I could. The *porteiro* would fend off the man, and I would jump in the elevator and get away.

When my stop came, I waited until the last person was on the bottom step. Then I bolted for the door. Out of the corner of my eye, I saw the man get up. As I jumped off the bus, I landed in the dark. Another power failure! Blindly, I ran through blackness, bumping into people and hearing their Portuguese swear words. I fell over a park bench and felt the concrete rake my knees. It hurt like hell. I stumbled up again and kept on running. As I got closer to my building I realized the elevator would be dead and I didn't know if I could run up thirteen floors. I couldn't even *think* about being caught in the stairwell with that man. Just then I saw the shape of a car parked on the sidewalk right in front of me. I dropped to my bloody knees, trying to ignore the pain, and half crawled, half slid under the car. I sprawled flat, panting like a dog. My heart was pounding so hard, it vibrated my whole body.

Even louder than the sound of blood rushing through my head was the sound of somebody running. It faded. But in a minute the same hard heels came clicking back and stopped near the car. Could he have seen me climb under there? I heard him walk away and come back again. Would I have to spend the whole night there? I shivered. The mosaics were hard and cold.

What if the car's owner came back and drove away? I thought of running to the building and finding the *porteiro.* But how could I find him in the dark? And how could I make him understand my lame Portuguese?

The lights came on. I waited, listening. I heard people return to the park, but the same click of heels did not come back. I inched my way to the edge of the car to look out. Either the man was gone or he was on the other side of the car. The chill of the tiles and the sting of my knees made me desperate to be home.

I decided to run for it. I dragged myself out and raced to the building. Inside, the *porteiro* looked at me curiously. I rushed to the elevator and leaned on the button, keeping my eyes glued to the entrance as the constant buzzing of the descending elevator got closer. *Finally* the door opened and an angry couple glared at me as they got out. I darted inside and pressed 13 for our floor. The door closed behind me.

When the elevator got to my floor, I stepped into the tiny foyer. My hand shook as I put my key in the door and let myself in.

My sisters and my mom were in the living room. They stared at me. "What happened to you?" they all asked. "You're covered with dirt, and your knees are all bloody."

"You'll never believe it," I said.

Chapter 50
Marilyn

Jack's return to Rio was marred by the news that Eva had rented our apartment. She wanted us out by June 15—no ifs, ands, or bribes. She found our friends unsavory—which we could not dispute—and she needed time to fumigate the apartment after the animals left. We wondered if there was anything she didn't know.

"The kids will still be in school," I said to Jack. "Lynne's graduation isn't until the twenty-first. What the hell are we supposed to do?"

"We'll go back to the Trocadero."

"It's too expensive. It would just be another cash drain."

"All right," he said heatedly, "you're the genius. You come up with an idea." The constant frustration was getting the best of him.

"I'll do that. Just give me time." I had to sleep on it. If I thought about it as I drifted off, I might wake up with an answer in the morning. It had worked before and I was hoping it would work again.

After the girls left for school the next day, Jack and I lingered at the breakfast table, having our first cigarette of the day. "I have an idea," I said. "I don't like it, but it's practical."

"Well," he said, more relaxed after a night's sleep, "let's hear it."

"Diane and Heather can leave school a week early. I'm sure *Escola Americana* would make arrangements for early tests or whatever. So. On the fifteenth, I'll take them and the animals back to New York."

"You'll miss Lynne's graduation."

I inhaled the smoke sharply and spit it out. "I know. It's an important milestone. My oldest daughter."

"Damn Jerry. I hate this." Jack shoved his chair away from the table and started pacing.

"You and Lynne and Evan can stay at the Trocadero, and it'll cost only half as much."

As I spelled out my plan, I watched Jack's face fill with hatred for Jerry Green.

"After graduation," I continued, "Lynne and Evan can fly home, and you . . ." That brought me to the next hurdle. "Have you found anyone to be your copilot?"

"Not yet."

"Jack, you can't fly alone! The way our luck is going, you'd end up at the bottom of the ocean."

"Thanks for the vote of confidence."

"It has nothing to do with your flying ability. But what happens if you get sick up there?"

"I won't."

"Oh, yeah? How can you be so sure? You could fall asleep from monotony or pass out from lack of oxygen. What if you can't get fuel from the French islands?" As I spoke, the hazards grew more ominous. "Why don't you just leave the damn plane. It isn't worth the risk."

I remembered times in the past, when Jack was working in New York and taking out his anger on the family, times when, in my secret innermost thoughts, I wouldn't have minded if he'd disappeared. Now, I couldn't bear the thought of losing him.

He covered my hand with his and squeezed it. "Mare, you know I can't just leave the Cessna. Please, forget that idea and don't worry about it. I'll work out something."

He usually did, I had to admit. "Okay. I won't worry. You'll take care of it." I brushed off my hands, symbolically erasing my concern. We exchanged a look, knowing it wouldn't work.

The next day, we received another setback: a letter from American Express, stating in part, ". . . *We regret to advise you that information received by us from someone other than a consumer reporting agency but whom we believe to be a reliable source has resulted in a decision to terminate the credit privileges extended to you . . .*"

"How can they do this?" I asked. "We've always paid our bill on time. We need that card now more than ever to get us all back to the States."

"I think I smell a rat," Jack said. "And his name is Jerry Green."

A cold fear stabbed at my chest. Was Jerry that powerful? "How can he do this? What kind of clout allows him to have somebody's credit card cut off?"

Jack's lips were tight as he stared out the living room window at the incessantly rolling ocean. "It's no surprise," he said quietly. Then he brightened. "Maybe it's a mistake."

A phone call to American Express resulted in a letter that told us it was no mistake. Nor would American Express enlighten us further. Nor would they rescind their action.

"How are we supposed to get plane tickets?" I asked after Jack had read the letter aloud. My voice was shaky. "We'll never get out of here. We'll end up on the sidewalk with the beggars."

Jack, unaccustomed to seeing his wife fall apart, put his arms around me. "It's okay, Mare. We'll work it out like we always do. We'll use cash. All we have to do is have it wired." He patted me on the back. "Don't worry. We'll get along without a credit card. People do, you know."

I laughed. "I feel so silly."

"It's okay, kid. You're entitled."

* * *

Jack had the necessary funds transferred from our bank in Greenwich to a local Brazilian bank. We picked up our money a few days later and exchanged the dollars at the bank for *cruzeiros.* Then we set about securing the necessary documents that would get us and the animals out of Brazil and back to the States.

"If we were going home in glory," I said, "all this drudge work would be easy. As it is, it's almost insurmountable."

Jack hugged me. "It's almost over. Just hang on a little longer."

It always seemed toughest when the end was in sight.

* * *

"Evan and I can fly home with you, Daddy." Lynne had her selling shoes on. "Evan can read charts, and I can help with the flying."

Jack put his arm around his oldest daughter and smiled affectionately at her. "Takeoffs and landings at Stormville Airport aren't quite the same as flying over the jungle and the ocean for hours at a stretch."

"I know, Daddy, but I've got almost twenty-two hours of lessons. I could fly solo if I had to." She put her hands on her father's shoulders and did a little dance of beseechment; her long straight hair, sun bleached to a pale gold, flopped up and down. "Come on, Daddy, say yes. Pleeeeeze?"

It wasn't a bad idea. In fact, it was the *only* idea. Jack and I exchanged glances.

I was thinking that Lynne would be a good copilot. She had an oldest child's strong sense of responsibility, plus a newfound maturity from her Brazil experience. And her tenacity would carry her through all kinds of situations. She could be an asset on the long flight home.

"How dangerous would it be?" I asked.

Jack was already pacing. "It wouldn't be dangerous. Not the way we'd do it. We'd take our time, no more than five hours a day in the air."

Lynne's hands now rested on my shoulders, and she gaily bounced from one foot to the other as she gave me a beguiling gaze. "Come on, Mom. It's a great idea! You know we could do it!"

I looked at my other daughter. "How do you feel about this, Evan?"

Evan grinned at Lynne with sisterly intimacy, her dimples blinking through scores of freckles. "If Lynne goes, I'll go."

Lynne hugged her, and they both squealed.

Jack gave me an endearing smile. "What do you think, Mom?"

"Well . . . If you're sure it's safe . . ."

"It is. I promise," he said.

"I hope I don't regret this." Lately it seemed I was having to let my two oldest daughters do things I never would have allowed in ordinary times. But these weren't ordinary times. Begrudgingly, I said, "I guess it's okay."

Lynne and Evan cheered like two cheerleaders whose team had just scored the winning goal.

"Of course, I'll be worried sick the whole trip," I had to add.

"Oh come on, Mom, lighten up." The sisters were already airborne.

* * *

I walked toward the Pan Am 727 with a heavy heart. Diane led the way, carrying Jasmine in her case. The girls had found homes with American school friends for all four kittens. Heather followed with Pom Pom on a leash. I turned for a last look at my darling husband and my two beloved oldest daughters. They waved eagerly, broad grins fixed on their faces. Their image seared into my mind, and I prayed I would see them again soon.

Chapter 51
Lynne

My graduation was small. Thirty-nine students and their families—except for my mom and two sisters—came to *Escola Americana's* auditorium. We wore royal blue caps and gowns. I was one of the two class princesses attending the class queen. I wished Mom could have been there.

Antonio Battista gave out the diplomas in a beautiful candlelit ceremony. Then our all-night party began. First the graduates went to an elegant midnight buffet at the penthouse of a Brazilian student on Ipanema Beach. Afterward, we all went out to celebrate. Evan and some other friends came with us. We went from one nightclub to the next, having a great time, and we ended up eating breakfast at a friend's apartment in Ipanema.

Through the window, I watched the sky turn from black to blue over Ipanema Beach as the sun rose. The waves started to light up and the beach looked golden. Two silhouettes in formal clothes and bare feet moved toward the water. They embraced lightly when they reached the hard sand that the tide had left, and then they danced a joyful, wild waltz. The girl's long full dress billowed in the strong sea breeze. When they turned, the sun lit their faces. I recognized the boy. He was in my class. His father worked for USIA. The boy's partner was Evan.

Not too shabby, Evan, I thought. *Dancing on the beach at sunrise in one of the most glamorous cities in the world.* As I watched Evan whirling through the sand, I thought of all the times we had shared during the past nine months. We were closer now than we had ever been.

I was excited, yet sad. I would miss Rio. I loved the energy of the city and I would always treasure the memories. But it didn't really matter where I lived. The world belonged to me. I had just graduated from high school!

Chapter 52
Jack

The following morning the girls and I stood in operations, our gear in tow. The day before I had moved the Cessna from Jacarapaqua to Galeao Airport, a secondary field on an island in the middle of Rio that had the necessary facilities for checking out of the country. My single-engine plane looked minute among the jets, yet it would have to carry us over islands and oceans all the way back to White Plains, New York, USA.

While I filed my flight plan, with Lynne as my translator, Evan watched two customs agents comb through our luggage. Against all odds, the departure seemed to be going without a problem. The girls' ebullience overflowed. "We're going home," they chanted. Their faces beamed. I began to relax, thinking about our homecoming.

My daydream was interrupted by a raucous outburst outside the door. In the next instant, Marcos da Matta, Ronaldo Nelson, and Deus Mar Brasil exploded into the room, highly incensed.

Da Matta shouted at me. "Kelley, you will not leave this country until you pay us our money." He looked as though he deeply wanted to be elsewhere.

The girls moved closer to me. Their celebration was over.

Ronaldo and Brasil had obtained the attention of two *Federales.* Their voices rose as they pointed at me and raved in Portuguese.

I was momentarily stunned, although I had sensed a change of attitude among our "friends" over the last few days. It was the reason I had not told them my exact time of departure. They must have tried to call me at the Trocadero. "Da Matta," I said, "what the hell is going on?"

Da Matta's amber skin had taken on its familiar gray tinge. He looked old and tired. "You are not going to escape without paying us, Kelley."

"Pay you?" I asked. "For what?"

"Why, for all the consulting. Hours, Kelley. We talked with you for many hours. I translated until I was ex*haus*ted."

Ronaldo joined da Matta. His thick body danced with agitation. "For my off-eese. We talk bee-uz-ness, one day and one day and one day. Many days. You must pay to me rent for my off-eese and my bee-uz-ness consult. And for eenformation I say on Jerry Green."

One *Federale* approached us with Brasil while the other rapidly dialed the phone. Deus Mar Brasil's usual sunny face was as dark as a hurricane. "Kel-lay, you pay. I bo-dy-guard. You in States, I guard wi-fee and *filias.* I hire bo-dy-guard for you!"

I looked at Brasil in disbelief. "Brasil, I never asked you to guard my family. You volunteered. I thought you did it as a friend."

"No friend." Brasil said adamantly. "You pay!" His glare was cold. He turned to the *Federale* and spoke rapidly. The officer glared at me and the girls as he listened to Brasil.

I leaned over and spoke quietly to my daughters. "Move very slowly. Pick up the gear. Take it to the plane and load it. Evan, you get in and lock both doors. Lynne, you come back, in case I need you to translate."

The girls did as they were told. No one tried to stop them. I would have gone myself and made a quick takeoff, but the officials still held our passports and the plane's registration.

Our former friends had put me in a difficult position. All I had to do to get out of it was pay them—how much was anybody's guess—a bribe for the privilege of leaving. From the looks of things, the *Federales* would probably side with their compatriots. They could confiscate the plane. Or even throw me in jail. I remembered tales of self-appointed judges who quietly "disposed" of prisoners.

Nervously I pointed to the phone on the counter and brought my fist to my ear. "Te-lay-phon-ay?"

One of the officers shrugged and slid the phone in my direction as Lynne returned to my side.

My hands trembled as I pulled the small phone book out of my pocket. I found the number of the American consulate and dialed. When I finally made contact with a representative, I told my story and asked him to intervene on my behalf. The man promised to call back as quickly as possible and hung up.

Da Matta, Ronaldo, and Brasil had grown quiet, but no less hostile. They stood together like a barrier between me and the plane. I knew that da Matta was harmless and Ronaldo wildly impetuous. But Brasil, exhibiting a side never before revealed, appeared cruel and calculating. I believed he and Ronaldo were capable of inflicting physical harm. On me. The girls. The plane. If da Matta somehow persuaded them to follow a less violent legal route, they could have the plane impounded and keep me and the girls in Brazil indefinitely. Or at least until I agreed to pay them.

I slid my hand into my right pocket and wrapped my fingers around my .45.

Chapter 53
Lynne

So slowly it was barely noticeable, Daddy pulled out his gun and pressed it into my hand. It was heavy. Then he spoke quietly to me. I listened hard and then turned away to slip the gun into the top of my jeans under my shirt. Trying to act cool, I walked slowly past the men and out the door toward the Cessna. As I got closer, a dart of panic shot through me. I couldn't see anyone inside. I rushed to the plane as fast as I dared and stared through the window. Evan was huddled on the floor in the back.

"Evan," I cried. "Open up. I want to give you something." Evan's hands shook as she undid the lock. I opened the door and handed her the pistol. "Keep this. Dad says if anybody tries to fool with the plane, don't be afraid to use it."

Evan nodded. Her face was pale and her eyes looked huge and full of fear.

"But only as a last resort!" I cautioned.

"But what about you and Daddy?" Her voice was a wavy ribbon of fright.

"We'll be back as soon as we can. Don't unlock the doors for anybody else!" Evan looked so scared. "Don't worry, we'll be back in a flash." I turned to leave and then gave her one last look and tried to smile.

Chapter 54
Jack

After Lynne came back, the phone rang. One of the two *Federales* answered it. He kept his eyes on me, with an occasional glance at my detainers, as he listened and nodded. The call seemed to last forever. When finally the officer hung up, he nodded at me.

Lynne translated the officer's message. "He says we can go. But first they must process our papers."

The officer's words fired new rage into our former friends. They crowded around Lynne and me at the desk, protesting loudly. I turned my back and rested both elbows on the desk, pretending to ignore them. This increased their anger.

As I watched the officers plow through their tedious job, my body was rigid, waiting for a quick fist in the kidneys or a blow to the back of the head. The Brazilians loved rubber stamps. They seemed to have one for every day of the week. The seconds ticked by to agitated shouts as each of the necessary stamps was ceremoniously pressed onto each of the many papers. At last, the labored exercise ended, and I quickly paid my landing fee.

I grabbed Lynne and we bolted for the plane.

Ronaldo and Brasil were at our heels. A small band of aroused Brazilian soldiers, somehow coerced into joining their cause, ran with them. It seemed to make no difference to my former friends that I had received federal clearance to leave the country. They wanted blood! Or to be more exact, money.

It took Lynne and me all of thirty seconds to reach the plane, yelling all the while, "Evan, unlock the doors. Unlock the doors."

Evan moved fast. We climbed inside and locked the doors behind us. My hands trembled uncontrollably as I turned the key. The engine rolled over twice and died. The propeller turned, stopped, made a half turn, and stopped again. "Come on!" I yelled. I turned the key again and the engine grumbled, the prop hesitated, stirred, and froze. Ronaldo and Brasil and their entourage had surrounded the plane. Lynne screamed, "Hurry up, Daddy!"

Ronaldo danced a wild jig. Brasil's mouth moved in an angry tirade, his arms punctuating his defamations. The soldiers stood behind them, legs apart, hands on holsters. Ready. My fear for my daughters' safety had momentarily flustered me. I turned the key again and pumped the choke. The engine coughed a cloud of oily exhaust as the prop made a slow arc, then a lazy spin, and finally a welcome blur. Skipping the formalities, I began my taxi for takeoff, scattering my pursuers. Their clothes flapped vigorously in the prop's wind. I drove the Cessna toward the runway, swerving through a maze of parked jets. After making a hasty visual check for incoming traffic, I pushed the throttle. The aircraft lurched forward, gained momentum, and sped down the runway. With sweaty palms, I gripped the wheel with all my might as if that in itself would ensure a safe getaway. The girls sat like statues.

It was history's shortest takeoff.

The Cessna lifted us, once again carrying her load out of harm's way. I tilted her nose to the sun and headed due east.

As we gained altitude, the scenery became more beautiful, but we took no time to enjoy it. Sugar Loaf was off to our right as we made a left-hand departure out of Galeao, skirting Rio's Santos Dumont Airport. We stayed low through Niteroy and slowly turned to the northeast.

Our destination was Caravelas, about 400 miles up the coast. Thanks to the send-off by our greedy friends—a perfect cap to the total Rio experience—we had gotten a late start. I was concerned about getting to the airport before dark. The field offered no nighttime service.

I glanced at my daughters. Lynne next to me in the front seat, a rosy flush on her cheeks, struggling to appear confident and able. Evan in back, eyes huge, pale as the clouds above us, silently working to collect herself. This was my crew for the long flight home, Lord help us. What they lacked in expertise they made up for in desire and grit. I glanced at my copilot and navigator, and my heart overflowed. "Everybody okay?"

"Yes."

"Uh-huh."

Their voices were thin.

With such precious cargo aboard, I was taking the longer route home along the coast, which provided more population, more convenience, and more relaxation—something we needed after our hair-raising departure from Rio.

* * *

Just as the sun's red glare was fading, we landed in Caravelas. The girls helped tie down the plane and then we caught a bus into town. It stopped frequently along the way, dispensing its load of laborers throughout the countryside. Forty-five minutes after we boarded, we were deposited in the heart of the city, three tired travelers.

Although Caravelas was on the ocean, it was a genuine frontier town with dirt roads and no sidewalks. Chickens, pigs, and a lone goat wandered loose.

Curious dark-skinned citizens surrounded us, staring openly and chattering among themselves. I put my hand in my pocket and let it rest on the .45. "Stay close to me," I said. The onlookers appeared harmless, but so did a lot of other people I knew. "Lynne, ask them where the hotel is."

"*Onde fica a hotel?*" Lynne's voice squeaked.

A man in front pointed down the road. As we began walking, the crowd parted to let us through, giving us plenty of space, as though we had leprosy.

"What's their problem?" Lynne asked.

"I don't think they see many white people," I said.

We walked down the main street, our arms touching, two chickens at our heels and part of the crowd following at a distance. We passed a line of wooden one-room shacks, each lit inside by a single overhead bulb. Soon we came to what we guessed was the hotel.

It was nothing more than a stable.

Inside, a man shyly greeted us, and Lynne asked him about rooms. He took us to a large box stall with dark, bare-beamed walls and one light bulb dangling from a cord on the ceiling. There were four cots with straw mattresses. Each had one short sheet and one pillow. The man watched as we set our gear on the floor.

"Ask him where we can get something to eat," I said.

When Lynne asked, the man smiled and beckoned for us to follow. He led us to the tack room, where three tables were covered with white cloths, and gestured for us to sit down. Our bodies dropped heavily into the rickety chairs as the impact of our traumatic morning finally hit with its full wallop.

I looked around. "This place reminds me of the Breezy Harbor Club," I said.

The girls were too tired to laugh.

About twenty minutes later, a careworn dark-skinned woman wearing a stained white apron shuffled in and placed our food in front of us. Lynne thanked her. Though we were hungry, we just stared at the plates. Each one held a small, gray cooked bird. A strange root vegetable sat next to it. It was white like the plate. "These must be cousins of the guys who followed us," I said.

"Come on, Daddy," Evan said. "It's bad enough."

When we had choked down enough of our meal to satisfy our hunger, we walked to the rear of the stable and an enclosed yard with six sinks in the middle. It seemed to be a popular gathering spot on that humid evening. Maybe the only place in town with running water. Following our noses to one side, we noticed three enclosed toilets.

We fetched our travel kits and returned to brush our teeth under the stars. The fascinated bystanders stood nearby and watched.

Our routine finished, we retired to our stall and fell onto our scratchy cots. Fully dressed, totally exhausted.

It took only a minute for the mosquitoes to find us. Yearning for sleep, we lay in wait, knowing that when the droning grew louder, a moment of silence would come. And then . . . the sting.

"Can't we shut the windows?" Evan asked.

Lynne slapped at her arms. "We'll smother."

"It's like a steam bath in here," I said. "I'm soaked already." I smacked myself behind the neck. "These guys are big enough to wear numbers on their wings."

All through the night we slapped at insects. We lay in our own sweat as we slipped in and out of sleep. Waiting for dawn to come.

* * *

It was not difficult to rise early. We ate a quick breakfast of coffee and rolls in the tack room and hitched a ride to the airport in the back of a dilapidated truck. I had topped off the fuel and checked the oil the night before. The Cessna was off the ground by 7:30 a.m.

Once we reached altitude, the engine hummed a lullabye and the sun warmed the cabin, and the girls drifted off to sleep. Lynne, a conscientious copilot, occasionally opened one eye to monitor the gauges.

We followed the coast to Ilhaus, never going farther than fifteen miles inland, beyond the edge of population. Three hundred miles out of Caravelas, we stopped to refresh ourselves at our next checkpoint, Salvador. Spread on a range of hills stretching along the seashore, Salvador was the oldest and one of the most attractive cities in Brazil, the fourth largest in population.

With a beautiful day in front of us, we chose to make the 900 mile trip to Fortaleza. Since the weather was good and the ride was smooth, Lynne took the wheel while I dozed. Without mosquitoes.

Fortaleza, appealing and sophisticated, was a neat, prosperous fishing port, exporting lumber and minerals and offering clean accommodations. A treat in which to delight. We had a decent dinner of what tasted like beef and an early bedtime.

Takeoff the next day was 6:30 a.m., with no air traffic. Destination Belèm, following the coast. Near Sao Luis, south-east of Belèm, we flew over a fifty-mile stretch of huge sand dunes where a mineralogical shift had created an astonishing imitation of Copacabana's black and white mosaic sidewalks.

When we landed in Belèm, the airport customs agent greeted me with a smile. "Your trip over the jungle was successful I see. Good. Good."

"Thank you for your help. This time I'm going to *Estadas Unidas.*"

"Oooh. A very long way. Good luck to all." He nodded at the girls.

"Thank you," I said. "I have a good crew."

The man laughed.

To add to the friendly ambiance—so unlike my last visit—the crew from a General Mills corporate jet gave us cans of meat and vegetables, concerned for me and my young crew on such a long trip in such a small plane.

Early the next morning we began the 618 mile trip to Paramaribo, Surinam, taking off over the Amazon River. From the air, the river looked like a fifty-mile-wide brown snake rushing to meet the Atlantic. Huge cumulus clouds drifted through a blue sky. We made our way above the mountains, dodging the gigantic moving puffs to avoid the rain and lightning they carried. When we flew over our checkpoints, Amapa and Rochambeau, I said, "Look down there, girls. That's where Che Gueverra planned to set up camp so he could spread his troops into South and Central America."

Evan asked how I knew that, and I explained that I had met some Brazilian officers at Jerry's house.

"They were proud to tell me how the Brazilian soldiers gave Che and his men a very unfriendly welcome."

"Wow!" said Lynne. "Things like that don't happen in the States. Americans don't know how lucky they are."

"Well, we know, don't we," I said.

"I can't wait to feel safe again," Evan said.

I reached around the back of my seat and patted her arm. "I know, honey. Me too. I feel so bad about everything."

"It's okay, Daddy," Lynne said. "We all survived."

My guilt for putting my family through so much turmoil was something I would never get over.

I gave Lynne a turn at the controls during the calm periods and was impressed by her confidence. The day's trip ended with a refreshing night in Paramaribo. The most memorable part of our visit was having a delicious Dutch and French dinner in the jungle. Or so it seemed. The hotel's huge restaurant surrounded us with tropical trees, plants, and colorful flowers. Live parrots squawked at us from their perches on nearby limbs—our dinner music.

The next day's first leg was to Piarco, Trinidad, for fuel, with a checkpoint of Georgetown, British Guiana. It was not a terribly long ride, though it turned out to be one of the most rugged and hazardous of my flying career. As we were passing over the Orinoco—one of the largest rivers in the world, with an uninhabitable, extremely dangerous delta running for hundreds of miles—we were hit by a sudden torrential rainstorm as only the tropics can give. I considered making a one-eighty, but I thought tropical storms lasted only a few minutes. We'd be out of it in no time. Unfortunately, this one was different. The sky wept as if it were the end of the world. I fought the punishing deluge as it pounded us, focusing on the instruments. *Needle, ball, air speed,* I kept repeating to myself. *Keep your eye on the needle, ball, and air speed.* That was the rule to stay level and steady: ignore the senses, those human reactions that battle constantly with the instrument panel. Your body might be telling you you're diving to the left, but your instruments indicate you're flying straight and level. Or the reverse could happen. The problem of "flying by the seat of your pants" in intense weather could lead a pilot dangerously astray. I concentrated on the instruments and kept the heading on Piarco. The girls were unnaturally quiet.

The rain was so strong it had penetrated the seals in the door and was coming in underneath the windscreen. A trace of water soon showed on the floor. I glanced at Lynne. She stared straight ahead, her body as still as a portrait. In that instant glance, I felt the plane dive and had a great urge to pull it up. *Needle, ball, air speed.* To my unbelieving eyes, the instruments told me the plane was still level, altitude good.

For the next interminable hour and a half, we were blinded by a steady barrage of silver bullets from all directions. Gushing streams of water clung to the windows, encasing us in our tiny cocoon. The puddle on the floor had grown. I couldn't go higher and wouldn't go lower. It took all I had to keep a steady course and follow the gauges while the Cessna rode the wind and battled the rain. The engine groaned noisily, but at least it kept going. My main concern was that the water would get behind the instrument panel and the instruments would short out. *Please, God,* I prayed, *get us through this abominable storm. Don't punish my daughters for my mistakes.*

The girls hadn't made a sound since the storm hit. "Evan, everything okay?" I yelled over the turbulence, wondering if she had passed out. Some people did in a panic situation. My voice roused Lynne, and she turned around to look at her sister. "She's okay, Daddy," Lynne said. My steadfast daughter's voice shook. I took a hand off the wheel long enough to give her arm a reassuring pat.

We plowed on, bucking and lunging like a skittish racehorse. I wondered how much longer the storm would last. More important, how much longer could the Cessna tolerate this steady, brutal abuse. The storm was testing both the body and the engine to the extreme, a test I would have given anything to have the girls forego. They were too quiet. I wished they'd scream or yell. Get their emotions out. Those poor kids. They had had enough misadventures for their young ages, on this trip alone.

Fatigue gnawed at my shoulders. My hands were cramping from holding the wheel so tightly. I began to think the storm must be covering all of South America, and we'd never reach the edge of it.

When it seemed the torture would never end, we broke out of it. In the blue and still at 8,500 feet! I had never been so happy to see the sun. The girls slowly came to life. Weak cheers that sounded like baby birds. I thanked God for keeping the instruments dry and the engine steady. Then I thanked myself for installing netting in the rear to keep the luggage from sliding and throwing the weight off balance or hitting someone.

We landed, somewhat shakily, in Piarco. This flight had to be the granddaddy of white-knuckle, sweaty-palm flights!

* * *

After fueling up in Piarco we took off again, heading for St. Croix on the US Virgin Islands, just southeast of Puerto Rico.

St. Croix customs officials put us through one of the most rigorous inspections of my experience, even removing the Cessna's panels. Driving a small plane, a popular vehicle for drug smuggling, with two girls of pot-smoking age aboard made us logical suspects.

After getting through customs, we left the plane at the airport and went to our condominium for some necessary rest, swimming, and decent food. When we had bought the condo in the late 60s, we'd had no inkling it would become a safe haven for my small-plane travels to Brazil and back. Though the Cruzans had brought home a hostile attitude against Americans from the Vietnam War, at least nobody was chasing us with pistols drawn. And they spoke English.

My present worry was the Cessna's engine. Real or imagined, I couldn't be sure, it seemed to have been running rough during the last leg of our trip. The only person I could think of to call was Charlie Blair, who owned the inter-island flying boat operation and was married to Maureen O'Hara, the beautiful Irish movie actress who often costarred with John Wayne. Charlie, an aviation pioneer and World War II hero, was gracious enough to offer the services of his head mechanic, Bunny, who, after his day of working on the Grumman Goose, drove to the airport to inspect the Cessna. I hadn't been hallucinating. One of the Cessna's two magnetos had to be replaced. No pilot would fly with only one magneto, especially over water. One magneto creates the energy for the ignition, and the other acts as the backup system. I wondered if I'd already used up my ration of luck for this trip.

The repairs kept us in St. Croix for an extra two days, and though it was an ideal place to be laid over—roaming the familiar streets and alleys of Christiansted, lying on the beach, relaxing and recovering from our unforgettable flight—we were eager to get home.

Finally, three days after we landed, we took off from St. Croix. We circled over Christiansted for one last look at the old Danish buildings sparkling in the sun and the brilliant turquoise sea lapping at the city's edge. Then we turned west and climbed to our cruising altitude of 8500 feet.

I went through the usual routine of making my checkpoints, where I intersected my two ADF (automatic direction finder) radio signals with my VOR (very high frequency omnidirectional range). I made my first checkpoint at Puerto Rico and then headed for South Caicos.

It would be a two-and-a-half-hour stretch, our longest passage over water, though we would see the Dominican Republic and Haiti along the way. This day we had perfect conditions: favorable winds and clear visibility with only the usual clouds hovering over the islands.

We hit South Caicos on the money and landed long enough to freshen up and top off our tanks. Then we made a beeline for Nassau, our next checkpoint.

Directly over Nassau, I reset the compass heading for West Palm Beach. As soon as we were close enough,

I contacted approach control and asked for customs clearance for entering the United States.

We stopped long enough to breeze through customs, and with perfect weather ahead, continued on to Savannah, Georgia.

St. Croix to Savannah was a long day's ride, most of it over water, to avoid landing in Martinique. But I felt it was worth the effort in case the gendarmes remembered our fast takeoff five months earlier with our tank full of golden fuel and our wallets full of dollars not spent there.

Savannah was the perfect place for our first night in the States. People went out of their way to be friendly, and the new Quality Inn was in a forest pungent with the smell of pine trees, a forgotten and sweetly comforting scent. We gorged on good old American hamburgers and then buried ourselves under fluffy comforters.

The next morning we were up at six, had the best ham and eggs we had ever tasted, and were airborne by 8:30. Later that day we would land at Westchester County Airport in White Plains, New York. It was the Fourth of July!

I smiled at my crew, feeling a deep closeness. My daughters and I had shared some harrowing experiences together. Evan had sat in back most of the time, reading, sleeping, studying charts. Lynne had performed well at the wheel and had developed a professional attitude toward the controls, applying discipline to maintain the course and the altitude. She had learned to trim properly and to let the plane fly itself, holding it steady and not over-controlling. My heart nearly burst with love and pride for my girls. They had shown their stuff, and it was beyond anything I could have hoped for.

"We're almost there," I said, and then concentrated on the final leg.

When we reached New York Center, air traffic control increased our altitude slightly to 9500 feet as we passed over Newark. The weather was ideal. Nobody said a word until we heard Westchester approach approve our descent for landing on runway 1-6. A cheer came from the backseat as we turned for our final approach and the airport came into view. Home at last!

Chapter 55
Evan

We could see places we remembered when Daddy lined up the plane for runway 1-6. When the wheels touched ground, Lynne and I exclaimed over and over, "Home on the Fourth of July!" Daddy taxied the plane to Westair, and we couldn't wait to get out of the tiny space where we had spent most of the last ten days. We all kissed the ground and then stood in a circle, hugging each other. I couldn't believe we were actually home.

"God bless America!" Lynne said. It didn't sound corny.

"The greatest country in the world!" I said.

Daddy had tears in his eyes. He hugged us tighter. "It's great to be home!"

Lynne took a deep breath. "I remember that smell. It smells like home."

Daddy had one arm around Lynne and one around me as we walked into the terminal to call Mom and get a tie down.

Then we went back to unload the Cessna. Daddy patted the wing like it was a good dog. "This little workhorse has served us well."

Lynne and I gave a cheer for the Cessna. It really had taken good care of us.

Chapter 56
Marilyn

Diane, Heather, and I attacked the travelers with hugs and kisses. Then all six of us piled into the The Honeymoon Express, the old maroon Plymouth station wagon the Warners used for hauling sails.

A twenty-minute ride of excited chatter put us in front of a small white colonial within walking distance of downtown. "This is it," I said, "the new homestead."

"I'm sorry it's not what everybody's used to," Jack said.

"It's a nice house." I was defending the house as well as my husband's ability as a provider. "It has personality."

"Wait'll you two see the room you have to share," Diane teased her older sisters. "It's tiny compared to your old ones."

Jack lowered his head, and I glared at Diane.

"It's really pretty though," she quickly added. A smile in her large mischievous eyes, she glanced at me. "I don't know why everybody's so uptight. Just because we don't have money."

As we walked toward the front door, I tried to prepare Jack, Lynne, and Evan for what was inside. "It's a little sparse, but at least we have beds. The piano fills a wall in the living room, and the girls still have their desks." I led the way up the steps to the small front porch and put the key in the door. "We're lucky nobody bought the dining room table. It fits, believe it or not, even with the buffet." I laughed. "Too bad we sold the chairs."

"Hindsight is twenty-twenty," Jack said, his voice quiet.

The girls took a quick run through the first floor and then went upstairs.

I put my hand in Jack's as we walked through the living room, our footsteps echoing on the bare wood floor. A fireplace stood on one wall, flanked by built-in bookcases that faced the piano. One end of the room opened onto a den. "It has charm," I said.

Jack looked pained. "I wish we hadn't sold our house."

"We had to. We needed the money." In my quiet moments, I longed for the old Victorian where we had raised our children, though I would never tell Jack that. "This is a nice house," I said firmly. "We can be happy here if we give it a chance. Besides." I smiled at my husband. "We still have each other."

He squeezed my hand.

From the den, we walked down a short hall across the back of the house and past a full bath to the kitchen, where Mother Kelley's card table and four folding chairs were set up.

"Vince Warner said he'd give us a deal on living room furniture from his showroom."

"The Warners are good friends."

"The best," I said. "By the way, they invited us to the club tonight for the Fourth of July cookout." I studied my husband's face. "We'd have to face everybody. Maybe you'd rather stay home. You must be tired."

"I'm not tired at all." His eyes met mine. "How about you? Are you ready for the firing line?"

"Well . . ." I chewed my lip. "We have to face these people sometime. Either we do it all at once and get blasted with both barrels, or we take the slow, painful route." I gave my husband a sad smile. "Choose your poison."

After a moment, Jack said, "Let's get it over with."

* * *

People in dressy summer casuals milled around on the rich green lawn while others sat on the sea wall. Some had gathered into small groups. Tables were set up at one end, their white covers waving lightly in Long Island Sound's warm breeze. In front of the dance floor, three chefs in tall hats flipped hamburgers, hot dogs, and chicken. The fat dripped onto red hot coals, sending delicious-smelling smoke curling through the air. Jack and I and our children huddled together at the edge of the crowd.

Jane Warner came to rescue us. She wore red, white, and blue like most of the members. "Here you are! Welcome home, you big rascal!" She threw her arms around Jack's middle in a great bear hug and gave him a light kiss on the lips. "You made it in one piece. Marilyn was worried sick."

Jack smiled with fondness at our friend. "You know Marilyn."

Jane hugged Lynne and Evan. "Did you ladies have a good trip?" The girls knew the Warners well, having spent many weekends sailing on Sea Canary, the Warner's yellow C&C 50 sailboat.

Knowing Mrs. Warner genuinely cared, Lynne and Evan told her their favorite anecdotes. Their younger sisters listened while they scanned the crowd for friends.

Vince Warner joined us and happily shook Jack's hand. "Welcome back, stranger! It's good to see your ugly face again! Now your wife can stop worrying about you."

Jack looked at me with mock impatience. "Marilyn worries about everything. Drives me nuts sometimes."

"She really loves you," Vince said, as though this was something wives didn't do.

This caught Jack off guard. His eyes sought mine. He blinked twice and I blinked back. "I hope you're not tired," Vince said to Jack. "We've got some serious drinking to catch up on." He looked at Jack with concern. "You'd do well to have a few libations under your belt. I'm afraid you're going to be bombarded."

Jack's jaw clenched. "What are people saying? What do they think happened?"

"Well . . ." Vince stared at the water. Two speedboats droned nearby like bumblebees.

"They're not really sure. But the basic story is that you got mixed up with a con man who enticed you to Brazil on a wild goose chase."

"That about sums it up, doesn't it?" Jack said, his tone bitter.

Vince wore a strange expression. "Well, not completely."

"Pray tell," Jack said with sarcasm, "what else could there be?"

Vince sighed. "Oh, there are a few, you know the type, the big know-it-alls, who say you may have been in cahoots with Jerry Green." Vince looked pained. "Maybe involved in something illegal." He gave Jack a weak smile. "You know how rumors go."

We knew all about rumors but weren't prepared for their sting. How could anybody believe such lies?

Jack made a loud effort to clear his throat. "I think I'll get a drink. How about you, Vince, you ready? Marilyn? Jane?" He and Vince headed for the bar; Jane and I followed. The girls left to join their friends.

At the bar, Jack came face to face with a number of old friends and acquaintances. Most welcomed him graciously, but some—an irritating minority—had to make the night unpleasant by getting in their quips.

"I knew from the beginning it was a cockamamie idea!" "Why would you ever go to Brazil?" "Don't tell me you made your fortune *already*, you lucky bastard. If that's true, show me the way to Brazil! Ha. Ha. Ha." "Well, pal, guess you're poorer but wiser now. Haw. Haw. Haw." "What are you gonna do for an encore? Har. Har. Har." "Your story'll keep the cocktail parties buzzing for months." "Come on, Kelley, fess up. What were you *really* doing in South America?" "Yeah, where'd you hide the stash?"

I hardly fared better. Over and over I heard, "I can't understand why you'd stay with Jack after what he's put you through. Most women would leave their husbands for *far* less."

The words surprised me. "It was my decision too," I said defensively. "He didn't exacty drag me off by the hair, kicking and screaming. I was supportive all the way." At times I was more aggressive. "At least we had the courage to go after something we believed in!"

That night, Jack's first night home, we lay on our new mattress and box spring, the only furniture in the bedroom. My clothes were stacked in neat piles against the wall. Two moving cartons served as bedside tables. I snuggled against Jack, and he put his arms around me.

"This feels a little bit like heaven," he said. As he stroked my hair in silence, I could sense that his thoughts were elsewhere.

Finally he said, "It could've worked, Mare. If only Jerry hadn't been so damn greedy!" He let go of me and turned away. "I'll never forgive him." His voice was thick. "I'll never forgive myself either. Why didn't I see the real side of Jerry? The kids did. I should have listened to them."

"Jack," I said gently, "you have to let go of the past. You have to look forward."

"I can't, Mare. I just can't."

I squeezed my eyes shut to hold back the tears. I had never felt so helpless, so totally inadequate.

Chapter 57
Marilyn

It was the summer of 1974, a year since Jack's first trip to Brazil. Our country was in flux, just as we were. Richard Nixon had succeeded in opening the door to communist China and making the Russians nervous, but he had lost his battle with the Watergate investigators and resigned in disgrace.

Jack was out of a job also, constantly hearing jokes at his expense.

His efforts to begin a new career were wearing him down, physically and emotionally, as we watched the remaining proceeds from the sale of our house slip away like the setting sun.

The girls were also struggling. Their Brazilian experience had given them an extra dimension. They no longer fit into their old niches. When school started, Heather, the youngest, slipped most easily into her old place among friends. Evan was in her senior year and had Jeff Perillo waiting for her, but in her heart nothing was the same. Lynne was making a new start as a freshman at Rochester University. She and Pete Sullivan had parted for college with no strings. Of all the children, Diane suffered most. She had given up the captainship of the gymnastic team and a spot as a cheerleader. Beginning her first year of high school, after being out of the mainstream for half a year, she found that everybody had moved on without her. Re-entry was a difficult endeavor.

I dispensed reassurances like Band-Aids, trying to heal crushed egos, hurt feelings and uncertainties, as well as build a new household on a limited budget.

Chapter 58
Jack

In an effort to avoid going back into broadcasting, I considered buying Stormville Airport, a country airfield near Poughkeepsie that sat among the hills of middle New York State, next to Green Haven Prison. It was owned by my cousin, Harry O'Connor. On weekends, the airport was like an amusement park. Long lines of small planes were tied down on the grass, while others flew over the runway for touch and goes. Colored parachutes from the jumping school drifted down, sometimes landing off target. Like, on rooftops. And once on electrical wires.

"The poor guy sizzled like bacon in a pan," Harry told fascinated listeners. He was the main attraction. He had lively blue eyes and wavy white hair. A vivid man who spoke vivid English. I was interested in buying the airport, and Harry, in his late sixties, was always willing to listen to offers. Encouraged by his enthusiasm, I made the two-hour round trip as often as three times a week, planning with him ways to improve business. We pored over records with his wife, Grace, a tyrant of a record keeper, and talked about a buyout plan wherein the O'Connors would finance the loan.

After two long months of amiable story swapping and earnest discussions, Harry stood by the gas pump one day, looking up and down the runway. "Ya know somethin,' Jackie?" he said. "I don't think I wanna sell this place."

* * *

Finally, I had a piece of luck. An acquaintance at the Breezy Harbor Club, who was executive vice president of marketing at Singer International Business Machines, called me. He said he'd heard I was a good salesman. Then he offered me a job as a consultant to work with his sales force. It was the right job at the right time. Though the money was less than I would have made in broadcasting, it met expenses. But there was an extra reward. Not only did I get to visit England, Germany, France, Italy, Belgium, and Luxembourg, I also met interesting—and honest—people.

Chapter 59
Marilyn

After taking care of everybody else's feelings, I realized *my* inner resources needed to be revived. Jack was commuting to New York and traveling to Europe in his new job at Singer. The girls were at school all day. Everybody "had a life" but me. I needed something to do, a reason to get up in the morning. After some thought, I came up with an idea. I'd get a job, even though few women I knew had one at the time.

"Jesus, Marilyn, how is that going to look?" Jack said. He and I were at the card table in the kitchen having an after-dinner cigarette. The kids were sitting on a borrowed couch in the den, watching the new TV. "I can't make enough money, so my wife has to go to work?" He jumped up and started pacing the small kitchen.

"You know something, Jack? I don't give a flying frig what people think anymore. I *need* a job. It's not for the money, though Lord knows we could use it. I need a job for myself. A diversion. Something to put some distance between me and our problems for a few hours a day. Maybe even have a laugh." I shrugged. "Just part-time. I know it's what I have to do."

"I swear, if I ever see Jerry Green again, I'll tear him apart."

"Jerry Green is in the past. And somewhere along the way, I lost my grasp of who I am. I need to be more than just somebody's wife and somebody's mother. I need to have my own identity." He shoved his hands in his pockets, and I hoped it was a sign he was giving in. "Can you understand what I'm trying to say?"

"I do." He sat down. "I hate the idea of your working. I guess I'm a chauvinist. I like the picture of my wife at home." He thought for a minute. "You'd be around other guys who admire you, maybe even go after you. That bothers me. A lot."

"I'm not interested in other guys."

"I think I should just disappear," he said in a surge of self-pity. "You and the girls would be better off without me." It was one of his frequent laments.

"That's not true, Jack. Stop talking that way."

"You'd be better off if I disappeared from your life. You could find somebody who's worthy of you."

"I won't listen to that kind of talk, so just cut it out." It was getting tiresome. "Besides," I said on a new tack, "after you, anybody else would be dull."

He came over and put his hands on my shoulders. "I don't know why you put up with me. You must be crazy."

For a second, I felt the old spark of fun. "Is there any doubt? I followed you to Brazil, didn't I?"

He laughed. It sounded strange. He hadn't laughed in a long time. It must have given him an odd sense of benevolence. He slid his arms around me and hugged me. "Go get a job, kid. Knock 'em dead!"

With my family's encouragement, I found a part-time job as a bookkeeper/secretary for a small communications firm in Greenwich. Somebody felt I was worth hiring. They were even willing to pay for my work. I floated two feet off the ground for a week.

Chapter 60
Jack

I enjoyed working at Singer. Meeting people of all nationalities, seeing their countries. The sales force was dynamic. It was a pleasure to work with them. Since language was not one of my high cards, it was fortunate they all spoke English.

Singer International Business Machines did well. So well, in fact, that a year and a half after I started working there, the company was sold and we were all out of a job.

I was still not ready for re-entry into broadcasting. Having always been intrigued by retail, I bought a liquor store in Greenwich. It was around 1976, a time when wine was becoming popular—the beverage of choice. Over the next two years, I built a large selection of good California wines. By a lucky coincidence, the New York Times's wine editor lived in Greenwich and often visited the store. He was kind enough to mention us more than once in his column. A big help in growing sales.

In order to pay for college tuitions and weddings, however, I eventually had to bite the bullet and try broadcasting again. I visited two headhunters. One was sufficiently impressed by my resumè to compile a half-inch-thick presentation on my behalf. I was immediately swept into a rush of interviews for a big job at one of the networks. I could almost smell the leather in the executive chair.

Then, without warning, the activity stopped. The headhunter was unable—or unwilling—to explain.

What had happened? I spent hours reviewing my recent past. Hours of careful examination always brought me to the same possibility. Rudy Schultz. Still holding court as president of Taylor. Still slandering me. Schultz had once given me high accolades. He would have looked like an ass to have let a good man get away. His over endowed ego would never allow it. It was a definite possibility.

But whatever the cause, I lacked the proof and the clout to do anything about it. To make matters worse, my concentration on the Big Job had wasted two months of valuable time.

I saw myself as a failure, yet I knew I couldn't quit. I had a family who counted on me to put food on the table. Keep a roof over their heads. Buy them a new pair of jeans once in a while. Some furniture to sit on. Pay tuition.

* * *

Finally. Two months after the Big Job fiasco, I sat in the president's office at Vista in New York City. My old friend, Gordon Naylor, leaned back in his tufted leather chair behind a huge antique desk. The image of success.

In our early careers, Gordon and I had worked together at a production company selling programs for syndication. Back then we'd both had the world by the gonads, and Gordon, the smart rascal, had never loosened his grip. At present he was the major shareholder of one of the largest TV program syndication companies in the business.

"I'm proud of you, you crafty Irishman," I said. "You done good!"

Gordon's face displayed a modest sense of well-being. "Luck and timing. Secret of success."

"Well, it couldn't happen to a better guy. You just proved it by giving me this job. Believe me, I appreciate it more than you know."

"Hell, I'm not doing you any favors, Kelley. I'm getting a damn good salesman."

"This job means a lot to me, Gordon. I promise, you won't regret it."

"Why do you think I hired you, you bastard? I know I'll get my money's worth. And as soon as there's an opening in management, you'll be a top contender."

I was happy to be back in broadcasting. In spite of the pitfalls and the ribbing about my misguided adventure, I enjoyed seeing my old pals, the friendships I hadn't realized I'd missed. And I enjoyed the comfort of knowing I could take care of my family.

Now if I could just get Jerry Green out of my mind, I might be able to enjoy life.

Chapter 61
Jack

Ever since we'd returned to the States, I'd been mentally replaying my many conversations with Jerry Green, searching for a clue. Any minute morsel to indicate that the whole thing had been a ruse. But *was* it a ruse? Jerry had taken me to Brazil. Shown me operational businesses. Introduced me to his associates. Had *they* been part of the scam? Or were they victims like me? Where did the truth end and the lies begin?

The gold business alone could have made both Jerry and me wealthy. My forty thousand would have been a mere pittance. So what happened? Where and when had I been asleep?

My weekly phone calls to the FBI, both in New York and in Washington, were fruitless, which aroused my suspicion. They had a file on Jerry. Why were they protecting him?

Out of total frustration, I called Clyde Williams, a friend in Boca Raton. Clyde, a good-looking bachelor, had been general manager of a Miami television station during my early days at Taylor. An offer to work in the broadcast department of the United States Information Agency, USIA, had lured him back into government service. Before his broadcast career, he had been the FBI's assistant director of Florida and the Caribbean. And an agent before that. Earlier in 1974, at age forty-five, he had completed his twenty-two years for Uncle Sam—during which time he earned a law degree—and was now semi-retired, doing occasional consulting work for the government.

My story intrigued Clyde. "I don't understand the Bureau's reticence," he said on the phone. "Being a government agent, *if* that's what Green is, doesn't give him a license to steal. At any rate, it doesn't look like they're going to help you. But there may be another way."

"I'm all ears," I said.

"Take your story to the Postal Department."

"The *Postal* Department?"

"The US Postal Department has a branch similar to the Bureau that handles mail-related crime. Since your friend mailed you an audio tape with all that phony business jazz on it, he committed fraud by mail. In my humble opinion, you have a case."

It was the first ray of light I had seen in months. "By God. One small tape, no bigger than my palm, could be Green's undoing. Thanks, Clyde. I'll check it out and let you know what happens."

The Postmaster of Greenwich reacted to my story with the same amazement as past officials. He made an appointment for Marilyn and me at the Bridgeport Branch of the US Postal Inspectors.

Three days later, Jimmie Lee Archer, head of the US Postal Inspection Department in Bridgeport, met Marilyn and me in his office. In his western boots, the twenty-eight-year-old towered a good three inches over me. He shook hands warmly. "It's good to meetcha," he drawled. He wore a suit and tie with a white shirt. "Come sit down." He indicated two old wooden armchairs as he sat behind his battered desk. "I hear you may be needing our services." His hair was short, his expression eager. "Why don't you start at the very beginning. And don't leave out a thing." He leaned back in his chair as though he were about to be royally entertained.

Constant repetition had fine-tuned my story. I took pains to include every detail and clue—or lack thereof—for the fascinated listener.

Soon Jimmie Lee Archer was leaning forward on both arms, completely captivated. After I finished my dissertation, with occasional comments from Marilyn, Jimmie Lee relaxed. "I just gotta tell ya, that Jerry Green is one smart character."

"I can't dispute that," I said.

"I also believe, Mr. Kelley, that you have a case. You do have a copy of that cassette tape, don't you?"

"As a matter of fact, I have three." I reached for my briefcase. "I brought one, along with other evidence and some snapshots of Jerry and his wife, Starr."

Jimmie Lee's face lit up. "That'll be a big help. I'd like to have everything I can git my hands on."

"Jimmie Lee, it's all yours. And believe me, I'll cooperate any way I can." What a great relief. Somebody who would help us. *Finally.*

"Okay, that's good," said Jimmie Lee. "Now here's what we gotta do. We'll get enough information together to prove to Larry Weinstein—he's the US Attorney—that there's due cause to prosecute Jerry Green. Which shouldn't be too difficult. Then Weinstein presents our case to the grand jury over at the US Attorney's office. If all goes well, they ought to give us an indictment. I don't think we'll have trouble getting one. And once we have the indictment, we can go after Green." He smiled broadly. "I don't mind admitting I'd sure love to match wits with this here Jerry Green. He's a sly one, all right." He looked at his watch. "My god, that's the fastest three hours I ever saw." He stood up. "Mr. and Mrs. Kelley, how would you like to join me for lunch?"

We rose. "Great idea, Jimmie Lee," I said. "But let's knock off the formalities. The names are Marilyn and Jack, and I'm buying." We walked out of the office. "Where are you from?" I asked.

"Alabama. A long ways from here. But don't you worry none. I'm working my way to a promotion, and I'll be down south again before ya know it. I gotta tell ya. Catching the likes of Jerry Green sure would get me there sooner."

"Well," I said, "it looks like the quicker you catch the bastard, the happier we'll both be." I put my hand on Jimmie Lee's shoulder. "Where's a good place to eat?"

* * *

The barrage of phone calls from Jimmie Lee Archer during the ensuing weeks demonstrated how deeply hooked he was on the pursuit of Mr. Jerry Green.

He took great pleasure in keeping me abreast of his progress. "Hey, Jack," he began one day. "I dug up some stuff here I thought ya'd be interested in knowing."

"What's that, Jimmie Lee?"

"Well, it looks like ole Jerry Green was conning some other folks too."

"Somehow that doesn't surprise me."

"And from what I could find out, they lost more'n you did. At least in money. They didn't pull up stakes and move outta the country."

"Hey, Jimmie Lee, that's great news! It should help our case."

"There's one problem."

"What's that?"

"Neither one of 'em is willing to testify."

"Why the hell not?"

"They're embarrassed. They don't want to admit in public that some crook outsmarted 'em."

"That's expensive pride. Do they know about us?"

"Yup. But this one guy's a big wheel at a fancy company in New York and he doesn't want any publicity. He's afraid it might cost him his job. Green bilked him outta two hundred and fifty thousand dollars."

"Holy shit! I guess I shouldn't feel so bad. But I don't understand why he wouldn't try to get his money back."

"Well, I guess he can make up his losses. It ain't worth it for him to go public."

"What about the other one?"

"Same story, only on a smaller scale."

"How did you find these people?"

"They filed complaints with the New York DA's office. That's their way of getting even."

"You're doing a great job, Jimmie Lee. Keep up the good work."

"You can count on it. By the way, Weinstein's gung ho."

* * *

Six weeks later, Marilyn and I stood with Jimmie Lee Archer in the second-floor hall of the Bridgeport Municipal Building, outside the room where Larry Weinstein was presenting our case to the grand jury. Before the hearing, we had met Weinstein, a dark-haired, dark-eyed, soft-spoken man about five foot ten. He looked intelligent, probably in his early thirties. Young for a district attorney, though Jimmie Lee assured us he was "sharp as a steel blade." "This won't take long," he said.

Forty-five minutes later, I paced back and forth through a haze of cigarette smoke. Too nervous to sit, I stood against a wall, staring at the dust balls in the corner. Marilyn said she'd already counted the ceiling tiles at least five times. Plus the hundred and ten holes in each one. And she had counted the black and white floor squares, worn gray along the center path. We had watched the same people walk in and out of a room down the hall. *Their* missions seemed to be accomplished.

"What's taking so long?" I asked Jimmie Lee. His frame filled half a slat-back wooden bench along one wall.

"Well, I don't know. But I wouldn't worry if I was you."

"I can't help it." I was afraid to even think about failing to get an indictment.

Noting my concern, Jimmie Lee rose. "I'll go see what I can find out." His footsteps echoed in the hall until he disappeared behind closed doors.

Marilyn and I occupied ourselves with another cigarette. I couldn't stop pacing.

Jimmie Lee reappeared. "There's nothing to worry about. They're just asking a lotta questions."

"Is that good or bad?" I asked.

"It don't make no never mind. I think we're gonna win it."

"We'd better," I said, "or I'll go after the bastard myself."

A half hour later, Larry Weinstein came out. He carried a tightly rolled paper. "Here it is. A federal indictment for mail fraud against Jerry Green."

* * *

Jimmie Lee Archer grabbed the indictment like a football and ran with it.

First he notified Interpol and alerted all passport checkpoints in the United States, especially New York and Florida. The job was complicated by Jerry's possession—as he had often bragged to me—of six passports with different names from at least three different countries.

Clyde Williams got Green's Miami address by passing Green's phone number to a friend at the FBI. Jimmie Lee uncovered two post office box numbers: one in Switzerland and one in Nassau. Combined with my list of Jerry's phone numbers, associates' names, his Belèm and Munich addresses, as well as photographs, Jimmie Lee Archer had a good start.

* * *

Jimmie Lee and I spoke often by phone. "You said Green told you he was born in Berlin, Connecticut?" Jimmie Lee asked one day.

"That's right," I said. "But probably not true."

"Well, it's half true. He was born in Berlin, Germany. Came to the US when he was fourteen."

"That would explain why he was so careful pronouncing his words, twisting his mouth like a contortionist. He was trying to hide his accent."

"You're probably right. The guy is smart. Weaving the truth in with the lies."

"Don't remind me."

* * *

Bits of information began to fit together like pieces of a jigsaw puzzle. On his next phone call, Jimmie Lee said, "Remember that Colonel what's-his-name down in Rio? The air attaché that Green claimed he had transferred back to Washington?"

"Colonel Eberly. What about him?"

"Well, it turns out the plans were already in the works for the good colonel to retire in the States. Green got hold of that information somehow and twisted it for his own purpose."

The depths of Jerry's inroads to power turned me cold. "How could Jerry get that kind of information?"

"It seems like Mr. Green has some good connections in Washington."

"Have you found out yet who they are?"

"Kelley, you're asking too many questions. Just be patient."

"'Patient' isn't in my dictionary."

"You'll find out everything soon enough. I gotta go out now and beat the bushes."

Sometimes Jimmie Lee frustrated the hell out of me. On the other hand, he had thrown himself into the case 150 percent and was coming up with results. That plus his colorful Southern manner made the association generally pleasant. Under the circumstances.

One day Jimmie Lee called me at my office in New York. "We heard from Jerry Green."

"Hey, Archer, you're not shittin' me, are you?"

Jimmie Lee let out a low, dirty laugh. "Now, Jack, would I do a thing like that?"

"For chris'sake, Jimmie Lee, I'm going crazy here."

"Weinstein got a letter from Jerry Green's lawyer. Green wants to settle. For twenty thousand."

"Twenty thousand? No deal! The cheap bastard crook."

"I knew y'all would say that."

"The snake finally raised his ugly head. We must be making life tough for old Jerry boy."

"Yup. We're doing that all right. He knows we're sniffing around, so he can't come and go like he used to." He lowered his voice. "Kelley, I gotta talk to you. ASAP."

"Well, it's Friday. How about dinner tonight? I know Marilyn would like to see you."

"Fine with me. Just tell me how to get there."

* * *

That night, Jimmie Lee Archer sat on one of our new kitchen stools at the butcher block counter we had installed. We were having a drink while Marilyn set out cheese and crackers. Evan, Diane, and Heather already had met the US Postal Inspector and gone out for the evening.

Jimmie Lee, not one to waste time, got right to business. "This here friend of yours, Jerry Green, is turning out to be a very interesting character." He reached inside his jacket and pulled out a paper. "This letter is from Green's attorney in Washington." He handed it to me and waited while I read it. "That there law firm's got a lot of clientele that enjoy the company of the Mafia," he said. "As a matter of fact, Jerry Green and Sam Giancana are using the same lawyer. Now, that doesn't prove that Green is mafioso, but based on what we already know about him, it surely does hint in that direction. He's connected with them somehow."

"The head of the Federal Ministry of Justice in Brazil suggested the same thing," I said.

"He stayed in our house with us!" Marilyn said.

"It was probably a nice little hideout for him," Jimmie Lee said. "Tucked away all safe and quiet. The thing is, if he's involved with the mob, it means the mob knows about the Kelleys. We're talking about some dangerous characters here. What I'm getting at, Jack, is you gotta protect yourself. You're making life tough for Jerry Green, and he's not the kind to take it sitting down."

"Oh, God!" Marilyn exclaimed. The snacks were forgotten.

"Good." I said. "Maybe we'll smoke him out."

Jimmie Lee's voice rose. "Jack, I'm not kidding. This is serious business." Then his voice dropped almost to a whisper. "Let me ask you. You got a gun?"

"I've got a .45."

"Well, you didn't hear it from me, but you better start carrying it." He turned to Marilyn. "D'you keep your house locked? I see your kids going in and out."

"We lock it when we go out, not when we're home," she said.

"Well, you better start locking your doors all the time. Windows too. Jerry Green's a dangerous man. You can't be too careful."

"Should we notify the police?" I asked.

"It wouldn't hurt."

Marilyn looked pale. "Are the girls in danger?"

"Not as long as they keep their eyes open and don't talk to strangers."

A dark mood settled in the kitchen. "Look, folks, I didn't mean to scare you. You can go on with your life the same as you always did. Just be careful, that's all."

Jimmie Lee's information put a damper on the rest of the night.

From then on, I carried my pistol wherever I went. And every morning I suffered the humiliation of crouching on the street to search under both cars for a bomb, cursing Jerry Green all the while.

* * *

One night I sat at the kitchen counter talking with Marilyn while she fixed dinner. Heather sat on a tall stool next to me. She was still thin and lanky at thirteen. She waited politely for a lull in the conversation and then asked, "Daddy, are you in the Mafia?"

Stunned, Marilyn and I exchanged looks. I said, "Of course I'm not in the Mafia. Where would you get an idea like that?"

"I don't know." All innocence.

"Yes, you do," I said. "Where did you hear that?"

Our youngest daughter shifted on the stool. "In school."

"From one of the kids?" Marilyn asked.

"Uh-huh."

"Who was it?" I asked.

Heather traced the lines of the butcher block with one finger. "Steve."

"The boy you like?" Marilyn asked.

"Uh-huh."

"Where would he get that idea?" I asked.

Heather squirmed in her seat. "His father told him."

I jumped up. "What?"

"Take it easy, Jack." Marilyn turned to Heather. "Do you know where his father heard that?"

"On the train."

I couldn't believe it. "Somebody on the train told Steve's father that I was in the Mafia?"

"Yep."

"What else did they say?" I demanded.

Heather faced me. "They said you went to Brazil to work for the Mafia, and now you're back here laundering money."

Marilyn let out a silent "oooh."

"God *damn*!" I pounded the counter with my fist and a spoon clattered on a plate. "What's Steve's last name? I want to call his father."

Heather jumped up. "No! Please don't, Daddy. I promised Steve I wouldn't tell."

"I'll talk to his father. Steve won't know anything about it."

"Please, Daddy! Steve'll get in trouble."

"Let's think about this first," Marilyn said. "We have to consider Heather too."

"Oh, this is wonderful." I said. "I'm being slandered and I can't defend myself. What am I supposed to do?"

"Nothing, for the time being." Marilyn looked at me, her lips pressed in a tight line.

"I'll sue him."

"Forget it, Jack. You'll only make it worse."

I rested both elbows on the counter and held my head in my hands. "God, Mare! It never ends."

Heather put her thin arm around me and patted my back, then she laid her head on my shoulder.

Chapter 62
Jimmie Lee Archer

There's always been competition between our guys and the FBI. Human nature, I reckon. The bureau claimed they didn't have anything on Green, but I didn't believe it for a minute. So I went to Miami to do some digging on my own.

Ray Bogden, my Miami counterpart, picked me up at the airport. Ray was clean-cut, neatly dressed, intelligent eyes, in his early thirties. He slowed the car as he drove onto a causeway leading to a small island in a wealthy Miami neighborhood. Green had an address there.

I whistled. "Pretty nice."

"Prime real estate," Ray said. He stopped in front of Green's place, a rambling white ranch house. The drapes were closed. It looked like nobody was home. "Let's give it a try," Ray said. We got out and took our time walking to the door so we could assess the expensive houses and the manicured yards. I rang the chimes and waited. No sound of life inside. Again, I rang and waited.

We were about to leave when the door slowly opened. A petite black-haired beauty stared at us with large doe-like eyes. She made a pretty picture in her cream-colored slacks and shirt. I smiled, momentarily forgetting the purpose of my trip.

"Good morning, ma'am. Is this the Green residence?"

"Yes." Her answer was more like a question.

"Are you, by any chance, Laura Green?"

She raised her eyebrows. "Yes, I am."

Her coloring was similar to Jerry's. "You wouldn't happen to be Jerry Green's daughter, now would you?"

She smiled, ever so slightly. "No," she said. "I'm his wife."

Ray came to life.

It was a surprise, that's for sure. I had always thought Starr was Jerry's wife. "I see," I said. "Well, ma'am, is your husband home?"

She became guarded. "No, he's not."

"Well, then, we'd like to ask *you* a few questions, if it's okay." I pulled out my ID and showed it to her. "I'm Jimmie Lee Archer and this here's Ray Bogden. We work for the US Postal Department."

She read our IDs. "Postal inspectors?"

"Yes, ma'am."

"I have nothing to say." The door began to inch closed.

"Please, ma'am. It'll just take a minute. I came all the way down here from Bridgeport, Connecticut."

She thought and then tilted her head back to look up at me. "I don't think so."

"Please, ma'am."

She frowned. "The US Postal Department. What's this about?"

"We have some questions we'd like to ask, that's all."

She was obviously curious. "Well, just for a minute."

As Ray and I followed her inside, her perfume surrounded us. With cat-like grace, she led us into an all-white living room and sat down. She motioned for us to sit on the matching sofa across from her.

I pictured Jerry Green in this fine room. Swarthy and cunning. Quite a contrast to the fancy white furniture. My respect for him grew as I admired the posh surroundings and the beautiful wife.

"So, you're Jerry Green's wife."

She looked straight ahead. "Yes."

"D'you expect him home soon?"

She inhaled deeply and lifted her chin. "No."

"Do you happen to know where he is?"

"No."

"Where do you think he might be?"

She faced me squarely. "I have no idea. His business takes him all over the world."

"That must be kinda tough on you. With him away so much." I wondered how Jerry could tear himself away from this gorgeous creature.

"Yes. It is tough."

"So, how do you keep busy?"

"I'm a flight attendant for Pan Am."

"Really! That must be interesting." *And it gives your husband international air travel for the mere price of taxes and fees.*

"It keeps me busy."

I leaned forward. "Ma'am, do you know there's a federal indictment against your husband for mail fraud?" I spoke quietly, so as not to alarm her.

She stiffened. "I do."

"Did he tell you that?"

"Yes, he did." She sat erect, hands folded.

Ray appeared relaxed. One arm stretched along the back of the couch.

"Did you know that he tried to settle out of court?" I asked.

She nodded.

"Did your husband ever tell you that he defrauded a Mr. Jack Kelley out of forty thousand dollars? That's alleged, of course."

She gasped and looked from me to Ray and back again. "He told me it was a loan."

"Then you *have* heard of Jack Kelley?"

"He's the one who has the indictment against my husband."

"That's right. Did your husband explain why Mr. Kelley would want to slap an indictment on him?"

"He said Mr. Kelley got impatient because things weren't happening fast enough. He claimed my husband had no intention of following through with their business plans."

"So you did know that your husband received money from Mr. Kelley."

Her pretty black brows curled in a frown. "Yes, but not in the way you suggest."

"Well, the way I heard the story is that your husband persuaded Mr. Kelley to invest forty thousand dollars in a gold business in Brazil. The problem is, Mr. Kelley never received the income your husband promised him. And through various events that occurred in Brazil, Mr. Kelley concluded that your husband never invested that money in the gold business and never intended to return it." Laura Green was paying close attention. I went on, "Now, when Mr. Green used the US mail to carry an audio tape promoting these alleged fraudulent business dealings with Mr. Kelley, he committed a felony, allegedly, which is why we have the indictment against him."

I leaned back and stretched my legs in front of me, smiling apologetically. "I have to give you fair warning, ma'am. If you know where your husband is, and you don't tell us . . . Well, you're harboring an alleged criminal. Which is conspiracy. And that's also a federal offense. Now let me ask you again. Are you sure you don't know where your husband is?"

Laura Green stared straight ahead. "I'm positive," she said coolly.

I pulled in my legs and leaned toward her. After pausing a moment, I asked, "Do you know anything about a woman named Starr?"

Her breath caught. "What about her?"

"I understand she's a friend of your husband's."

Laura's expression darkened. "That's true," she said, her tone quiet.

"Do you think she might travel with him on occasion?" I asked, as gently as possible.

Laura was silent, her mouth drawn tight. She nodded in the affirmative.

I turned to Ray and said under my breath, "Oh, Lord, I hate this."

Ray winked.

"She's not the only one." Laura's voice was choked.

"Aw, now, maybe that's not true. How would you know that?"

Ray leaned forward so as not to miss a word. As they say, a woman scorned has no limit to her fury.

Laura cleared her throat and pulled herself up straight. "I know it's true. I've spoken to them on the phone. He's got women all over the world. There's one in Munich." Her laugh was bitter. "One in Raleigh. Another one in Canada. Toronto, I believe." She ran a hand through her short dark hair. "His first wife lives in upstate New York. She's the mother of his children. I'm not sure he ever divorced her, but I don't think he sees her anymore."

Ray's and my eyes met for a second.

I was thinking Jerry Green must be quite a man. "So, ole Jerry might be a bigamist."

"There's no question about it. Plus the other women. And then there's Starr."

"Whew. How do you know all this?"

"He gave me phone numbers where I could reach him if an important message came in." Laura's voice had grown deeper to hide the emotion, but it still came through. "Whenever I called Raleigh, or Toronto, or even Munich, a female voice answered. And not an office voice. I can tell the difference." Her hands fidgeted in her lap. "I believe he was having affairs with all these women." She laughed loudly, without humor. "Yes. You might say Jerry is a grade A philanderer."

Jerry was full of surprises. I worked to conceal a smile. "That's too bad," I said.

But Laura Green wasn't finished. She seemed relieved to be unburdening herself. "I don't think he ever married the woman in Munich." Her smile was close to a grimace. "You could call her a glorified housekeeper. With fringe benefits. But Starr. Starr's the one who has it made." Her tone was resentful. "She sees more of Jerry than any of us. The mistress always does, I suppose." She vigorously flicked an invisible speck off her slacks as though that would eliminate Starr.

I leaned forward and spoke gently. "Do you think he's staying with one of these other women now?"

Laura ran a hand through her hair. "No, I don't think so. It's too risky." She looked pained. "I have no idea where he is. Or when I'll hear from him again."

I scratched my head, trying to envision Jerry's hidden life, wondering where Laura ranked in the lineup. "I hope you don't mind my asking this, but if you know about all these women, why do you stay with the guy?"

She stared for a minute at the white drapes drawn against the Florida sun. "This may be hard to believe," she said, "but . . . I love him." She searched our faces, as if begging us to understand. "He's the most exciting man I've ever known. Brave. Important. Mysterious. Traveling all over the world. And yet when we're together, I'm all he cares about. He's kind and generous and hopelessly charming." The mere thought of him brought a smile to her face, the other women momentarily forgotten. "My husband is a very complex man, Mr. Archer. Did you know he was a World War II hero?"

"Yes, ma'am, I did."

"Are you aware that he's been working with the US government for over ten years?"

Ray drew in a quick breath.

"I'd heard he did some consulting work," I said.

Laura looked off into space. "I remember one time I had to drive him to a marina in Miami. A boat was picking him up there." She smiled. "You'll never guess who was in that boat."

"No, ma'am."

"Henry Kissinger," she said proudly. "Henry Kissinger and a group of Secret Service men."

I dared not talk or breathe. Laura Green had just confirmed her husband's story to Jack Kelley.

Her face was flushed. "Do you know where that boat went?"

"I surely don't."

"That boat, with my husband on it, went to Key Biscayne to rendezvous with a yacht. The yacht was carrying President Nixon." Ray and I exchanged glances. Laura went on. "Only a certain breed of man has clandestine meetings with the president of the United States. Jerry thrives on living on the edge. With his work. And with his women. I happen to find that kind of man irresistible." She gave a sigh of acceptance. "His sins are part of the package, I'm afraid."

"I guess I can understand that. You gotta take the bad with the good. But getting back to that meeting. Do you happen to know what your husband and the president talked about?"

"Oh, no. Jerry's very closemouthed about business. But the day he met the president, he was so excited, he had to share it with somebody." She looked directly at me. "And I was there."

I saw a glint of triumph in her eyes. She was the one Jerry trusted. I acknowledged her status with a slight nod. Then I asked, "Do you know about any other meetings Jerry might have had?"

"Only that he met Castro once, back in the sixties."

"He didn't tell you anything else?"

"Nothing."

"How about his other businesses? Do you know anything about the gold or the beef and the fish?"

"Jerry never talked much about business." She looked into the distance, the hint of a smile on her face. "We never had time."

"What about working with the Brazilian government? Did he ever talk about that?"

"He mentioned it once or twice. He didn't go into detail."

"Did he ever talk about Jack Kelley?"

"Only after the indictment. Jerry said Jack Kelley got nervous and jumped the gun. Jerry tried to settle with him, but Mr. Kelley wouldn't take the twenty thousand dollars he offered. It was all Jerry could scrape together at the time. Five thousand of it was mine. I think Mr. Kelley hit him at a low point. Jerry seems to be either very rich or very poor."

"And you say you have no idea where Jerry is now."

She shook her head, her mouth drawn. "He said he wouldn't be back for a while. He didn't say where he was going."

I believed her. In a way, Laura Green was a victim too. I wished I'd known her before she met Jerry. I rose to leave, and Ray did the same. "Well, ma'am, we'll be going now," I said. "I appreciate your talking to us." As we walked to the door, I took one last look at the beautiful face. It was full of worry. "Good luck, ma'am," I said as I stepped outside.

Ray and I walked to the car in silence and got in. Ray put the key in the ignition. "I'd say this trip was worthwhile."

"God almighty *damn*," I said. "It's beginning to look like Jerry Green's one of the mafiosa who's been working with the CIA. The pieces are falling together. Green *told* Kelley about meeting Kissinger in Florida. I didn't believe it."

Ray was pale. "God. Kind of chills the bones, doesn't it? Henry Kissinger, Richard Nixon, and Jerry Green taking a boat ride together."

"Oh, there's more than that. Green knew about the Bay of Pigs too. Stuff that never made the press. And Castro. He mentioned there were plans kicking around to get rid of the bastard."

"I'd heard that," Ray said.

"Looking back, Green was pretty talkative with Kelley. He must've trusted him. Kelley was staying with him in Belèm when Allende was assassinated. Kelley said Green was on the phone all the time and went into town a lot. Green told Kelley that pretty soon they wouldn't have to worry about Allende anymore. Four days later, Allende was dead."

"Jesus!"

"Knowing the rumors about the CIA being in on Allende's assassination, and after talking to Mrs. Green, it's easy to put two and two together. I'd bet a year's pay that Green's working for the CIA. That could explain how he got the info on Colonel Eberly."

"Some connections!" Ray said.

"Yeah. That's probably why the Bureau wouldn't help us. I'm still curious about that. I'm gonna do some more digging when I get back." I looked out the window, thinking. "I wonder if I'll ever get Jerry Green."

"It's a hell of a challenge."

"I love a challenge," I said. "And I do believe that any man who can keep five women happy is worth meeting face to face."

Chapter 63
Jack

Jimmie Lee told us Jerry Green was an informant for the FBI. He said it had taken some intense persuading to get that information from a friend at the Bureau who owed him a favor. He learned Jerry might be one of the Mafia who had been working with the CIA. "It makes a lot of sense," he said, "but it sure doesn't make our job any easier with him working both sides of the law."

I remembered Jerry had talked about staying with Starr at the Jockey Club in Miami. He liked to drop the name Meyer Lansky, a prominent member of the Mafia, who he said hung out there. Perhaps Jerry had been playing with us, giving us a clue to his Mafia connection. But with what we knew at the time, it had never occurred to us. A US undercover agent hanging with the Mafia?

Jimmie Lee also told us about Jerry's harem. We pictured the two main players: Starr, his mistress, staying at the Jockey Club in Miami, and Laura Green, his wife, living a few miles away. It fit the familiar mold of deceit. Our only comfort—though small—was the grim reaffirmation that we weren't the only fools in the world.

When my friend in Miami, former FBI agent Clyde Williams, heard about Jerry's connection with the FBI and his involvement with the CIA, he said they got a rotten apple now and then. He called his pals at the Bureau to ask if they knew him.

The answer gave us more than we had expected. One of Clyde's friends learned from a contact at the SNI—Brazil's FBI counterpart—that a Belèm newspaper, *O'Liberal*, had dubbed Pedro Da Silva The King of Contraband and Drugs.

Jerry's little flunky? I couldn't believe it. He was such a sycophant.

Clyde said apparently he was a good actor.

Academy Award material, I'd say.

I could have been in Belèm when that newspaper came out. Unfortunately, I couldn't read Portuguese. Jerry's friends must have had a good laugh.

* * *

Faced with the further challenge of Jerry's FBI-CIA connection, Jimmie Lee attacked the case with extra vigor. One of his first acts was to consult the new central computer for information on Jerry Green's whereabouts.

I devoured every crumb of news from him like a starving man. In truth, Jimmie Lee Archer wasn't far behind me. He said he knew more about Jerry Green than he knew about his closest friends. And the better he knew him, the more fascinated he became.

Finally, he called me. "Kelley, I got good news and bad news."

"Give me the good news."

"Well, the good news is that we've located your friend."

"Where is the bastard?"

"He's living in Curacao."

"Familiar territory for Jerry. What time is the next plane?"

"Now, Jack, you just cool your heels."

"Let's go get him. What the hell are we waiting for?"

"That's the bad news. Curacao's in the Dutch Antilles, as y'all know. We only have extradition rights for murder and kidnapping with the Dutch. Mail fraud just doesn't cut it. And knowing Jerry Green like I do, you better believe he's well aware of that."

"The slimy bastard! So, what does that mean? We sit here and stew while he sits in Curacao and laughs?"

"Don't worry, Kelley. I want him almost as bad as you. And bet your buttons, I'll get him. Know why?"

"Why?"

"'Cause I'm good, that's why."

There was no doubt that Jimmie Lee was good. But Curacao's extradition laws gave him a handicap he couldn't beat.

* * *

Over time our phone calls dwindled. Occasionally, Jimmie Lee checked with Interpol and the FBI, but they reported no new activity. Obviously, Jerry Green was avoiding the United States.

I often thought about my former partner with a strong desire for retribution. It wasn't so much the money anymore. I just wanted to see Jerry punished for what he had done to our family.

So, what were the damages? We lost forty thousand dollars. We gave up a year's worth of income to pursue phony business ventures. We uprooted the girls and unknowingly exposed them to the Mafia. We had several harrowing experiences, some due to world events, some due to our "friends," some due to the elements.

But there were rewards. Our shared adventures brought our family closer. Marilyn and I saved our marriage. Our daughters have a support system between them that makes them a formidable force—intimidating at times, according to their peers. And after living under a military dictatorship in a foreign country, we all came to realize that the freedom and amenities Americans enjoy, and sometimes take for granted, are a precious gift. The United States truly is the greatest country in the world.

Epilogue I
Marilyn

In 1986, Jimmie Lee Archer, now based in Texas, came to Greenwich to pursue a mail-fraud suspect. He invited us to dinner. Of course, the subject of Jerry Green came up, which for Jimmie Lee was like waving the scent of a fox in front of a hound dog.

Within a few months, he had learned through the Bureau that, since our indictment, Jerry Green had tried to slip into New York to visit his mother. Jimmie Lee didn't know if he made it.

Even more interesting, Jimmie Lee located Starr, living in Colorado. He paid her a visit. This time, the quiet, reticent Starr was quite talkative. She said Laura Green and Jerry had divorced. She claimed that Jerry had died of a liver ailment. (Could that be why he never drank alcohol?) At the time of his death, according to Starr, Jerry was living in his native Germany with a woman—marital status unknown—who carried his child. Starr traveled to Germany to visit his gravesite. (A good man is hard to forget.) Jimmie Lee believed Jerry was dead. The FBI told him Green's file was closed.

At the time, I had my doubts about Jerry's death. Call me skeptical (a little late).

One thing I know for sure. Our indictment against him inhibited his travel into the United States and probably changed his entire *modus operandi.* That is satisfying.

* * *

We kept the Cessna for a while. Jack had floats put on it. To cover expenses, he chartered it to a group of Long Island businessmen for their commute to Wall Street, as well as to two movie stars for their vacations on Nantucket and Martha's Vineyard. Our family and friends also enjoyed Jack's enterprise. On weekends we would fly over the Sound to watch the tall ships or our sailing friends, or we'd go to Block Island or the Vineyard for lobster and a swim. There's nothing like taking off with salt spray rushing by before lifting into the air. It was a sad day for all of us when the rising cost of insurance forced Jack to sell the plane. A woman who was a bush pilot in Alaska was the lucky new owner. We like to picture our powerful little green and white bird carrying its new riders to safety.

* * *

Occasionally Jack and I talk about whether we could have succeeded in Brazil if we had been more patient. The gold mine alone could have kept us going in good form. But Jerry Green was a talented con man. He skillfully mixed the truth with the lies. And he spent half our investment furnishing his Belèm pied-à-terre. When we get to that point, we know it never would have worked.

* * *

As for our family: after a number of years, Jack became vice president and general sales manager of another TV program syndication company. In 1983—nine years after we returned from Brazil—we were able to buy a house in Riverside, part of Greenwich.

At the time, Lynne was married to a local boy and had a son, with another soon to follow. Evan was newly married to her second husband, a friend of Lynne's husband. Diane was co-host of *Movieloft and Company* on WSBK-TV in Boston. Later she had a decorating segment on WCVB-TV's *The Good Day Show* and a spot as a reporter in the pilot for *The Andy Griffith Show.* Heather, who had been homecoming queen at Greenwich High and ridden a white stallion in the parade, was at UConn with her horse, Quartermain, a descendant of Bold Ruler she had bought "off the track" while working on a thoroughbred racehorse breeding farm in Maryland. He became a favorite in steeplechase races.

And I began to write.

Epilogue II
Jack

In the late seventies, we learned that while he was involved with us, Jerry Green allegedly had been—among other escapades—transporting stolen bearer bonds to Germany through a contact at Franklin National Bank in New York. The bonds ended up in a complex money-laundering scheme that went through the Vatican with the help of Bishop Marcincus, an American priest who worked at the Vatican. This "enterprise" was reported in *The Vatican Connection*, by Richard Hammer, a National Book Award nominee, which details the investigative work of Detective Sergeant Joe Coffee at the NYPD. Jerry Green's name was not mentioned.

In June of 2000, the national broadcast news reported that in the 1960s and '70s, the CIA had hired unsavory characters to help in their undercover work during the cold war. We believe Jerry Green was one of them, participating in South America's fight against communism.

After 9/11, people suggested the United States start using the underworld again to act as undercover agents in our fight against the terrorists. I agree. They're good at deceit.

Acknowledgements

Fortunately, I began writing this story in 1983 when everyone's memories were still fresh.

I couldn't have put it all together without help from so many great people. First of all, I want to thank my family for sharing their adventures and making this a richer narrative. Their gentle nudging and never-failing support kept me moving forward. Also, a thank you to Martha Barron Barrett, who invited me to Molasses Pond, a marvelous writer's retreat where I met kindred spirits whose friendship I enjoyed for many years in a writer's group. Karin Lium, Dick Roberts, Andrew Martin, and Janet Taylor patiently read chapter after chapter and gave me invaluable critique. In the homestretch, and after countless edits, Karin and Dick were still critiquing and Tom Chase had joined them. Their willingness to help outdid anything I could have wished for.

I first wrote this story as fiction in order to describe the scenes where I was not present. When I balked at portraying my husband and daughters as acting out of character, my loyal group suggested I make the story creative non-fiction. The only way to achieve this was to write in the voices of my family. I am grateful to Sue Wheeler, a dear friend, who helped me write in a man's voice and was supportive throughout. She generously read the entire manuscript and some parts twice. Her enthusiasm kept me going. And finally, kudos to my editor, Elizabeth Barrett, who did a remarkable job.

The wonderful generosity of all these people was not only heartwarming but beyond measure.

A gigantic thank you to everyone. You are the greatest.

About The Author

Marilyn Kelley and her husband raised four daughters. After their adventures in Brazil, she worked at a satellite communications company, taught a fitness program, and began writing.

In 1993, she and her husband moved to Portsmouth, New Hampshire where she continued teaching exercise and attended writers' workshops. She is currently working on a romantic comedy called "Waltz Me Around Again, Willie," and a children's book. She and her husband have seven grandchildren and two great grandchildren.